Enhanced Edition

BIG COMPUTER GAMES

I0487695

1984 EDITION

David H. Ahl – Editing

Patrick Calkins – Art Direction

*Eugene Bicknell, Chris DeMilia, Peter Kelley, Diana Negri Rudio –
Illustrations and Production*

2022 ENHANCED EDITION

Brian Wiser – Editing, Layout, Remastering

Bill Martens – Scanning

David H. Ahl – Preface

 Apple PugetSound Program Library Exchange

Big Computer Games: Enhanced Edition

www.callapple.org

Paperback ISBN: 978-1-387-85401-1
Hardback ISBN: 978-1-387-85398-4

ACKNOWLEDGEMENTS

Thanks to David H. Ahl for his support and new preface for this *Enhanced Edition*. Produced in coordination with and permission from David H. Ahl. Special thanks to the original authors, artists, and publisher for this wonderful view into the past.

This new edition is copyright by A.P.P.L.E. as the publisher. No claim to copyright over *Big Computer Games* is created outside of those portions created by A.P.P.L.E..

PRODUCTION

Big Computer Games: Enhanced Edition → © 2022 Apple Pugetsound Program Library Exchange

Brian Wiser   → Layout, Editing, Remastering of Cover, Art, and Pages
Bill Martens → Scanning
David H. Ahl → Preface

Big Computer Games → © 1984 Creative Computing Press

David H. Ahl   →   Editing
Patrick Calkins →   Art Direction
Eugene Bicknell, Chris DeMilia, Peter Kelley, Diana Negri Rudio → Illustrations and Production

DISCLAIMER

About David H. Ahl

David H. Ahl is the author or editor of 22 how-to books, including *Basic Computer Games* (the first million-selling computer book), *Dad's Lessons for Living*, and *Dodge M37 Restoration Guide*. In 1974, he founded *Creative Computing* magazine – the world's first personal computing magazine – and was the publisher and editor-in-Chief of *Creative Computing* magazine and six others from 1974 to 1985. He is a frequent lecturer and workshop leader at educational and professional conferences.

David holds a MS and BS degree in Electrical Engineering from Cornell University, an MBA from Carnegie-Mellon University, and has done further work in educational psychology at the University of Pittsburg.

He served in the Army Security Agency, was a consultant with Management Science Associates and a senior research fellow with Educational Systems Research Institute. In 1967, David devised the first computer model for forecasting the success of new consumer products. In early 1970, he joined Digital Equipment Corporation. As education product line manager, he formulated the concept of an educational computer system consisting of hardware, software and courseware and helped guide DEC into a leading position in the education market.

David joined AT&T in 1974 as education marketing manager and was later promoted to manager of marketing communications for the unit later to become American Bell. Concurrent with this move, he started *Creative Computing* as a hobby in late 1974. It was the first personal computing magazine in the world. As *Creative Computing* grew, David left AT&T in 1978 to devote full time to it. In 1984, *Creative Computing* magazine was Number 1 in software and applications.

He has also written more than 1,000 articles on technology, automotive restoration, marketing, Bible, logic puzzles, travel, market research, financial planning and investment analysis. Among computer games, he created *Lunar Lander, Subway Scavenger, Orient Express*, and 50 others.

David's hobbies include racing 1950s Triumph sports cars, collecting and exhibiting WWII patriotic stamped covers and classic first day covers, and collecting toy tow trucks. He is an award-winning photographer, restores historic military trucks, hikes, and sails. And he is a softball pitcher and coach, collects antique and historic Bibles and leafs, and repairs anything! Read more about David at: https://swapmeetdave.com. Some of his favorite quotes include:

"Learn from the past; live for the future."

"You can never have too many bungee cords, AA batteries, or rolls of duct tape."

"The circles around you can include or exclude ideas, people, and events.
Draw large circles."

About the Producers

Brian Wiser

Brian Wiser is a producer of books, films, games, and events, as well as a long-time consultant, enthusiast and historian of Apple, the Apple II and Macintosh. Steve Wozniak and Steve Jobs, as well as *Creative Computing*, *Nibble*, *InCider*, and *A+* magazines were early influences.

Brian designed, edited, and co-produced dozens of books including: *Nibble Viewpoints: Business Insights From The Computing Revolution*, *Cyber Jack: The Adventures of Robert Clardy and Synergistic Software*, *Synergistic Software: The Early Games*, *The Colossal Computer Cartoon Book: Enhanced Edition*, *All About Applesoft: Enhanced Edition*, *Graphically Speaking: Enhanced Edition*, *What's Where in the Apple: Enhanced Edition*, and *The WOZPAK: Special Edition* – an important Apple II historical book with Steve Wozniak's restored original, technical handwritten notes. Brian is also the author of *The Etch-a-Sketch and Other Fun Programs*.

He passionately preserves and archives all facets of Apple's history, and noteworthy companies such as Beagle Bros and Applied Engineering, featured on AppleArchives.com. His writing, interviews and books are featured on the technology news site CallApple.org and in *Call-A.P.P.L.E.* magazine that he co-produces as an A.P.P.L.E. board member. Brian also co-produced the retro iOS game *Structris*.

In 2005, Brian was cast as an extra in Joss Whedon's movie *Serenity*, leading him to being a producer and director for the documentary film *Done The Impossible: The Fans' Tale of Firefly & Serenity*. He brought some of the *Firefly* cast aboard his Browncoat Cruise and recruited several of the *Firefly* cast to appear in a film for charity. Throughout these experiences, he develops close personal relationships with many actors, authors, and computer industry luminaries. Brian speaks about his adventures to large audiences at conventions around the country.

Bill Martens

Bill Martens is a systems engineer specializing in office infrastructures and has been programming since 1976. The DEC PDP 11/40 with ASR-33 Teletypes and CRT's were his first computing platforms with his first forays in the Apple world coming with the Apple II computer.

Influences in Bill's computing life came from *Byte* magazine, *Creative Computing* magazine, and *Call-A.P.P.L.E.* magazine as well as his mentors Samuel Perkins, Don Williams, Joff Morgan, and Mike Christensen.

Bill is the author of *ApPilot/W1*, *The Anatomy of an EAMON*, and multiple EAMon adventure games, as well as a co-producer of many books including *What's Where in the Apple: Enhanced Edition*, *The WOZPAK: Special Edition*, *Nibble Viewpoints: Business Insights From The Computing Revolution*, and co-programmer for the iOS version of the retro game *Structris*. He has written many articles which have appeared in user group newsletters and magazines such as *Call-A.P.P.L.E.*.

Bill worked for Apple Pugetsound Program Library Exchange (A.P.P.L.E.) under Val Golding and Dick Hubert as a data manager and programmer in the 1980s, and is the current president of the A.P.P.L.E. user group established in 1978. He reorganized A.P.P.L.E. and restarted *Call-A.P.P.L.E.* magazine in 2002. He is the production editor for the A.P.P.L.E. website CallApple.org, writes science fiction novels in his spare time, and is a retired semi-pro football player.

CONTENTS

 Dedicated to Ken Uston, a good friend and gamester extraordinaire who, to this day, claims he would have beaten me for Gamester of the Year (1983) if only he had a better joystick.

Preface – 2022

    Big Computer Games was originally published in 1984 and included 12 games, some of which were written much earlier on large time-sharing systems. Now that personal computers had more memory, the games could run on those systems. This was an interesting time in the world of computers and video games. Just take a look at what was happening. A decade earlier in 1971, *Computer Space* created by Nolan Bushnell and Ted Dabney was the first coin-op video game and possibly the first commercially available video game. However, *Computer Space* itself was a derivative of the 1962 computer game *Spacewar* developed by Slug Russell and some outer guys at MIT.

    How about the mass market in homes? The Atari Video Computer System (VCS) was launched in 1977 with nine simple, low-resolution games in 2 KB cartridges. The system's first killer app was the home conversion of Taito's arcade game *Space Invaders* in 1980. In Japan a few years later in 1983 Nintendo released the Family Computer, commonly known as the Famicom, a year later to become the Nintendo Entertainment System when released in the U.S. And then there was *Super Mario Kart* in 1992 for the Super Nintendo now in version 8, recipient of the Best Family Game Award in 2014.

    Anyway, do you see what's happening here? Relative crude computer games of the 1960s on million dollar computers became popular arcade coin-op games on dedicated machines in the 1970s, got ported to $3,000 personal computers in the early 1980s, and then converted to run on mass market $200 home game systems a few years later. The technology gets more advanced, faster and cheaper at an accelerating rate. And has continued to do so in the next three decades and will continue further. Personally, I feel that this is a mixed blessing. You won't be seeing new books like my four games books with each game written by an individual programmer. Games like *Sniper Elite*, *The Stanley Parable*, *Warhammer 40,000*, or *Citizen Sleeper* require an army of writers, designers, and programmers to produce. A game like *Grand Theft Auto* has as many as 800,000 lines of code, so the listing would require a book of more than 10,000 pages and require four feet of shelf space. So a programmer of today is very specialized and has a very different job than a programmer of 50 years ago who came up with a concept and wrote the code for a complete and finished game.

But for the game player, there are big advantages. Many of the latest games can be played on pretty much any platform home game system or computer. Oh, maybe you want a fast graphics card or special VR goggles, but they're affordable too. Also, compared to 50 years ago, a game player has a lot more to choose from and gets a superb product at a reasonable cost.

In the first 1984 edition of *Big Computer Games*, I noted I had been on a radio show in 1976 and was asked to make some predictions about the next 100 years of computing. I said I couldn't do it and even 25 years was too far out. So I made some guesses as to the next 10 years. Most were spectacularly wrong.

But going out on a limb again, in the preface I speculated on the future direction of computer technology. Perhaps 10 years of publishing *Creative Computing* and spending a good bit of time with the movers and shakers of the industry helped, but this time my projections were much closer to the mark. I saw knowledge-based systems (AI) becoming more important, more realistic and comprehensive games on the horizon, natural language processing, and much improved graphics and sound coming soon. Pretty much what happened, although I definitely missed the advent of VR and I was totally off base about writing another games book 5 or 10 years down the road (especially since 10 years later, I was publisher and editor of *Military Vehicles* magazine)!

At 83 years old, I don't want to make any more predictions other than *Super Mario Kart 10* will probably be played wearing VR goggles.

David H. Ahl   Morristown, New Jersey   June 2022

Preface

It seems thay my games books come out at about five-year intervals. The first version of *Basic Computer Games* was published in July 1973. *More Basic Computer Games* made its debut in June 1979. And here we are some five years later with *Big Computer Games*. So what is significant about that? Not much at all, except that it gives you an historical perspective on computer games, specifically ones written in Basic.

Years ago, most games in Basic were very short, reflecting of course, the limited memory available in most computers. Indeed, my first lunar lander program was written to fit in a computer with 4K of memory in which the Basic interpreter occupied nearly 3.5K. Thus the program was less than 500 bytes long. In the first book I edited, *Basic Computer Games*, nearly one-half of the 101 programs were less than 40 lines long. Some of them were mighty interesting programs, although there wasn't much room for the rules, error checking, or user-friendly features.

On the other hand, years ago people who had access to large timesharing systems were writing long, elaborate programs with all sorts of extended features. Unfortunately, these weren't of much use to early microcomputer owners who felt lucky to be able to afford 4K, or maybe 8K if they splurged.

Times have changed. Today, memory is cheap. When I talk to kids at schools, they can't imagine a computer with less than 48K and another two to four times that on disk. Consequently, although many of the programs in this book were originally developed on large timesharing systems, today they will run on the average microcomputer. Actually, most of them don't require much more than 16K (some timesharing systems limited users to a 16K partition). Of course, some of the programs in this book were initially developed on microcomputers.

So, as a result of the relentless march of technology, today we are able to run programs on a small computer that ten years ago required a $100,000 system. Furthermore, many of the programs being written today on small computers are more elaborate than those written on larger machines.

I wish I could say that these advances in technology have led to higher quality programming; they have in some cases, but certainly not across the board. Valdocs and Lotus 1-2-3 are certainly masterful pieces of code; most of the programs in this book are not. Some of the programs almost cry out for improvement, but for that you must first get them into your computer.

Don't Call Us

After you have spent the better part of a week typing one of these long programs into your computer and it doesn't work, then what? Don't call us. Chances are, we can't help you, nor are we prepared to answer calls or letters.

But perhaps I can take a leaf from my experience with some of the million purchasers of the two earlier games books who had problems.

First of all, every program in the book runs. The listings have not been typeset—they came directly out of the computer. In other words, there are no typos. The major reasons for readers' programs not running in the past were typos—yours, not ours. So, check your listings against the ones in the book very carefully.

Second, although all these programs are in Microsoft Basic, there are several slightly different dialects of Microsoft Basic. We tried not to use any of the unusual or extended features, but that dosen't mean that the implementation on your computer is identical to the one we used. Moreover, we used four different computers to prepare these programs, so there may be minor incompatibilities.

Let me stress, that any language incompatibilities between versions of Microsoft Basic are truly minor, RND versus RND (1) for example. In general, the syntax error checking in the language will identify these problems.

If you have a computer with a Basic interpreter other than Microsoft, you will have to make some conversions. In the previous games books, I included a section on converting to other Basics. It is not in this book because there are now more than 30 different versions of Basic; to include conversion instructions for all of them would require an inordinate amount of space.

Moreover, when I put together the first book of games, one of the primary reasons for doing so was for instructional purposes. I never expected people to copy the programs blindly and run them. I expected people to modify them, improve them, and learn something about programming in the process. Indeed, the first edition of *Basic Computer Games* deliberately included programs in four distinctly different versions of Basic (DEC PDP-8, DEC PDP-11, Honeywell, and HP).

How difficult is it to convert these programs to a significantly different version of Basic such as Commodore, Atari, or TI? Not too difficult at all. We took two programs in the book and converted them to all three in a few days. You might want to get a book on Microsoft Basic—there are scores of them—and use it along with the manual for your computer to ease the job. However, the conversions can be done without a book on Microsoft if you have a good understanding of the basics of Basic.

Not All Games

In addition to the 11 ready-to-run games in this book, there is a chapter about writing your own adventure games. The first article in this chapter, "How to Write an Adventure" describes how to construct an overall framework for an adventure game and a structure for storing data, and how to parse the commands entered by the player.

The chapter also includes the listing of an adventure game framework—in Applesoft Basic—which uses some of these principles.

In addition, this chapter includes a description and listing of an adventure game which uses a videodisc. The game can be used without the videodisc routines, but as it was designed to demonstrate the videodisc, it is a rather simple adventure. Nevertheless, it is included to show the sort of game that might be coming along in the future. Five years from now, we will probably look back and judge it as a very primitive effort, but at least it is a start.

The Next Step

Some years ago, during the American bicentennial, I was the guest on a radio show. The commentator asked me to speculate on the next hundred years in computing. I begged off and said I couldn't possibly forecast 25 years, much less 100. So I made some guesses about ten years down the road.

Eight years have now passed, and I can say with certainty that most of my forecasts were wrong—either they happened much sooner than I predicted, or the technology has gone in a different direction. Nevertheless, I'm going to go out on a limb again.

In the future, I see knowledge-based expert systems looming much more important than they are today. The development of such systems will not only have implications for industry, medical, governmental, educational, and professional applications, but for entertainment and games as well. Future games and simulations will be much more realistic and comprehensive. Natural language processing will simplify the interaction with players while graphics and sound will make the output easier to understand.

Will a games book written five or ten years from now use these approaches? Probably, although to what extent I cannot say. Nevertheless, the field is ripe for improvement, and I for one am excited about the possibilities.

Morristown, New Jersey   David H. Ahl
May, 1984

The Games

Cribbage

The computer game of **Cribbage** was written by Sheppard Yarrow in IBM Basic for a 370/158. It appeared in this form in *Creative Computing*, May 1979. For this book, it was converted to Microsoft Basic by Steve Williams.

If you happen to be a cribbage fanatic, you know the frustration of wanting to play but not being able to find an opponent. Well, never again; Cribbage will always be willing to accept the challenge. If you don't happen to be a cribbage player, this program provides a good way to learn the game.

Rules of Cribbage

Cribbage is a two-player game. A regular deck of cards is used. The cards are used chiefly as numbers; the suits have practically no role in the game. Each player receives six cards on the deal. From his hand, each player selects two cards for discard; these four cards are placed face down and are known as the crib, an extra hand which belongs to the dealer.

After the crib is laid down, the nondealer cuts the rest of the pack and the dealer turns up the top card of the lower portion. This card is the starter or up card. If it is a jack, the dealer scores 2 points. This operation is done automatically by the program.

In normal play of the game, a cribbage board is used to keep track of the scores, a function performed by the computer in this game. The game is won when one player has traversed twice around the board (121 or more points).

The nondealer begins by playing any card; face cards and the ten have a point value of 10. The dealer then plays a card and announces the sum of the two cards thus far played. Play continues alternately, the new sum being announced each time, until one player is unable to play without carrying the total over 31. He must then say "go" and his opponent pegs (or scores) for go. The player who called the go must lead again for a new series of plays. The count begins again at zero, and again the total must not be carried beyond 31.

After go is called, the other player must play additional cards if he can do so without exceeding 31. Thus, the same player may play two or three times in succession. For making exactly 31, the player scores 2; for a go at less than 31, he scores 1. Playing the last card of the eight in play counts 1 point, or 2 if it makes the sum 31.

Scoring During Play

In addition to the points for go's and playing the last card, other points are awarded as follows:

Fifteen. For making the sum 15, score 2.

Pairs. For playing a card of the same rank as just played by your opponent (i.e., king, king, or 8, 8), score 2. Playing the third card of a rank scores 6, and the fourth scores 12.

Runs. For playing a card in sequence with two or more just played, score the number of cards in the run (or sequence). The cards need not be played in sequential order to score for a run, for example, if the cards played are 5, 7, 6, the last player scores 3 for the run.

Scoring A Hand

In cribbage, scoring a hand is known as showing. The hands are shown in order: nondealer, dealer, and crib. The starter (or up card) is treated as a fifth card belonging to each of these three hands. The combinations that score are as follows:

Fifteen. For each combination of cards that total 15, score 2. Thus, a hand with 9, 8, 7, 7, and 6 has three combinations of 15: 9 and 6, 8 with one 7, and 8 with the other 7.

Multiples. For a pair, score 2; for three of a kind, score 6; for four of a kind, score 12.

Runs. For each combination that makes a run of three or more, score the number of cards in the run. In the hand, 9, 8, 7, 7, 6, there are 8 points for two runs of four, using one 7 in each run.

Flush. For four cards in the hand (excluding the up card) of the same suit, score 4, or 5 if the up card is also the same suit. For crib and up card of the same suit, score 5; there is no score for a four-flush in the crib alone.

His Nobs. For a jack in the hand of the same suit as the up card, score 1.

Muggins

If a player overlooks a score to which he is entitled, either in playing or showing, his opponent may call "Muggins!" and take the score himself. Since the computer keeps playing scores automatically and always counts his own hand correctly, the only time that Muggins is used in this game is against you when you score your hand or the crib hand.

Specifics of the Computer Version

To the question, "Cut for deal?" you should enter a number between 1 and 52 which is where the shuffled deck will be cut. The cards in your hand are numbered 1 to 6; any entries representing cards should use these numbers, not the value(s) of the card. If you must say go, simply type it instead of a card number on your turn.

The computer will shuffle, deal, generate the starter (up card), keep track of the running scores, and credit all points earned during play. It will not let you exceed 31, but it dosen't check to see if you could have played a card if you respond with go. It is up to you to score your hand and the computer will call *Muggins* without mercy if you have counted incorrectly.

The program uses a very simple playing strategy of keeping the cards that yield the most points or playing the card which will score the most points. There are much more involved strategies of play that can be found in any good book of card games.

Good playing!

Cribbage

```
10 REM ****************************
20 REM *       CRIBBAGE          *
30 REM *  in Microsoft BASIC     *
40 REM ****************************
50 CLS:CLEAR 1000
60 PRINT "************** CRIBBAGE **************"
70 PRINT:INPUT "Enter a number from 1 to 500";NT
80 IF NT>500 OR NT<0 THEN 70
90 FOR X=1 TO NT:YU=RND(1):NEXT X
100 DIM D(52,4),C$(52),I(52),W(5,4)
110 DIM M(6,4),Y(6,4),C(4,4),D$(6),S(4)
120 DIM V(15,7),Q(11,6),R(4,5),J(52)
130 FOR X=1 TO 15:FOR Y=1 TO 7
140 READ V(X,Y):NEXT Y:NEXT X
150 FOR X=1 TO 11:FOR Y=1 TO 6
160 READ Q(X,Y):NEXT Y:NEXT X
170 FOR X=1 TO 4:FOR Y=1 TO 5
180 READ R(X,Y):NEXT Y:NEXT X
190 FOR X=1 TO 4:READ S(X):NEXT X
200 FOR X=1 TO 6:READ D$(X):NEXT X
210 FOR I=1 TO 13
220 READ C$
230 C$(I)=LEFT$(C$,4)+" of Spades    "
240 C$(I+13)=LEFT$(C$,4)+" of Diamonds "
250 C$(I+26)=LEFT$(C$,4)+" of Hearts   "
260 C$(I+39)=LEFT$(C$,4)+" of Clubs    "
270 NEXT I
280 PRINT:PRINT
290 S1=0:S2=0
300 REM ** SHUFFLE DECK & CUT FOR DEAL
310 GOSUB 5850
320 GOSUB 6020
330 REM ** SUFFLE AND DEAL
340 GOSUB 5850
350 GOSUB 6280
360 REM ** FIND BEST 4 CARDS
370 GOSUB 3480
380 REM ** DISCARDS
390 I1=V(B9,5)
400 I2=V(B9,6)
410 PRINT
420 PRINT "Your discards";
430 INPUT I3,I4
440 IF I3<1 THEN 460
450 IF I3<7 THEN 470
460 PRINT "Invalid input":GOTO 420
470 IF INT(I3)<>I3 THEN 460
480 IF I4=I3 THEN 460
490 IF I4<1 THEN 460
500 IF I4>6 THEN 460
510 IF I4<>INT(I4) THEN 460
520 REM ** CRIB
530 FOR J=1 TO 4
540 C(1,J)=M(I1,J)
550 C(2,J)=M(I2,J)
560 C(3,J)=M(I3,J)
570 C(4,J)=Y(I4,J)
580 NEXT J
590 REM ** GENERATE THE UPCARD
600 GOSUB 4320
610 REM ** PLAY OF THE HAND
620 GOSUB 1510
630 IF M=0 THEN 670
640 PRINT "You score first "
650 X1=1
660 GOTO 890
670 PRINT "I score first "
680 X1=2
690 GOTO 1160
700 PRINT "The crib cards are"
710 PRINT
720 FOR I=1 TO 4
730 PRINT C$(C(I,1))
740 NEXT I
750 FOR I=1 TO 4:FOR J=1 TO 4
760 W(I,J)=C(I,J)
770 NEXT J:NEXT I
780 C=1
```

```
790 W(5,4)=T9
800 GOSUB 4530
810 ON X1 GOTO 820,870
820 PRINT
830 PRINT P;"points"
840 S1=S1+P
850 IF S1>=121 THEN 1420
860 GOTO 1370
870 X1=3
880 GOTO 1010
890 K=1
900 FOR I=1 TO 6
910 IF I=I3 THEN 970
920 IF I=I4 THEN 970
930 FOR J=1 TO 4
940 W(K,J)=Y(I,J)
950 NEXT J
960 K=K+1
970 NEXT I
980 W(5,4)=T9
990 C=0
1000 GOSUB 4530
1010 PRINT "How many points ";
1020 INPUT P9
1030 D=P-P9
1040 IF D>=0 THEN 1070
1050 PRINT "Not with that hand"
1060 GOTO 1020
1070 S2=S2+P9
1080 IF S2>=121 THEN 1460
1090 IF D=0 THEN 1150
1100 S1=S1+D
1110 PRINT
1120 PRINT "Muggins for";D;"points"
1130 PRINT
1140 IF S1>=121 THEN 1420
1150 ON X1 GOTO 1160,700,1370
1160 FOR K=1 TO 4
1170 L=V(B9,K)
1180 FOR J=1 TO 4
1190 W(K,J)=M(L,J)
1200 NEXT J
1210 NEXT K
1220 PRINT "My cards are"
1230 PRINT
1240 FOR K=1 TO 4
1250 L=W(K,1)
1260 PRINT C$(L)
1270 NEXT K
1280 W(5,4)=T9
1290 C=0
1300 GOSUB 4530
1310 S1=S1+P
1320 IF S1>121 THEN 1420
1330 PRINT
1340 PRINT P;"points"
1350 PRINT
1360 ON X1 GOTO 700,890
1370 PRINT
1380 PRINT "I have";S1;"points."
1390 PRINT "You have";S2;"points."
1400 PRINT
1410 GOTO 330
1420 PRINT
1430 PRINT "I win";S1;"to";S2
1440 PRINT
1450 STOP
1460 PRINT
1470 PRINT "You win";S2;"to";S1
1480 PRINT
1490 STOP
1500 REM **
1510 REM ** PLAY OF THE HAND
1520 REM **
1530 Y5=0:M5=0:C=0:S9=0:G=0
1540 IF M=0 THEN 1940
1550 IF Y5<>4 THEN 1580
1560 IF M5=4 THEN 2570
```

```
1570 GOTO 1940
1580 PRINT "Your play ";
1590 INPUT C$
1600 IF C$="go" OR C$="GO" THEN 1940
1610 FOR C6=1 TO 6
1620 IF C$=D$(C6) THEN 1660
1630 NEXT C6
1640 PRINT "Invalid play"
1650 GOTO 1590
1660 IF C6=I3 THEN 1880
1670 IF C6=I4 THEN 1880
1680 IF Y5=0 THEN 1720
1690 FOR J=1 TO Y5
1700 IF I(10+J)=C6 THEN 1900
1710 NEXT J
1720 IF S9+Y(C6,2)>31 THEN 1920
1730 S9=S9+Y(C6,2)
1740 Y5=Y5+1
1750 I(10+Y5)=C6
1760 C=C+1
1770 J(C)=Y(C6,4)
1780 GOSUB 3020
1790 PRINT "You played the ";C$(Y(C6,1))
1800 PRINT "Sum =";:PRINT USING"##";S9;
1810 PRINT ", Points =";:PRINT USING"###";P
1820 F=1
1830 S2=S2+P
1840 IF S2>121 THEN 1460
1850 IF S9<>31 THEN 1940
1860 F=0:C=0:S9=0:G=0
1870 GOTO 1940
1880 PRINT "You discarded that card."
1890 GOTO 1590
1900 PRINT "Already played"
1910 GOTO 1590
1920 PRINT "That totals more than 31"
1930 GOTO 1590
1940 IF M5<>4 THEN 2110
1950 IF Y5=4 THEN 2570
1960 IF C$<>"go" AND C$<>"GO" THEN 1550
1970 PRINT
1980 IF F=2 THEN 2050
1990 PRINT "You get one point for the last card."
2000 PRINT
2010 S2=S2+1
2020 IF S2>=121 THEN 1460
2030 F=0:C=0:S9=0
2040 GOTO 1550
2050 PRINT "I get one point for the last card."
2060 PRINT
2070 S1=S1+1
2080 IF S1>=121 THEN 1420
2090 F=0:C=0:S9=0
2100 GOTO 1550
2110 K9=0:P9=0
2120 C9=C
2130 C=C+1
2140 H9=S9
2150 FOR I9=1 TO 6
2160 I(I9)=0
2170 IF I9=I1 THEN 2310
2180 IF I9=I2 THEN 2310
2190 IF M5=0 THEN 2230
2200 FOR J9=1 TO M5
2210 IF I9=I(20+J9) THEN 2310
2220 NEXT J9
2230 IF H9+M(I9,2)>31 THEN 2310
2240 K9=K9+1
2250 S9=H9+M(I9,2)
2260 J(C)=M(I9,4)
2270 GOSUB 3020
2280 IF P>P9 THEN P9=P
2290 I(I9)=P
2300 I(K9+30)=I9
2310 NEXT I9
2320 C=C9
2330 S9=H9
2340 IF K9<>0 THEN 2690
```

```
2350 IF C$<>"go" AND C$<>"GO" THEN 2440
2360 IF G=1 THEN 2450
2370 PRINT
2380 PRINT "I get 1 point for the last card."
2390 PRINT
2400 C=0:S9=0
2410 S1=S1+1
2420 IF S1>121 THEN 1420
2430 GOTO 1550
2440 IF Y5<>4 THEN 2530
2450 PRINT
2460 PRINT "I'll give you 1 point for last card."
2470 PRINT
2480 S2=S2+1
2490 IF S2>=121 THEN 1460
2500 C=0:S9=0:G=0
2510 C$=""
2520 GOTO 1940
2530 IF G=1 THEN 1550
2540 PRINT "Go"
2550 G=1
2560 GOTO 1550
2570 IF F=0 THEN 2670
2580 PRINT
2590 IF F=1 THEN 2640
2600 PRINT "I get 1 point for the last card."
2610 S1=S1+1
2620 IF S1>121 THEN 1420
2630 GOTO 2670
2640 PRINT "You get 1 point for the last card."
2650 S2=S2+1
2660 IF S2>=121 THEN 1460
2670 PRINT
2680 RETURN
2690 C=C+1
2700 M5=M5+1
2710 IF C<>1 THEN 2840
2720 FOR J9=1 TO 4
2730 I9=V(B9,J9)
2740 REM ** DON'T PLAY A 5 FIRST
2750 IF M(I9,2)=5 THEN 2810
2760 I(M5+20)=I9
2770 J(C)=M(I9,4)
2780 P9=0
2790 S9=M(I9,2)
2800 GOTO 2910
2810 NEXT J9
2820 L=V(B9,1)
2830 GOTO 2760
2840 FOR J9=1 TO K9
2850 I9=I(J9+30)
2860 IF I(I9)=P9 THEN 2880
2870 NEXT J9
2880 I(M5+20)=I9
2890 J(C)=M(I9,4)
2900 S9=S9+M(I9,2)
2910 PRINT "My card is the ";C$(M(I9,1))
2920 PRINT "Sum =";:PRINT USING"##";S9;
2930 PRINT ", Points =";:PRINT USING"###";P9
2940 F=2
2950 S1=S1+P9
2960 IF S1>121 THEN 1420
2970 IF S9<>31 THEN 3000
2980 F=0:C=0:S9=0
2990 GOTO 1550
3000 IF C$="go" OR C$="GO" THEN 1940
3010 GOTO 1550
3020 REM **
3030 REM ** CHECK FOR 15 OR 31 OR
3040 REM ** 2,3,4 OF A KIND RUNS
3050 REM **
3060 P=0
3070 IF C=1 THEN 3300
3080 IF S9<>15 THEN 3110
3090 P=P+2
3100 GOTO 3140
3110 IF S9<>31 THEN 3140
3120 P=P+2
```

```
3130 UY=2:IF C-2>2 THEN UY=C-2
3140 FOR I=C TO UY STEP -1
3150 IF J(I)<>J(I-1) THEN 3230
3160 ON C-I+1 GOTO 3170,3190,3210
3170 P=P+2
3180 GOTO 3220
3190 P=P+4
3200 GOTO 3220
3210 P=P+6
3220 NEXT I
3230 REM ** RUNS
3240 IF C=2 THEN 3300
3250 R9=0
3260 FOR I=3 TO C
3270 GOSUB 3310
3280 NEXT I
3290 P=P+R9
3300 RETURN
3310 FOR J=1 TO C
3320 J(J+10)=J(C-J+1)
3330 NEXT J
3340 FOR K=1 TO I
3350 FOR L=K+1 TO I
3360 IF J(K+10)<J(L+10) THEN 3400
3370 X=J(K+10)
3380 J(K+10)=J(L+10)
3390 J(L+10)=X
3400 NEXT L
3410 NEXT K
3420 FOR K=1 TO I-1
3430 IF J(K+10)<>J(K+11)-1 THEN 3460
3440 NEXT K
3450 R9=I
3460 RETURN
3470 REM **
3480 REM ** FIND THE BEST 4 CARD HAND
3490 REM **
3500 P9=0
3510 FOR Z9=1 TO 15
3520 I1=V(Z9,1)
3530 I2=V(Z9,2)
3540 I3=V(Z9,3)
3550 I4=V(Z9,4)
3560 FOR J=1 TO 4
3570 W(1,J)=M(I1,J)
3580 W(2,J)=M(I2,J)
3590 W(3,J)=M(I3,J)
3600 W(4,J)=M(I4,J)
3610 W(5,J)=25
3620 NEXT J
3630 REM ** EVALUATE THE HAND
3640 C=0
3650 GOSUB 4530
3660 V(Z9,7)=P
3670 IF P>P9 THEN P9=P
3680 NEXT Z9
3690 REM ** FIND ALL HANDS WITH MAX
3700 REM     SCORE (P9)
3710 J=0
3720 FOR I=1 TO 15
3730 IF V(I,7)<>P9 THEN 3760
3740 J=J+1
3750 I(J)=I
3760 NEXT I
3770 IF J>1 THEN 3810
3780 REM ** THIS IS SINGLE BEST HAND
3790 B9=I(1)
3800 RETURN
3810 REM ** NO SINGLE BEST HAND,
3820 REM     SEARCH FOR KEY CARDS
3830 REM ** CHECK FOR FIVES
3840 C9=5
3850 Z=1
3860 GOTO 4080
3870 REM ** CHECK FOR EIGHTS
3880 C9=8
3890 Z=2
3900 GOTO 4080

3910 REM ** CHECK FOR SEVENS
3920 C9=7
3930 Z=3
3940 GOTO 4080
3950 REM ** CHECK FOR JACKS
3960 C9=11
3970 Z=4
3980 GOTO 4080
3990 REM ** CHECK FOR ACES
4000 C9=1
4010 Z=5
4020 GOTO 4080
4030 REM ** RANDOMLY CHOOSE A HAND IF
4040 REM     WE REACH THIS POINT
4050 FOR WQ=1 TO NT:B9=INT(J*RND(1))+1:NEXT WQ
4060 B9=I(B9)
4070 RETURN
4080 REM ** BEST HAND WILL BE THAT
4090 REM     WHICH HAS MOST OF CARD C9
4100 P9=0
4110 FOR I=1 TO 15
4120 J(I)=0
4130 NEXT I
4140 FOR I=1 TO J
4150 FOR K=1 TO 4
4160 L=V(I(I),K)
4170 IF M(L,4)<>C9 THEN 4190
4180 J(I)=J(I)+1
4190 NEXT K
4200 IF J(I)>P9 THEN P9=J(I)
4210 NEXT I
4220 K=0
4230 FOR I=1 TO J
4240 IF J(I)<>P9 THEN 4270
4250 K=K+1
4260 B9=I(I)
4270 NEXT I
4280 IF K<>1 THEN 4300
4290 RETURN
4300 ON Z GOTO 3870,3910,3950,3990,4030
4310 REM **
4320 REM ** GENERATE THE UP CARD
4330 REM **
4340 U=INT(38*RND(1))+14
4350 PRINT
4360 PRINT "The up card is the ";C$(D(U,1))
4370 PRINT
4380 FOR I=1 TO 4
4390 W(5,I)=D(U,I)
4400 NEXT I
4410 T9=W(5,4)
4420 IF W(5,4)<>11 THEN 4510
4430 IF M=0 THEN 4480
4440 PRINT "2 points to me "
4450 S1=S1+2
4460 IF S1>=121 THEN 1420
4470 RETURN
4480 PRINT "2 points to you "
4490 S2=S2+2
4500 IF S2>121 THEN 1460
4510 RETURN
4520 REM **
4530 REM ** SCORE THE 5 CARD HAND
4540 REM **
4550 REM     CHECK FOR A JACK OF SAME
4560 REM     SUIT AS UP CARD, EXCEPT CRIB
4570 P=0
4580 IF C=1 THEN 4650
4590 FOR I=1 TO 4
4600 IF W(I,4)<>11 THEN 4640
4610 IF W(I,3)<>W(5,3) THEN 4640
4620 P=P+1
4630 GOTO 4650
4640 NEXT I
4650 REM ** CHECK FOR A 4 OR 5 CARD
4660 REM     FLUSH
4670 FOR I=1 TO 3
4680 IF W(I,3)<>W(I+1,3) THEN 4790
```

```
4690 NEXT I
4700 REM ** CRIB SCORES ONY FOR A 5
4710 REM     CARD FLUSH
4720 IF C<>0 THEN 4770
4730 P=P+4
4740 IF W(4,3)<>W(5,3) THEN 4790
4750 P=P+1
4760 GOTO 4790
4770 IF W(4,3)<>W(5,3) THEN 4790
4780 P=P+5
4790 REM ** CHECK FOR 2 CARD SUMS OF 15
4800 FOR I=1 TO 4
4810 FOR J=I+1 TO 5
4820 IF W(I,2)+W(J,2)<>15 THEN 4840
4830 P=P+2
4840 NEXT J
4850 NEXT I
4860 REM ** CHECK FOR 3 CARD SUMS OF 15
4870 FOR I=1 TO 3
4880 FOR J=I+1 TO 4
4890 FOR K=J+1 TO 5
4900 IF W(I,2)+W(J,2)+W(K,2)<>15 THEN 4920
4910 P=P+2
4920 NEXT K
4930 NEXT J
4940 NEXT I
4950 REM ** CHECK FOR 4 CARD SUMS OF 15
4960 FOR I=1 TO 2
4970 FOR J=I+1 TO 3
4980 FOR K=J+1 TO 4
4990 FOR L=K+1 TO 5
5000 IF W(I,2)+W(J,2)+W(K,2)+W(L,2)<>15 THEN 5020
5010 P=P+2
5020 NEXT L
5030 NEXT K
5040 NEXT J
5050 NEXT I
5060 REM ** CHECK FOR 5 CARD SUMS OF 15
5070 S=0
5080 FOR I=1 TO 5
5090 S=S+W(I,2)
5100 NEXT I
5110 IF S<>15 THEN 5150
5120 P=P+2
5130 REM ** CHECK FOR PAIRS AND THREE
5140 REM     OR FOUR OF A KIND
5150 FOR I=1 TO 13
5160 J(I)=0
5170 NEXT I
5180 FOR I=1 TO 5
5190 J=W(I,4)
5200 J(J)=J(J)+1
5210 NEXT I
5220 FOR I=1 TO 13
5230 ON J(I)+1 GOTO 5270,5270,5260,5250,5240
5240 P=P+6
5250 P=P+4
5260 P=P+2
5270 NEXT I
5280 REM ** SORT HAND INTO ASCENDING
5290 REM     SEQUENCE
5300 FOR I=1 TO 5
5310 FOR J=1 TO 5
5320 IF W(I,4)<=W(J,4) THEN 5360
5330 K=W(I,4)
5340 W(I,4)=W(J,4)
5350 W(J,4)=K
5360 NEXT J
5370 NEXT I
5380 REM ** CHECK FOR A 5 CARD RUN
5390 D=W(1,4)-Q(I,1)
5400 FOR I=1 TO 11
5410 FOR J=1 TO 5
5420 Q(I,J)=Q(I,J)+D
5430 NEXT J
5440 NEXT I
5450 FOR I=1 TO 11
5460 FOR J=1 TO 5
5470 IF W(J,4)<>Q(I,J) THEN 5520
5480 NEXT J
5490 REM ** A 5 CARD RUN
5500 P=P+Q(I,6)
5510 RETURN
5520 NEXT I
5530 REM ** CHECK FOR A 4 CARD RUN
5540 FOR L=1 TO 2
5550 D=W(L,4)-R(1,1)
5560 FOR I=1 TO 4
5570 FOR J=1 TO 4
5580 R(I,J)=R(I,J)+D
5590 NEXT J
5600 NEXT I
5610 FOR I=1 TO 4
5620 FOR K=1 TO 4
5630 IF W(K+L-1,4)<>R(I,K) THEN 5680
5640 NEXT K
5650 REM ** A 4 CARD RUN
5660 P=P+R(I,5)
5670 RETURN
5680 NEXT I
5690 NEXT L
5700 REM ** CHECK FOR A 3 CARD RUN
5710 FOR L=1 TO 3
5720 D=W(L,4)-S(1)
5730 FOR I=1 TO 3
5740 S(I)=S(I)+D
5750 NEXT I
5760 FOR I=1 TO 3
5770 IF W(L+I-1,4)<>S(I) THEN 5820
5780 NEXT I
5790 REM ** A 3 CARD RUN
5800 P=P+S(4)
5810 RETURN
5820 NEXT L
5830 RETURN
5840 REM **
5850 REM ** SHUFFLE THE DECK
5860 REM **
5870 FOR I=1 TO 52
5880 I(I)=0
5890 NEXT I
5900 FOR I=1 TO 52
5910 J=INT(52*RND(1))+1
5920 IF I(J)<>0 THEN 5910
5930 D(I,1)=J
5940 D(I,3)=INT((J-1)/13)+1
5950 D(I,4)=J-13*INT((J-1)/13)
5960 UY=10:IF D(I,4)<UY THEN UY=D(I,4)
5970 D(I,2)=UY
5980 I(J)=1
5990 NEXT I
6000 RETURN
6010 REM **
6020 REM ** CUT FOR DEAL.
6030 REM **
6040 PRINT "Please cut for deal";
6050 INPUT I
6060 IF I<1 THEN 6080
6070 IF I<53 THEN 6100
6080 PRINT "Enter the card number to cut."
6090 GOTO 6040
6100 IF I<>INT(I) THEN 6080
6110 I1=D(I,1)
6120 PRINT "Your card is the ";C$(I1)
6130 J=INT(52*RND(1))+1
6140 IF J=1 THEN 6130
6150 J1=D(J,1)
6160 PRINT "  My card is the ";C$(J1)
6170 IF D(I,4)<D(J,4) THEN 6240
6180 IF D(J,4)<D(I,4) THEN 6210
6190 PRINT "Cut again"
6200 GOTO 6050
6210 REM ** COMPUTER DEALS
6220 M=0
6230 RETURN
6240 REM ** PLAYER DEALS
```

Cribbage

```
6250 M=1
6260 RETURN
6270 REM **
6280 REM ** DEAL
6290 REM **
6300 IF M=0 THEN 6330
6310 PRINT "You are dealing."
6320 GOTO 6340
6330 PRINT "I am dealing."
6340 M=1-M
6350 Y=1-M
6360 PRINT
6370 PRINT "Your cards are:"
6380 FOR I=1 TO 6
6390 K=2*I-Y
6400 L=2*I-M
6410 FOR J=1 TO 4
6420 REM ** COMPUTER'S HAND
6430 M(I,J)=D(K,J)
6440 REM ** PLAYER'S HAND
6450 Y(I,J)=D(L,J)
```

```
6460 NEXT J
6470 PRINT USING"###";I;
6480 PRINT") ";C$(Y(I,1))
6490 NEXT I
6500 RETURN
6510 DATA 1,2,3,4,5,6,0,1,2,3,5,4,6,0,1,2,3,6,4,5,0
6520 DATA 1,2,4,5,3,6,0,1,2,4,6,3,5,0,1,2,5,6,3,4,0
6530 DATA 1,3,4,5,2,6,0,1,3,4,6,2,5,0,1,3,5,6,2,4,0
6540 DATA 1,4,5,6,2,3,0,2,3,4,5,1,6,0,2,3,4,6,1,5,0
6550 DATA 2,3,5,6,1,4,0,2,4,5,6,1,3,0,3,4,5,6,1,2,0
6560 DATA 1,1,1,2,3,9,1,1,2,2,3,12,1,1,2,3,3,12
6570 DATA 1,1,2,3,4,8,1,2,2,2,3,9,1,2,2,3,3,12
6580 DATA 1,2,2,3,4,8,1,2,3,3,3,9,1,2,3,3,4,8
6590 DATA 1,2,3,4,4,8,1,2,3,4,5,5
6600 DATA 1,1,2,3,6,1,2,2,3,6,1,2,3,3,6,1,2,3,4,4
6610 DATA 1,2,3,3
6620 DATA "1","2","3","4","5","6"
6630 DATA " A"," 2"," 3"," 4"," 5"," 6"," 7"," 8"
6640 DATA " 9","10"," J"," Q"," K"
6650 END
```

```
************** CRIBBAGE ***************

Enter a number from 1 to 500? 485


Please cut for deal? 26
Your card is the  4 of Spades
  My card is the  5 of Clubs
You are dealing.

Your cards are:
   1)   K of Clubs
   2)   2 of Clubs
   3)   5 of Clubs
   4)   4 of Diamonds
   5)   A of Spades
   6) 10 of Spades

Your discards? 2,1

The up card is the  6 of Spades

My card is the  A of Hearts
Sum = 1, Points =  0
Your play? 5
You played the  A of Spades
Sum = 2, Points =  2
My card is the  5 of Hearts
Sum = 7, Points =  0
Your play? 6
You played the 10 of Spades
Sum =17, Points =  0
My card is the 10 of Diamonds
Sum =27, Points =  2
Your play? 4
You played the  4 of Diamonds
Sum =31, Points =  2
My card is the  A of Hearts
Sum = 1, Points =  0
Your play? 3
You played the  5 of Clubs
Sum = 6, Points =  0

You get 1 point for the last card.

I score first
My cards are

  5 of Hearts
  A of Hearts
  9 of Clubs
 10 of Diamonds

  6 points
```

```
How many points? 6
The crib cards are

  J of Hearts
  6 of Clubs
  5 of Hearts
  K of Clubs
How many points? 5

Muggins for 1 points


I have 9 points.
You have 16 points.

I am dealing.

Your cards are:
   1)   A of Clubs
   2) 10 of Spades
   3)   8 of Hearts
   4)   2 of Clubs
   5)   3 of Diamonds
   6)   9 of Diamonds




************** CRIBBAGE ***************

Enter a number from 1 to 500? 259


Please cut for deal? 23
Your card is the  6 of Clubs
  My card is the  5 of Hearts
I am dealing.

Your cards are:
   1)   3 of Clubs
   2)   9 of Diamonds
   3)   9 of Spades
   4)   4 of Hearts
   5)   7 of Spades
   6)   3 of Diamonds

Your discards? 1,2

The up card is the  2 of Spades

Your play? 5
You played the  7 of Spades
Sum = 7, Points =  0
```

8

Cribbage

My card is the 7 of Diamonds
Sum =14, Points = 2
Your play? 3
You played the 9 of Spades
Sum =23, Points = 0
My card is the 6 of Clubs
Sum =29, Points = 0
Your play? 6
That totals more than 31
? 60
My card is the 2 of Clubs
Sum =31, Points = 2
Your play? GO
My card is the 6 of Clubs
Sum = 6, Points = 0

I get one point for the last card.

Your play? 4
You played the 4 of Hearts
Sum = 4, Points = 0
Your play? GO

You get one point for the last card.

Your play? 4
Already played
? 3
Already played
? GO

You get one point for the last card.

Your play? GO

You get one point for the last card.

Your play? GO

You get one point for the last card.

Your play? GO

You get one point for the last card.

Your play? 1
You discarded that card.
? go

You get one point for the last card.

Your play? go

You get one point for the last card.

Your play? 5
Already played
? 6
You played the 3 of Diamonds
Sum = 3, Points = 0

You get 1 point for the last card.

You score first
How many points? 10

Not with that hand
 10

Not with that hand
 5

Not with that hand
 3

Not with that hand
 1

Muggins for 1 points

My cards are

 6 of Clubs
 7 of Diamonds
 2 of Clubs
 9 of Hearts

 8 points

The crib cards are

 3 of Spades
 5 of Clubs
 6 of Clubs
 9 of Diamonds

 2 points

I have 16 points.
You have 9 points.

You are dealing.

Your cards are:
    1)   K of Clubs
    2)   2 of Clubs
    3)   5 of Clubs
    4)   4 of Diamonds
    5)   A of Spades
    6) 10 of Spades

Your discards? 5,2

The up card is the Q of Diamonds

My card is the A of Hearts
Sum = 1, Points = 0
Your play? 1
You played the K of Clubs
Sum =11, Points = 0
My card is the 5 of Hearts
Sum =16, Points = 0
Your play? 4
You played the 4 of Diamonds
Sum =20, Points = 0
My card is the 9 of Clubs
Sum =29, Points = 0
Your play? 6
That totals more than 31
? GO

I get 1 point for the last card.

Your play? 6
You played the 10 of Spades
Sum =10, Points = 0
My card is the 10 of Diamonds
Sum =20, Points = 2
Your play? 3
You played the 5 of Clubs
Sum =25, Points = 0

You get 1 point for the last card.

I score first
My cards are

 5 of Hearts
 A of Hearts
 9 of Clubs
10 of Diamonds

 6 points

How many points? 3

Cribbage

Muggins for 3 points

The crib cards are

  J of Hearts
  6 of Clubs
  9 of Clubs
  2 of Clubs
How many points? 3

Not with that hand
 1

Muggins for 1 points

I have 29 points.
You have 14 points.

*************** CRIBBAGE ***************

Enter a number from 1 to 500? 68

Please cut for deal? 36
Your card is the 9 of Clubs
  My card is the K of Diamonds
You are dealing.

Your cards are:
  1) 4 of Spades
  2) 6 of Clubs
  3) 5 of Clubs
  4) 5 of Hearts
  5) 3 of Clubs
  6) 5 of Spades

Your discards? 2,3

The up card is the 4 of Diamonds

My card is the 7 of Spades
Sum = 7, Points = 0
Your play? 1
You played the 4 of Spades
Sum =11, Points = 0
My card is the 7 of Hearts
Sum =18, Points = 0
Your play? 6
You played the 5 of Spades
Sum =23, Points = 0
My card is the 8 of Clubs
Sum =31, Points = 2
Your play? GO
My card is the 7 of Spades
Sum = 7, Points = 0

I get one point for the last card.

Your play? 5
You played the 3 of Clubs
Sum = 3, Points = 0
Your play? 4
You played the 5 of Hearts
Sum = 8, Points = 0

You get 1 point for the last card.

I score first
My cards are

7 of Spades
7 of Hearts
8 of Clubs
5 of Diamonds

 6 points

How many points? 2

Muggins for 2 points

The crib cards are

  K of Clubs
  6 of Spades
  7 of Hearts
  5 of Clubs
How many points? 4

I have 11 points.
You have 7 points.

I am dealing.

Your cards are:
  1) Q of Clubs
  2) 5 of Spades
  3) 3 of Clubs
  4) K of Spades
  5) K of Diamonds
  6) 3 of Diamonds

Your discards? 3,4

The up card is the 10 of Spades

Your play? 4
You discarded that card.
? 5
You played the K of Diamonds
Sum =10, Points = 0
My card is the J of Spades
Sum =20, Points = 0
Your play? 2
You played the 5 of Spades
Sum =25, Points = 0
Go
Your play? 6
You played the 3 of Diamonds
Sum =28, Points = 0
Your play? 3
You discarded that card.
? 2
Already played
? 1
That totals more than 31
? GO

I'll give you 1 point for last card.

My card is the J of Spades
Sum =10, Points = 0

Dukedom

Hammurabi by Rick Merrill and David Ahl (1969) is the original computerized land management game. It was expanded by Lee Schneider and Todd Voros as **Kingdom** (1974) and then by Vince Talbot as **Dukedom** (1976). It was further revised by Jamie Hanrahan and finally converted to Microsoft Basic by Richard Kaapke. This final version first appeared in *Creative Computing*, February 1980.

You are one of several Dukes chosen by the High King to help run the Kingdom. Your Duchy is not in the best of shape, and your job is to build up its population, land holdings, and grain reserves. Your secret ambition is to become powerful enough to overthrow the High King.

The game cycles on an annual basis, and it is now fall and the harvest has just been completed. Each year at this time the computer will display the current population, land and grain totals, followed by a detailed report of the previous year's events. Note that land and grain are measured in metric units hectares (HA.) and hectoliters (HL.), respectively.

Each year you will have to make the following decisions:

Grain for Food

You must decide how much grain to feed the peasants. 14 HL. of grain will just adequately feed one peasant; 13 will cause some hunger and decrease the peasants' fighting ability, and 12 or fewer will cause

some starvation. The peasants will complain if you try to starve then excessively and they know that you are holding back grain. If you feed the peasants more than 14 HL. each (up to a maxinum of 18) they will appreciate the boom and fight better in any war the following summer. A long term memory keeps track of the peasants' cumulative attitude (it fades slowly with time) and if you create sufficient bad will (by underfeeding them, for instance) they will depose you. You may enter the quantity of grain for the peasants in two ways: Numbers less than 100 are interpreted as hectoliters-per-peasant, while an entry of 100 or more represents the total amount for the entire population.

Land to Buy

Enter the number of hectares of land you want to buy. The prices offered vary from about 4 hectoliters/hectare to about 30, depending primarily on last year's crop yield. If you don't want to buy any land, enter 0. You will then be given the option of selling your land at a price one unit lower than the buying price. Enter the number of hectares you want to sell, or enter 0 if you don't want to sell any.

Land to Plant

Enter the number of hectares you wish to plant. Each hectare planted will require 2 hectoliters of grain to seed it. Also, remember that each peasant can plant and care for no more than 4 hectares. There is no fertilizer and no alternate crop, so land used many years in a row becomes depleted. The annual report lists the number of hectares you have of each of six classes from 100% yield to 0%. In any given year, land used in any class moves 1 step closer to being totally depleted while unused land moves two steps closer to fallow (100%). The best quality land will always be planted first. The yield for fallow land is calculated each year at random (variances in the weather) and ranges from 4 to 13 hectoliters of grain harvested for each hectare planted. The actual yield obtained will be the average generated by the various qualities of land used.

Special Operating Instructions

When a response is prompted by a "?", a Y or N may be given for Yes or No, respectively. A simple return will be assumed to be a "N" response.

When a response is prompted by a "*", a non-negative integer is required. Any fraction will be trimmed from input, and a simple return will be interpreted as an entry of 0.

General Information

Running totals are maintained by the computer. All additions and subtractions are made at once and further transactions are limited by the current balance. No credit is allowed (with one exception).

One hectare of land equals about 2.5 acres. One hectoliter of grain equals about 2.8 bushels.

It is (usually) necessary to gamble occasionally to win. Most gambles consist of buying land you can't afford at very low prices and gambling that yield will be high and there won't be a war. If the gamble fails, you will spend the next ten years recovering (if you survive, that is).

Food Allocation

By overfeeding the peasants when possible, you can build up good will among the population. This may save your life as it can counteract unavoidable resentment in the future (during times of famine, for instance). Judge Lynch never sleeps!

Land Trading

When you buy land you always receive 60% quality. When you sell land the machine sells your 60% land until it's used up, then the 80% quality, and finally the 100% if you sell that much. You can never sell 40% (or poorer) quality land; no buyers will accept it.

There is another limit on land sales: You cannot sell more than 4000 HL. worth in any one year. That's all the grain available to pay you with.

Crop Hazards

Sometimes the rats get into the granary and eat up to 10% or so of your reserve grain. Rats never eat field grain—field grain is eaten by the seven year locusts. They eat half of all your crop in the years that they appear The yield printed in these years already includes locust losses.

The King's Peasant Levy

Occasionally rats will eat so much of the High King's grain that some of his workers starve to death. When this happens, the King will require some peasants from each of his Dukes as replacements. You may supply them as requested or pay an alternate amount of grain.

Wars

Neighboring Dukes may attack you, hoping to obtain some land. This is more portable in years of poor crop yield. It is no secret, and you can attack first if you wish. This means that you and your peasants go over there some night and burn a few huts and generally make a great din. If your attack is impressive, the nearby Duke may cancel his war plans. This depends on the size of your attack force and the size of his current defense force. You will certainly lose some peasants in such an attack.

If your first attack fails, or if you do not elect to attack first, the war will occur. You had better hire some mercenaries since your enemy is doing the same. A mercenary is worth about 8 peasants in fighting power. Mercenaries cost 40 HL. each, and there is a maximum of 75 mercenaries available to you. If your fighting power (mercenaries & peasants) exceeds your enemy's, you win; otherwise he wins. The winner acquires land from the loser in ratio to the size of the win. How much you fed the peasants last fall is now important and may occasionally make the difference between a win and a loss.

The winner also picks up some grain from the captured land and is able to harvest the captured land along with his own (at the same yield as his original land). The land acquired (or lost) will appear in next year's land quality table evenly distributed between the 100%, 80%, and 60% categories.

Since the mercenaries are horse mounted and the peasants are on foot, the mercenaries attack first. Thus, a large number of mercenaries will keep down your peasant losses whether you win or lose. The mercenaries must be paid after the battle. You can use granary reserves and the actual grain captured from acquired land (the one exception to the no-credit rule), but not the anticipated harvest (the mercenaries want their pay NOW).

If you can't pay all the mercenaries, they will attack your peasants, killing them and collecting grain from their huts until fully paid. Since the peasants don't have much grain left this late in the season, even a small default may cost you a lot of peasants. Incidentally, if the mercenaries do turn on the peasants, they also rape every female in the Duchy, making next year's birth rate very high. (We ignore the fact that the women deliver only a few months later—these are no ordinary mercenaries.) All peasant deaths from war cause resentment to build up against you. Attack by your own mercenaries is quite heavily resented.

Plagues and Poxes

The plague will kill off a third of the population, but in so doing it confers a 13-year immunity on the survivors. Therefore the plague cannot occur again for at least 13 years.

The pox is less deadly; it kills 10% or fewer peasants but confers no immunity. It can occur several years in a row.

Taxes and Expenses

The High King charges a tax of ½ HL. of grain for each HA. of land you possess (after war gains or losses). You had better be able to pay.

After the grain is harvested it must be milled. The castle granary can mill a maximum of 4000 HL. during the year. Additional harvest must be sent to the village miller at a charge of 10% of the amount milled. This amount is added to the castle overhead, which is fixed at 120 HL. per year.

Births and Deaths

During the year, some natural deaths and numerous births have occurred. Both are lumped together as if they occur just after the fall harvest.

The computer now prints out the results for the year, and you start over again with the peasant's food decision.

Winning the Game

Through astute land management, profitable real-estate trading, winning a few wars, and lots of luck, you may be able to build up your Duchy. If instead you let it decline, the High King may take it away

from you and select a new manager. An unemployed Duke can find employment as a mercenary in somebody else's game.

Prosperity brings its risks. If you get too prosperous, the High King may become worried and begin to subsidize wars against you. These subsidies get larger as the game progresses.

If you should persevere, you may eventually beat some Duke so badly that you succeed in taking over his entire Duchy. In addition to the more 400 HA. of land you will obtain, you get all of his surviving peasants (your war casualties will be positive) and the remaining contents of his granary. This poses a real threat to the crown, and the High King will begin planning a direct attack against you. At the beginning of the following year the King will demand twice the usual tax. You may pay it and continue the game as usual, or you may refuse. You will never be rid of the double tax once it starts unless you refuse to pay it. This constitutes defiance of your Liege Lord, and the King has his excuse for attacking you directly. The rest of the year will go as usual except that there will be no tax at all (no peasant levies either) and there will be no war threats (nobody dares).

The following year the King will attack just before planting time. You will have to hire as many foreign mercenaries as possible at 100 HL. each, grain in advance (the loser won't be in any position to pay). The program will automatically hire as many mercenaries as you can afford at the time. There is no limit to the number of foreign mercenaries you can hire except your current grain holdings. Each mercenary has as much fighting power as 8 peasants. If your total fighting strength is greater than the King's, you win. 250 to 300 mercenaries ought to be enough, depending on how many peasants you have.

Either way, the game is over. Good Luck!

Historical Waiver

No historical accuracy is implied in any way by this game. Except for the grain yields and planting requirements, the game is almost pure fiction. There were few mercenaries, Dukes did not often fight each other nor readily buy and sell land, the church was a power to be feared. The metric system had not yet been developed and the seven year locusts were not so reliable.

A Duke would have as his lord not a King but a Count or Earl and would have under him Barons or Marquises. Their various nobles were the fighting force of the Kingdom (peasants did not fight). Taxes were paid not in grain but in periods of military service. (Yes, the National Guard was a medieval invention—at the latest.)

```
10 REM        DUKEDOM-MICROSOFT BASIC
20 REM
30 Q1%=1
40 CLS:PRINT
50 CLEAR 400
60 DEF FNR%(Q1%,Q2%)=RND(1)*(1+Q2%-Q1%)+Q1%
70 DEF FNX%(Q1%)=FNR%(-F3%,F3%)+ R(Q1%)
80 GOTO 440:' skip subroutine def
90 REM
100 REM       SUBPROGRAM DEFINITIONS
110 REM
120 DIM P(8),L(3),G(10),S(6),U(6),R(8),P$(8),L$(8),G$(10)
130 REM PARTIALLY GAUSSIAN RANDOM #
140 Q3%=FNR%(Q1%,Q2%)
150 Q3%=FNR%(Q1%,Q2%)
160 IF FNR%(Q1%,Q2%)>5 THEN G0%=(Q3%+FNR%(Q1%,Q2%))/2 ELSE G0%=Q3%
170 RETURN
180 REM
190 REM      READ YES/NO
200 REM
210 LINE INPUT V$:V$=LEFT$(V$,1)
220 IF LEN(V$)=0 THEN V$="N" ELSE IF ASC(V$) > 95 THEN V$=CHR$(ASC(V$)-32)
230 IF V$="Y" OR V$= "N" THEN RETURN ELSE PRINT "Please anser yes or no:";
240 GOTO 210
250 REM
260 REM     INPUT NUMERIC RESPONSE
270 REM
280 LINE INPUT V$:V=INT(VAL(V$))
290 IF V>= 0 THEN RETURN ELSE PRINT "Pleas enter a non-negative #:";
300 GOTO 280
310 REM
320 REM     COMMON MESSAGES
330 REM
340 PRINT "But you don't have enough grain":PRINT"You have"G"HL. of grain left,"
350 IF X1>=4 THEN PRINT "Enough to buy"INT(G/X1)"HA. of land":RETURN
360 PRINT "Enough to plant"INT(G/2) "HA. of land":RETURN
370 PRINT "But you don't have enough land"
380 PRINT "You only have"H"HA. of land left":RETURN
390 PRINT "But you don't have enough peasants"
400 PRINT "Your peasants can only plant"4*P"HA. of land":RETURN
410 REM
420 REM     INTRO TO THE GAME
430 REM
440 PRINT "D U K E D O M":PRINT:PRINT " SV Microsoft Basic Version"
450 PRINT " Converted By":PRINT "        Bob Anderson"
460 F3%=2:M=1.95:REM ONCE ONLY INIT
470 PRINT "Do you want to skip detailed reports ?"::GOSUB 210:R$=V$
480 REM
490 REM     START NEW GAME
500 REM
510 READ Y%,C1,U1,U2,K%,D,P,L,G
520 FOR I%=1 TO 8:READ P(I%):NEXT
530 FOR I%=1 TO 3:READ L(I%):NEXT
540 FOR I%=1 TO 10:READ G(I%):NEXT
550 FOR I%=1 TO 6:READ S(I%):NEXT
560 FOR I%=1 TO 8:READ P$(I%):NEXT
570 FOR I%=1 TO 3:READ L$(I%):NEXT
580 FOR I%=1 TO 10:READ G$(I%):NEXT
590 RESTORE
600 DATA 0,3.95,0,0,0,0,100,600,4177,96,0,0,0,0,0
610 DATA -4,8,600,0,0,5193,-1344,0,-768,0,0,0,1516,-120,-300,216,200,184,0,0,0
620 REM
630 REM     INIT RANDOM BASE TABLE
640 REM
650 Q1%=4:Q2%=7:GOSUB 140:R(1)=G0%:Q2%=8:GOSUB 140:R(3)=G0%:Q2%=6:GOSUB 140
660 R(3)=G0%:Q1%=3:GOSUB 140:R(4)=G0%:Q1%=5:GOSUB 140
670 R(5)=G0%:Q1%=3:Q2%=6:GOSUB 140:R(6)=G0%
680 Q2%=8:GOSUB 140:R(7)=G0%:Q1%=1:GOSUB 140:R(8)=G0%
690 REM
700 REM     DISPLAY LAST YEARS RESULTS
710 REM
720 PRINT:PRINT:PRINT "Year"Y%"Peasants"P"Land"L"Grain"G :PRINT
730 IF R$="Y" THEN 830
740 FOR J1%=1 TO 8:IF P(J1%)<>0 OR J1%=1 THEN PRINT P$(J1%);TAB(25);P(J1%)
750 NEXT J1%:PRINT "Peasants at end";TAB(25);P:PRINT
760 FOR J1%=1 TO 3:IF L(J1%)<>0 OR J1%=1 THEN PRINT L$(J1%);TAB(25);L(J1%)
770 NEXT J1%:PRINT "Land at end of year";TAB(25);L:PRINT
780 PRINT "100% 80%  60%  40%   20%  Depl":PRINT USING "#####";S(1);
```

```
790 FOR J1%=2 TO 6:PRINT USING "#####";S(J1%);:NEXT J1%:PRINT:PRINT
800 FOR J1%=1 TO 10:IF G(J1%)<>0 OR J1%=1 THEN PRINT G$(J1%);TAB(25);G(J1%)
810 NEXT J1%:PRINT "Grain at end of year";TAB(25);G
820 IF Y%<=0 THEN PRINT "(Severe crop damage due to seven":PRINT" year locusts)"
830 PRINT:PRINT:Y%=Y%+1
840 FOR I%=1 TO 8:P(I%)=0:NEXT:FOR I%=1 TO 3:L(I%)=0:NEXT
850 FOR I%=1 TO 10 :G(I%)=0:NEXT:P(1)=P:L(1)=L:G(1)=G
860 REM
870 REM    TEST FOR END OF GAME
880 REM
890 IF P>= 33 THEN 910 ELSE PRINT "You have so few peasants left that"
900 PRINT"the High King has abolished your Ducal":PRINT"right":GOTO 2430
910 IF L>= 199 THEN 920 ELSE PRINT "You have so little land left that":GOTO 930
920 IF U1>88 OR U2>99 THEN 930 ELSE IF G>=429 THEN 950
930 PRINT "The peasants tired of war and stavation"
940 PRINT"You are deposed":PRINT:GOTO 2430
950 IF Y%> 45 AND K=0 THEN PRINT "You have reached the age of retiremant":GOTO 2430
960 U1=0:IF K%>0 THEN PRINT "The King demands twice the royal tax in" ELSE GOTO 1020
970 PRINT"THE HOPE TO PREVOKE WAR. WILL YOU PAY";: GOSUB 210
980 K%=2:IF V$="N" THEN K%=-1
990 REM
1000 REM    FOOD FOR PEASANTS
1010 REM
1020 PRINT "Grain for food =";:GOSUB 280 :V=-V*(V>=100)-V*P*(V<100)
1030 IF V>G THEN GOSUB 340:GOTO 1020
1040 IF V/P<11 AND V<>G THEN PRINT "The peasants demonstrate before the":PRINT "castle"
1050 G(2)=-V:G=G+G(2)
1060 X1=V/P
1070 IF X1<13 THEN PRINT "Some peasants have starved":P(2)=-INT(P-V/13):P=P+P(2)
1080 X1=X1-14:X1=-X1*(X1<=4)-4*(X1>4):U1=U1-3*P(2)-2*X1
1090 IF U>88 THEN 930 ELSE IF P<33 THEN 890
1100 REM
1110 REM    LAND BUY/SELL
1120 REM
1130 C=C1:X1=INT(2*C+FNX%(1)-5):X1=-X1*(X1>=4)-4*(X1<4)
1140 PRINT "Land to buy at"X1"HL./HA. = ";:GOSUB 280:G(3)=-V*X1
1150 IF -G(3) > G THEN GOSUB 340:GOTO 1140
1160 L(2)=V:S(3)=S(3)+V:IF V>0 THEN 1270 ELSE X2=S(1)+S(2)+S(3)
1170 FOR J1%=1 TO 3:X1=X1-1:PRINT "Land to sell at"X1"HL./HA. = ";:GOSUB 240
1180 IF V>X2 THEN PRINT "But you only have"X2"HA. of good land":GOTO 1210
1190 G(3)=V*X1:IF G(3)<= 4000 THEN 1220
1200 PRINT "No buyers have that much grain try less"
1210 NEXT J1%:PRINT "Buyers have lost inerest":V=0:G(3)=0
1220 L(2)=-V
1230 FOR J1%=3 TO 1 STEP -1:IF V<=S(J1%) THEN 1260
1240 V=V-S(J1%):S(J1%)=0:NEXT J1%
1250 PRINT "Land selling loop error":STOP
1260 S(J1%)=S(J1%)-V
1270 L=L+L(2):IF L<10 THEN 910
1280 IF L(2)<0 AND X1<4 THEN 1290 ELSE GOTO 1310
1290 G(3)=INT(G(3)/2):PRINT "The High King appropiates half"
1300 PRINT"of your earnings as punishment":PRINT"for selling at such a low price"
1310 G=G+G(3)
1320 REM
1330 REM    WAR WITH THE KING
1340 REM
1350 IF K%<> -2 THEN 1460
1360 PRINT "The King's army is about to attack"
1370 PRINT"your duchy":X1=INT(G/100):PRINT"at 100 HL. each (pay in advance)"
1380 PRINT "You have hired"X1"foreign mercinaries":IF B*X1+P>2399 THEN 1400
1390 PRINT "Your head is placed atop of the":PRINT "castle gate.":GOTO 2430
1400 PRINT "Wipe the blood from the crown - you"
1410 PRINT"are High King! A near by monarchy"
1420 PRINT"THREATENS WAR; HOW MANY ........":PRINT:PRINT:PRINT:END
1430 REM
1440 REM    GRAIN PRODUCTION
1450 REM
1460 PRINT "Land to be planted = ";:GOSUB 280:IF V>L THEN GOSUB 370:GOTO 1460
1470 G(4)=-2*V:IF -G(4) > G THEN GOSUB 340:GOTO 1460
1480 G(8)=V:G=G+G(4)
1490 FOR I%=1 TO 6:U(I%)=0:NEXT
1500 FOR J1%=1 TO 6:IF V<=S(J1%) THEN 1530
1510 V=V-S(J1%):U(J1%)=S(J1%):S(J1%)=0:NEXT J1%
1520 PRINT "LAND TABLE ERROR":STOP
1530 U(J1%)=V:S(J1%)=S(J1%)-V:S(1)=S(1)+S(2):S(2)=0
1540 FOR J1%=3 TO 6:S(J1%-2)=S(J1%-2)+S(J1%):S(J1%)=0:NEXT J1%
1550 FOR J1%=1 TO 5:S(J1%+1)=S(J1%+1)+U(J1%):NEXT J1%:S(6)=S(6)+U(6)
1560 REM
```

```
1570 REM    CROP YEILD AND LOSS
1580 REM
1590 C=FNX%(2)+9:IF INT (Y%/7)*7=Y% THEN PRINT "Seven year locusts":C=INT(C*.65)
1600 X1=0
1610 FOR J1%=1 TO 5:X1=X1+U(J1%)*(1.2-.2*J1%):NEXT J1%:IF G(8)=0 THEN C1=0:C=0:GOTO 1630
1620 C1=INT((C*(X1/G(8)))*100)/100:C=C1
1630 PRINT "Yield ="C"HL./HA.":X1=FNX%(3)+3:IF X1 < 9 THEN 1750
1640 G(5)=-INT((X1*G)/83):G=G+G(5)
1650 PRINT "Rats infest the gainery":IF P < 67 OR K%=-1 THEN 1750
1660 X1=FNX%(4):IF X1> P/30 THEN 1750
1670 PRINT "The king requires"X1"peasants for":PRINT"his estate and mines.Will you supply"
1680 PRINT"them (Y)es or pay"X1*100"HL.of"
1690 PRINT"grain instead (N)o ? ";:GOSUB 210
1700 IF V$="N" THEN G(10)=-100*X1:G=G+G(10):GOTO 1750
1710 P(3)=-X1:P=P+P(3)
1720 REM
1730 REM    WAR
1740 REM
1750 IF K%<>-1 THEN 1780
1760 PRINT "The High King calls for peasant levies"
1770 PRINT"and hires many foreign mercenaries":K%=-2:GOTO 2180
1780 X1=INT(11-1.5*C):X1=-X1*(X1>=2)-2*(X1<2)
1790 IF K%<>0 OR P<=109 OR 17*(L-400)+G<= 10600 THEN 1820
1800 PRINT "The High King grows uneasy and may"
1810 PRINT "be subsidizing wars against you": X1=X1 +2:X2=Y%+5:GOTO 1830
1820 X2=0
1830 X3=FNX%(5):IF X3>X1 THEN 2180
1840 PRINT "A near by Duke threatens war; ";:X2=INT(X2+85+18*FNX%(6))
1850 X4 = 1.2-U1/16:X5=INT(P*X4)+13:PRINT "Will you attack first ? ";:GOSUB 210
1860 IF V$="Y" THEN 1920
1870 IF X2>=X5 THEN 1890 ELSE PRINT "Peace negotiations successful"
1880 P(4)=-X1-1:X2=0:GOTO 1910
1890 PRINT "First strike failed - you need"
1900 PRINT"professionals":P(4)=-X3-X1-2:X2=X2+3+P(4)
1910 P=P+P(4):IF X2<1 THEN U1=U1-2*P(4)-3*P(5):GOTO 2180
1920 PRINT "How many mercenaries will you hire":PRINT"at 40 HL. each = ";:GOSUB 280:IF V>75 THEN PRINT
     "There are only 75 available for hire":GOTO 1920
1930 X2=INT(X2*M):X5=INT (P*X4)+7*V+13:X6=X2-4*V-INT(.25*X5)
1940 X2=X5-X2:L(3)=INT(.8*X2)
1950 IF -L(3)<=.67*L THEN 1970
1960 PRINT "You have been over run and have lost":PRINT"you entire Dukedom":GOTO 1390
1970 X1=L(3)
1980 FOR J1%=1 TO 3:X3=INT(X1/(4-J1%)):IF -X3<=S(J1%) THEN X5=X3 ELSE X5=-S(J1%)
1990 S(J1%)=S(J1%)+X5:X1=X1-X5:NEXT J1%
2000 IF L(3)<399 THEN 2050
2010 PRINT "You have overrun the enemy and annexed":PRINT"his entire Dukedom"
2020 G(7)=3513:G=G+G(7):X6=-47:X4=.55:IF K%>0 THEN 2090
2030 K%=1:PRINT "The King fears for his throne and"
2040 PRINT"may be planning direct action": GOTO 2090
2050 IF X2<1 THEN 2070
2060 PRINT "You have won the war":X4=.67:G(7)=INT(1.7*L(3)):G=G+G(7):GOTO 2080
2070 PRINT "You have lost the war":X4=G(8)/L
2080 IF X6<=9 THEN X6=0 ELSE X6=INT(X6/10)
2090 X6=-X6*(X6<=P)-P*(X6>P):P(4)=P(4)-X6:P=P-X6:G(8)=G(8)+INT(X4*L(3)):X6=40*V
2100 IF X6<=G THEN G(6) = -X6:GOTO 2130
2110  G(6)=-G:P(5)=-INT((X6-G)/7)-1
2120 PRINT "There isn't enough grain to pay the":PRINT"mercenaries"
2130 G=G+G(6):P(5)=-P(5)*(-P(5)<=P)+P*(-P(5)>P)
2140 P=P+P(5):L=L+L(3):U1=U1-2*P(4)-3*P(5)
2150 REM
2160 REM    PLAGUE,BIRTH,DEATH
2170 REM
2180 X1=FNX%(8)+1:IF X1>3 THEN 2240
2190 IF X1<>1 THEN 2230
2200 IF D>0 THEN 2240
2210 PRINT "The BLACK PLAGUE has struck the area":D=13:X2=3
2220 P(6)= -INT(P/X2):P=P+P(6):GOTO 2240
2230 PRINT "A POX EPIDEMIC has broken out": X2=X1*5:P(6)=-INT(P/X2):P=P+P(6)
2240 X1=FNX%(8)+4:X1=-X1*(P(5)=0)-4.5*(P(5)<>0)
2250 P(8)=INT(P/X1):P(7)=INT(.3-P/22):P=P+(7)+P(8):D=D-1
2260 G(8)=INT(C*G(8)):G=G+G(8):X1=G(8)-4000
2270 G(9)=-G(9)*(X1<=0)+INT(.1*X1)*(X1>0):G(9)=G(9)-120:G=G+G(9)
2280 IF K%<0 THEN 2360 ELSE X1=-INT(L/2)
2290 X1=-X1*(K%<2) -2*X1*(K%>=2)
2300 IF -X1<=G THEN 2320
2310 PRINT "You have insufficient grain to pay":PRINT"the royal tax":GOTO 2430
2320 G(10)=G(10)+X1::G=G+X1
2330 REM
```

Dukedom

```
2340 REM   UPDATE COUNTER AND CONTINUE
2350 REM
2360 U2=INT(U2*.85)+U1:GOTO 720
2370 DATA "Peasants at start","Starvations","King's levy","War casualties"
2380 DATA "Looting victims","Disease victims","Natural deaths","Births"
2390 DATA "Land at start","Bought/sold","Fruits of war"
2400 DATA "Grain at start","Used for food"
2410 DATA "Land deals","Seeding","Rat losses","Mercenary hire"
2420 DATA "Fruits of war","Crop yield","Castle expense","Royal tax"
2430 PRINT "Do you wish to play again ? ";:GOSUB 210:IF V$="Y"THEN 510
```

```
D U K E D O M

 SV Microsoft Basic Version
 Converted By
      Bob Anderson
Do you want to skip detailed reports ?


Year 0 Peasants 100 Land 600 Grain 4177

Peasants at start          96
Natural deaths             -4
Births                      8
Peasants at end           100

Land at start             600
Land at end of year       600

100%  80%  60%  40%  20%  Depl
 216  200  184    0    0    0

Grain at start           5193
Used for food           -1344
Seeding                  -768
Crop yield               1516
Castle expense           -120
Royal tax                -300
Grain at end of year     4177
(Severe crop damage due to seven
 year locusts)


Grain for food =12
Some peasants have starved
Land to buy at 7 HL./HA. = 200
Land to be planted = 400
Yield = 9.08 HL./HA.


Year 1 Peasants 113 Land 800 Grain 3889

Peasants at start         100
Starvations                -7
Natural deaths             -4
Births                     13
Peasants at end           113

Land at start             600
Bought/sold               200
Land at end of year       800

100%  80%  60%  40%  20%  Depl
 400  216  184    0    0    0

Grain at start           4177
Used for food           -1200
Land deals              -1400
Seeding                  -800
Crop yield               3632
Castle expense           -120
Royal tax                -400
Grain at end of year     3889
```

```
Grain for food =12
Some peasants have starved
Land to buy at 18 HL./HA. =
Land to sell at 17 HL./HA. =
Land to be planted = 400
Yield = 11 HL./HA.
Rats infest the gainery
The king requires 3 peasants for
his estate and mines.Will you supply
them (Y)es or pay 300 HL.of
grain instead (N)o ? y
A POX EPIDEMIC has broken out


Year 2 Peasants 119 Land 800 Grain 5386

Peasants at start         113
Starvations                -8
King's levy                -3
Disease victims            -6
Natural deaths             -5
Births                     16
Peasants at end           119

Land at start             800
Land at end of year       800

100%  80%  60%  40%  20%  Depl
 400  400    0    0    0    0

Grain at start           3889
Used for food           -1356
Seeding                  -800
Rat losses               -187
Crop yield               4400
Castle expense           -160
Royal tax                -400
Grain at end of year     5386


Grain for food =12
Some peasants have starved
Land to buy at 21 HL./HA. = 50
Land to be planted = 400
Yield = 9 HL./HA.
Rats infest the gainery


Year 3 Peasants 132 Land 850 Grain 4910

Peasants at start         119
Starvations                -9
Natural deaths             -5
Births                     15
Peasants at end           132

Land at start             800
Bought/sold                50
Land at end of year       850

100%  80%  60%  40%  20%  Depl
 450  400    0    0    0    0
```

```
Grain at start          5386
Used for food          -1428
Land deals             -1050
Seeding                 -800
Rat losses             -253
Crop yield             3600
Castle expense         -120
Royal tax              -425
Grain at end of year   4910


Grain for food =13
Land to buy at 20 HL./HA. =
Land to sell at 19 HL./HA. =
Land to be planted = 450
Yield = 9 HL./HA.



Year 4 Peasants 153 Land 850 Grain 5794

Peasants at start       132
Natural deaths           -6
Births                   14
Peasants at end         153

Land at start           850
Land at end of year     850

100%  80%  60%  40%  20%  Depl
 400  450    0    0    0     0

Grain at start          4910
Used for food          -1716
Seeding                 -900
Crop yield             4050
Castle expense         -125
Royal tax              -425
Grain at end of year   5794


Grain for food =13
Land to buy at 17 HL./HA. = 50
Land to be planted = 400
Yield = 11 HL./HA.
Rats infest the gainery
The king requires 5 peasants for
his estate and mines.Will you supply
them (Y)es or pay 500 HL.of
grain instead (N)o ? y




Year 5 Peasants 171 Land 900 Grain 5712

Peasants at start       153
King's levy              -5
Natural deaths           -7
Births                   16
Peasants at end         171

Land at start           850
Bought/sold              50
Land at end of year     900

100%  80%  60%  40%  20%  Depl
 500  400    0    0    0     0

Grain at start          5794
Used for food          -1989
Land deals             -850
Seeding                 -800
Rat losses             -233
Crop yield             4400
Castle expense         -160
Royal tax              -450
Grain at end of year   5712
```

```
Grain for food =13
Land to buy at 21 HL./HA. = 50
Land to be planted = 500
Yield = 9 HL./HA.
Rats infest the gainery
The king requires 4 peasants for
his estate and mines.Will you supply
them (Y)es or pay 400 HL.of
grain instead (N)o ? y
The High King grows uneasy and may
be subsidizing wars against you




Year 6 Peasants 197 Land 950 Grain 5138

Peasants at start       171
King's levy              -4
Natural deaths           -8
Births                   23
Peasants at end         197

Land at start           900
Bought/sold              50
Land at end of year     950

100%  80%  60%  40%  20%  Depl
 450  500    0    0    0     0

Grain at start          5712
Used for food          -2223
Land deals             -1050
Seeding                -1000
Rat losses             -156
Crop yield             4500
Castle expense         -170
Royal tax              -475
Grain at end of year   5138


Grain for food =12
Some peasants have starved




Land to buy at 18 HL./HA. =
Land to sell at 17 HL./HA. =
Land to be planted = 550
Seven year locusts
Yield = 6.74 HL./HA.
Rats infest the gainery
The king requires 3 peasants for
his estate and mines.Will you supply
them (Y)es or pay 300 HL.of
grain instead (N)o ? y
The High King grows uneasy and may
be subsidizing wars against you




Year 7 Peasants 205 Land 950 Grain 4605

Peasants at start       197
Starvations             -15
King's levy              -3
Natural deaths           -8
Births                   19
Peasants at end         205

Land at start           950
Land at end of year     950

100%  80%  60%  40%  20%  Depl
 400  450  100    0    0     0
```

Dukedom

```
Grain at start          5138
Used for food          -2364
Seeding                -1100
Rat losses              -181
Crop yield              3707
Castle expense          -120
Royal tax               -475
Grain at end of year    4605


Grain for food =12
Some peasants have starved
Land to buy at 12 HL./HA. =
Land to sell at 11 HL./HA. =
Land to be planted = 450
Yield = 7.82 HL./HA.
Rats infest the gainery
The king requires 3 peasants for
his estate and mines.Will you supply
them (Y)es or pay 300 HL.of
grain instead (N)o ? y
```

```
Year 8 Peasants 220 Land 950 Grain 4019

Peasants at start         205
Starvations               -15
King's levy                -3
Natural deaths             -9
Births                     26
Peasants at end           220

Land at start             950
Land at end of year       950

100%  80%  60%  40%  20%  Depl
 500  400   50    0    0    0

Grain at start           4605
Used for food           -2460
Seeding                  -900
Rat losses               -150
Crop yield               3519
Castle expense           -120
Royal tax                -475
Grain at end of year     4019


The peasants tire of war and stavation
You are deposed

Do you wish to play again ? n
```

Eliza

Eliza was originally written by Joseph Weizenbaum in LISP at MIT. The first version in Basic was written by Jeff Shrager in 1973 and converted to MITS 8K Basic (later to become Microsoft Basic) by Steve North in 1977. It originally appeared in *Creative Computing*, July/August 1977.

Introduction

Eliza is a program which accepts natural English as input and carries on a reasonably coherent conversation based on the non-directive psychoanalytic techniques of Carl Rogers. You will have to forgive Eliza for her awkward English. You will find it is best not to use punctuation (especially commas and contractions) in your input and keep each line of input to one main idea. Since Eliza is a non-directive therapist, you will have to carry the conversation; nevertheless, that can lead some mighty interesting results. You may end your conversation by typing in "SHUT UP" (or just "SHUT").

How It Works

In order to do what it does, Eliza must: (1) get a string from the user and prepare it for further processing; (2) find the keywords in the input string; (3) if a

keyword is found, take the part of the string following the keyword and "translate" all the personal pronouns and verbs ("I" becomes "YOU", "ARE" becomes "AM", etc.); (4) finally, look up an appropriate reply based on the keyword which was found, print it and, if necessary, the "translated" string. ELIZA uses four types of program data to accomplish this:

(1) 36 keywords, such as "I AM", "WHY DONT YOU", and "COMPUTER". The keywords are in order of priority, so Eliza will key on "YOU ARE" before "YOU".

(2) 12 strings used for the translation or conjugation process. These are in pairs such that if one member of the pair is found, the other is substituted for it. Examples: "I", "YOU", "AM", "ARE", etc.

(3) 112 reply strings. The strings are arranged in groups corresponding to the keywords. There is no fixed number of different replies for each keyword. Replies ending in a "*" are to be followed by the translated string, while the strings ending in normal punctuation are to be printed alone.

(4) Numerical data to determine which replies to print for each keyword. For each keyword there is a pair of numbers signifying the start of reply strings and the number of reply strings. Thus the fifth pair of numbers, (10, 4), means that the replies for the fifth keyword ("I DONT") start with the tenth reply string and that there are four replies.

Name	Usage
R(X),S(X),N(X)	See text.
I$	Input string
K$	Keyword string
C$	Translated or conjugated string
F$	Reply string, also used to save K$ in scanning for keyword
R$,S$	Strings used in conjugation process
P$	Previous input string
Z$	Sratch (used for simulating RESTORE NNNN statement)
N1	Number of keywords
N2	Number of conjugation strings
N3	Number of replies
K	Keyword number
S,T	Used to save K and L when scanning for keyword
X,L	X,L Scratch. X is generally used for looping, while L is used for scanning through strings.
V	Used for scanning for keyword string.

Detailed Explanation

Lines 10–160: Intialization. Arrays and strings are dimensioned. N1, N2, and N3, which represent the number of keywords, number of translation strings, and number of replies, respectively, are defined. Then the arrays are filled. S(keyword number) is the ordinal number of the start of the reply strings for a a given keyword, R(keyword number) is the actual reply to be used nest, and N(keyword number) is the last reply for

that keyword. Finally, an introduction is printed.

Lines 170–255: User input section. This part of the program gets a string from the user, places one space at the start of the string and two at the end (to make it easier to correctly locate keywords and to prevent subscripting out of bounds), throws out all the apostrophes (so DONT and DON'T are equivalent), and stops if the word SHUT is found in the input string (which it takes to mean SHUT UP). Eliza also checks for repetitive input by the user.

Lines 260–370: Keyword-finding section. Eliza scans the input string for keywords and saves the keyword of highest priority temporarily in S, T, and F$. If no keyword is found, the keyword defaults to number 36, NOKEYFOUND (which causes Eliza to say something noncommital) and it skips the next section.

Lines 380–555: Translation or conjugation section. The part of the input string following the keyword is saved. Then pairs of translation strings, as described above, are read, and upon the occurrence of one of these strings, the other is substituted for it. When this is done Eliza makes sure there is only one leading space in the translated string.

Lines 560–640: Reply printing section. Using R(keyword number), S(keyword number), and N(keyword number), the correct reply is located. The pointer for the next reply is bumped and reset if it is too large. If the reply string ends in a "*" it is printed with the translated string, otherwise it is printed alone. The previously entered input string is saved to permit checking for repetitive input, and then Eliza goes back for more input.

Modifications

You can easily add, change, or delete any of the keywords, translation words, or replies. Remember, you will also have to change N1, N2, N3, and/or the numerical data. Just as a suggestion, if you decide to insert "ME" and "YOU" in the translation string list, put a nonprinting (control) character in YOU to prevent Eliza from substituting I→YOU→ME. This means that YOU will always be assumed to be the subject of a verb, never the object, but resolving that difficulty is a whole different problem.

What It All Means

We'll leave this to you. Although this program is an inferior imitation of the original, it does work. It is pretty far-fetched to believe that a psycholanalyst is nothing but a sentence-input-keyword-finder-conjugator-reply finder, but if you really think so, you can buy your computer a speech-recognition unit, a Computalker, and a green couch, and charge $75 per hour. My computer, the doctor!

Eliza

```
10 REM
20 REM     ELIZA/DOCTOR
30 REM     CREATED BY JOESEPH WEIZENBAUM 40 REM    THIS VERSION BY JEFF SHRAGER
50 REM     EDITED BY BOB ANDERSON
60 REM     CREATIVE COMPUTING
70 REM
80 REM --- INITIALIZATION ---
90 DIM C$(72),I$(72),K$(72),F$(72),S$(72),R$(72),P$(72),Z$(72)
100 DIM S(36),R(36),N(36)
110 N1=36:N2=12:N3=112
120 FOR X=1 TO N1+N2+N3:READ Z$:NEXT X
130 FOR X=1 TO N1
140 READ S(X),L:R(X)=S(X):N(X)=S(X)+L-1
150 NEXT X
160 PRINT "Hi! I'm Eliza. What is your problem?"
170 REM
180 REM --- USER INPUT ---
190 REM
200 INPUT I$
210 I$=" "+I$+"   "
220 REM
230 FOR L=1 TO LEN (I$)
240 IF MID$(I$,L,1)="'" THEN I$=LEFT$(I$,L-1)+RIGHT$(I$,LEN(I$)-L):GOTO 240
250 IF L+4 <= LEN(I$) THEN IF MID$(I$,L,4)="SHUT" THEN PRINT "Shut up...":END
260 NEXT L
270 IF I$=P$ THEN PRINT "PLEASE DON'T REPEAT YOURSELF!":GOTO 170
280 REM
290 REM --- FIND KEYWORD ---
300 REM
310 RESTORE
320 S=0
330 FOR K=1 TO N1
340 READ K$
350 IF S>0 THEN 390
360 FOR L=1 TO LEN(I$)-LEN(K$)+1
370 IF MID$(I$,L,LEN(K$))=K$ THEN S=K:T=L:F$=K$
380 NEXT L
390 NEXT K
400 IF S>0 THEN K=S:L=T:GOTO 430
410 K=36:GOTO 630
420 REM
430 REM  TAKE RIGHT PART OF STRING
440 REM  AND CONJUGATE CORRECTLY
450 REM
460 RESTORE:FOR X=1 TO N1:READ Z$:NEXT X
470 C$=" "+RIGHT$(I$,LEN(I$)-LEN(F$)-L+1)
480 FOR X=1 TO N2/2
490 READ S$,R$
500 FOR L=1 TO LEN(C$)
510 IF L+LEN(S$)>LEN (C$) THEN 560
520 IF MID$(C$,L,LEN(S$))<>S$ THEN 560
530 C$=LEFT$(C$,L-1)+R$+RIGHT$(C$,LEN(C$)-L-LEN(S$)+1)
540 L=L+LEN(S$)
550 GOTO 600
560 IF L+LEN(R$)>LEN(C$)THEN 600
570 IF MID$(C$,L,LEN(R$))<>R$ THEN 600
580 C$=LEFT$(C$,L-1)+S$+RIGHT$(C$,LEN(C$)-L-LEN(R$)+1)
590 L=L+LEN(S$)
600 NEXT L
610 NEXT X
620 REM
630 REM --- GET REPLY ---
640 REM
650 RESTORE:FOR X=1 TO N1+N2:READ Z$:NEXT X
660 FOR X=1 TO R(K):READ F$:NEXT X
670 R(K)=R(K)+1:IF R(K)>N(K) THEN R(K)=S(K)
680 IF RIGHT$(F$,1)<>"*" THEN PRINT F$:P$=F$:GOTO 170
690 PRINT LEFT$(F$,LEN(F$)-1);C$
700 P$=F$:GOTO 170
1000 REM
1010 REM --- PROGRAM DATA ---
1020 REM
1030 REM --- KEYWORDS ---
1040 REM
1050 DATA "CAN YOU","CAN I","YOU ARE","YOURE","I DONT","I FEEL"
1060 DATA "WHY DONT YOU","WHY CANT I","ARE YOU","I CANT","I AM","IM "
1070 DATA "YOU ","I WANT","WHAT","HOW","WHO","WHERE","WHEN","WHY"
1080 DATA "NAME","CAUSE","SORRY","DREAM","HELLO","HI ","MAYBE"
```

```
1090 DATA "NO","YOUR","ALWAYS","THINK","ALIKE","YES","FRIEND"
1100 DATA "COMPUTER","NOKEYFOUND"
1200 REM
1210 REM --- CONJUGATION DATA ---
1220 REM REM
1230 DATA " ARE "," AM ","WERE ","WAS "," YOU "," I ","YOUR ","MY "
1240 DATA " IVE "," YOUVE "," IM "," YOURE "
1300 REM
1310 REM --- REPLIES ---
1320 REM
1330 DATA "DON'T YOU BELIEVE THAT I CAN*"
1340 DATA "PERHAPS YOU WOULD LIKE TO BE ABLE TO*"
1350 DATA "YOU WANT ME TO BE ABLE TO*"
1360 DATA "PERHAPS YOU DON'T WANT TO*"
1370 DATA "DO YOU WANT TO BE ABLE TO*"
1380 DATA "WHAT MAKES YOU THINK I AM*"
1390 DATA "DOES IT PLEASE YOU TO BELIEVE THAT I AM*"
1400 DATA "PERHAPS YOU WOULD LIKE TO BE*"
1410 DATA "DO YOU SOMETIMES WISH YOU WERE*"
1420 DATA "DON'T YOU REALLY*"
1430 DATA "WHY DON'T YOU*"
1440 DATA "DO YOU WISH TO BE ABLE TO*"
1450 DATA "DOES THAT TROUBLE YOU?"
1460 DATA "TELL ME MORE ABOUT SUCH FEELINGS."
1470 DATA "DO YOU OFTEN FEEL*"
1480 DATA "DO YOU ENJOY FEELING*"
1490 DATA "DO YOU REALLY BELIEVE I DON'T*"
1500 DATA "PERHAPS IN GOOD TIME I WILL*"
1510 DATA "DO YOU WANT ME TO*"
1520 DATA "DO YOU THINK YOU SHOULD BE ABLE TO*"
1530 DATA "WHY CAN'T YOU*"
1540 DATA "WHY ARE YOU INTERESTED IN WHETHER OR NOT I AM*"
1550 DATA "WOULD YOU PREFER IF I WERE NOT*"
1560 DATA "PERHAPS IN YOUR FANTASIES I AM*"
1570 DATA "HOW DO YOU KNOW I CAN'T*"
1580 DATA "HAVE YOU TRIED?"
1590 DATA "PERHAPPS YOU CAN NOW*"
1600 DATA "DID YOU COME TO ME BECAUSE YOU ARE*"
1610 DATA "HOW LONG HAVE YOU BEEN*"
1620 DATA "DO YOU BELIEVE IT IS NORMAL TO BE*"
1630 DATA "DO YOU ENJOY BEING*"
1640 DATA "WE WERE DISCUSSING YOU-- NOT ME."
1650 DATA "OH, I*"
1660 DATA "YOU'RE NOT REALLY TALKING ABOUT ME, ARE YOU?"
1670 DATA "WHAT WOULD IT MEAN IF YOU GOT*"
1680 DATA "WHY DO YOU WANT*"
1690 DATA "SUPPOSE YOU SOOM GOT*"
1700 DATA "WHAT IF YOU NEVER GOT*"
1710 DATA "I SOMETIMES ALSO WANT*"
1720 DATA "WHY DO YOU ASK?"
1730 DATA "DOES THAT QUESTION INTEREST YOU?"
1740 DATA "WHAT ANSWER WOULD PLEASE YOU THE MOST?"
1750 DATA "WHAT DO YOU THINK?"
1760 DATA "ARE SUCH QUESTIONS ON YOU MIND OFTEN?"
1770 DATA "WHAT IS IT YOU REALLY WANT TO KNOW?"
1780 DATA "HAVE YOU ASKED ANYONE ELSE?"
1790 DATA "HAVE YOU ASKED SUCH QUESTIONS BEFORE?"
1800 DATA "WHAT ELSE COMES TO MIND WHEN YOU ASK THAT?"
1810 DATA "NAMES DON'T INTEREST ME."
1820 DATA "I DON'T CARE ABOUT NAMES. GO ON."
1830 DATA "IS THAT THE REAL REASON?"
1840 DATA "DON'T ANY OTHER REASONS COME TO MIND?"
1850 DATA "DOES THAT REASON EXPLAIN ANYTHING ELSE?"
1860 DATA "WHAT OTHER REASON MIGHT THERE BE?"
1870 DATA "PLEASE DON'T APOLOGIZE."
1880 DATA "APOLOGIES ARE NOT NECESSARY."
1890 DATA "WHAT FEELINGS DO YOU GET WHEN YOU APOLOGIZE."
1900 DATA "DON'T BE SO DEFENSIVE!"
1910 DATA "WHAT DOES THAT DREAM SUGGEST TO YOU?"
1920 DATA "DO YOU DREAM OFTEN?"
1930 DATA "WHAT PERSONS APPEAR IN YOUR DREAMS?"
1940 DATA "ARE YOU DISTURBED BY YOUR DREAMS?"
1950 DATA "HOW DO YOU DO... PLEASE STATE YOUR PROBLEM."
1960 DATA "YOU DON'T SEEM QUITE CERTAIN."
1970 DATA "WHY THE UNCERTAIN TONE?"
1980 DATA "CAN'T YOU BE MORE POSITIVE?"
1990 DATA "YOU AREN'T SURE?"
2000 DATA "DON'T YOU KNOW?"
```

Eliza

```
2010 DATA "ARE YOU SAYING THAT JUST TO BE NEGATIVE?"
2020 DATA "YOU ARE BEING A BIT NEGATIVE."
2030 DATA "WHY NOT?"
2040 DATA "ARE YOU SURE?"
2050 DATA "WHY NO?"
2060 DATA "WHY ARE YOU CONCERNED ABOUT MY*"
2070 DATA "WHAT ABOUT YOUR OWN*"
2080 DATA "CAN YOU THINK OF A SECIFIC EXAMPLE?"
2090 DATA "WHEN?"
2100 DATA "WHAT ARE YOU THINKING OF?"
2110 DATA "REALLY, ALWAYS?"
2120 DATA "DO YOU REALLY THINK SO"
2130 DATA "BUT YOU ARE NOT SURE YOU*"
2140 DATA "DO YOU DOUBT YOU*"
2150 DATA "IN WHAT WAY?"
2160 DATA "WHAT RESEMBLENCE DO YOU SEE?"
2170 DATA "WHAT DOES THE SIMILARITY SUGGEST TO YOU?"
2180 DATA "WHAT OTHER CONNECTIONS DO YOU SEE?"
2190 DATA "COULD THERE REALLY BE SOME CONNECTION?"
2200 DATA "HOW?"
2210 DATA "YOU SEEM QUITE POSITIVE."
2220 DATA "ARE YOU SURE?"
2230 DATA "I SEE."
2240 DATA "I UNDERSTAND."
2250 DATA "WHY DO YOU BRING UP THE TOPIC OF FRIENDS?"
2260 DATA "DO YOUR FRIENDS WORRU YOU?"
2270 DATA "DO YOUR FRIENDS PICK ON YOU?"
2280 DATA "ARE YOU SURE YOU HAVE ANY FRIENDS?"
2290 DATA "DO YOU IMPOSE ON YOUR FRIENDS?"
2300 DATA "PERHAPS YOUR LOVE FOR FRIENDS WORRIES YOU?"
2310 DATA "DO COMPUTERS WORRY YOU?"
2320 DATA "ARE YOU TALKING ABOUT ME IN PARTICULAR?"
2330 DATA "ARE YOU FRIGHTENED BY MACHINES?"
2340 DATA "WHY DO YOU MENTION COMPUTERS?"
2350 DATA "WHAT DO YOU THINK COMPUTER HAVE TO DO WITH YOUR PROBLEM?"
2360 DATA "DON'T YOU THINK COMPUTERS CAN HELP PEOPLE?"
2370 DATA "WHAT IS IT ABOUT MACHINES THAT WORRIES YOU?"
2380 DATA "SAY, DO YOU HAVE ANY PSYCOLOGICAL PROBLEMS?"
2390 DATA "WHAT DOES THAT SUGGEST TO YOU?"
2400 DATA "I SEE."
2410 DATA "I'M NOT SURE I UNDERSTAND YOU FULLY."
2420 DATA "COME COME ELUCIDATE YOUR THOUGHTS."
2430 DATA "CAN YOU ELABORATE ON THAT?"
2440 DATA "THAT IS QUITE INTERESTING."
2500 REM
2510 REM --- REPLY FINDING DATA ---
2520 REM
2530 DATA 1,3,4,2,6,4,6,4,10,4,14,3,17,3,20,2,22,3,25,3
2540 DATA 28,4,28,4,32,3,35,5,40,9,40,9,40,9,40,9,40,9,40,9
2550 DATA 49,2,51,4,55,4,59,4,63,1,63,1,64,5,69,5,74,2,76,4
2560 DATA 80,3,83,7,90,3,93,6,99,7,106,6
```

```
Hi! I'm Eliza. What is your problem?
? I'M AN IBM 370
DID YOU COME TO ME BECAUSE YOU ARE AN IBM 370
? YES I WANT A NEW LINE PRINTER
WHAT WOULD IT MEAN IF YOU GOT  A NEW LINE PRINTER
? ABOUT 1200 LPM
SAY, DO YOU HAVE ANY PSYCOLOGICAL PROBLEMS?
? HOW WOULD YOU KNOW YOU'RE A SPECTRAVIDEO
WHAT MAKES YOU THINK I AM  A SPECTRAVIDEO
? IT SAYS SO ABOVE YOUR KEYBOARD
WHY ARE YOU CONCERNED ABOUT MY  KEYBOARD
? CAUSE THAT IS WHAT I'M TYPING ON
HOW LONG HAVE YOU BEEN TYPING ON
? SINCE I TYPED RUN
WHAT DOES THAT SUGGEST TO YOU?
? YOU'RE THE SHRINK
DOES IT PLEASE YOU TO BELIEVE THAT I AM  THE SHRINK
? DON'T YOU KNOW
WE WERE DISCUSSING YOU-- NOT ME.
? I AM BEGINNING TO WONDER ABOUT YOU
DID YOU COME TO ME BECAUSE YOU ARE  BEGINNING TO WONDER ABOUT I
? I DIDN'T START TO WONDER ABOUT YOU UNTIL AFTER I CAME TO YOU
```

Lost & Forgotten Island

Lost & Forgotten Island was passed along to us by Ken Modesitt of Texas Instruments and converted to Microsoft Basic by Jeffery Yaun. It first appeared in *Creative Computing*, March 1980.

Lost & Forgotten Island is a game of survival for one to three players. Unlike other similar games, to survive requires cooperation and joint decision-making among players.

In the scenario, you and all the other players have been shipwrecked and are now stranded on a remote island in the Pacific Ocean. Also on the island is a pirate's cache of buried treasure and, of course, your damaged ship. To complicate matters, a typhoon is approaching.

On each turn, each player must make a decision as to whether to do repair work on the ship or to dig for gold. The longer you remain on the island collecting treasure, the higher the risk that the typhoon will catch up with your ship when you leave the island.

In addition to your race against the approaching typhoon, you will encounter other problems—mainly injuries from mishandling your tools or explosives. You may trade tools among players for either other tools or gold. Certain tools will perform two functions, although using a tool for the wrong function will diminish its ability to perform its main function. For example, using an axe to dig dulls it and makes it less useful for cutting down trees for ship repairs.

There are several ways in which the game can end, some of which are not at all pleasant. But with persistence, sensible decisions, and cooperation among players, you can all make it back to safety with enough gold to buy a fleet of Rolls Royces. Good Luck!

Lost & Forgotten Island

```
10 REM-LOST AND FORGOTTEN ISLAND
20 REM-REV. 6/8/84
30 DIM T$(12),T2(3,9),T3(3,15),V1(3,9),V2(3,9),N$(3),C1(4)
40 DIM V3(3,9),V4(3,9),C3(4),I$(2),J$(9),W(4),G1(4),G2(4)
50 DIM N3(2),B$(2)
60 REM INSTRUCTIONS
70 REM ADAPTED FROM "COMPUTERS AND SOCIETY" VOL.7-NO.3,FALL,1976
80 PRINT"WELCOME TO THE LOST AND FORGOTTEN ISLAND."
90 PRINT"WOULD YOU LIKE SOME INSTRUCTIONS";
100 INPUT Z$
110 IFZ$="YES"THEN150
120 IFZ$="NO"THEN250
130 PRINT"INVALID ANSWER, PLEASE RETYPE. YES OR NO"
140 GOTO 100
150 PRINT"LOST AND FORGOTTEN ISLAND IS A SURVIVAL GAME BASED ON"
160 PRINT"COOPERATION. IT CONTAINS A MIXTURE OF LIFE'S VALUES."
170 PRINT"IMAGINE:"
180 PRINT"        YOU HAVE BEEN SHIPWRECKED ON A REMOTE ISLAND."
190 PRINT"YOU HAVE THE CHOICE OF DIGGING FOR GOLD AND/OR BUILDING"
200 PRINT"A SHIP TO SURVIVE THE APPROACHING HURRICANE."
210 PRINT"CAN YOU SURVIVE?  IF SO, WITH HOW MUCH GOLD?"
220 PRINT
230 PRINT"        GOOD LUCK"
240 PRINT
250 T8=RND(1)
260 FORI=1TO3
270 FOR J=1TO9
280 T2(I,J)=0
290 T3(I,J)=0
300 V1(I,J)=0
310 V2(I,J)=0
320 NEXTJ
330 NEXTI
340 FOR I=1TO2
350 N3(I)=0
360 NEXTI
370 FOR I=1TO4
380 W(I)=0
390 G1(I)=0
400 G2(I)=0
410 C3(I)=0
420 C1(I)=0
430 NEXT I
440 N$(3)="STORAGE"
450 FOR I=1 TO 9
460 READT$(I)
470 NEXT I
480 PRINT
490 REM NUMBER OF PLAYERS
500 PRINT"HOW MANY PEOPLE (1/2/3) ARE PLAYING";
510 FOR U1=1TO3
520 FORU2=1TO9
530 T2(U1,U2)=0
540 NEXT U2
550 NEXT U1
560 INPUT N1
570 PRINT
580 IFN1<1THEN 600
590 IFN1<=3THEN710
600 PRINT"YOU MUST PLAY WITH 1,2 OR 3 PLAYERS"
610 PRINT
620 GOTO 500
630 E=0
640 FOR H=1TON1
650 G1(H)=0
660 C3(H)=0
670 C1(H)=0
680 W(H)=0
690 NEXT H
700 C2=0
710 FOR I=1TON1
720 PRINT"PLAYER ";I;"WHAT NAME ARE YOU USING";
730 INPUTN$(I)
740 PRINT
750 FOR J=1TO3
760 IF J=I THEN 810
770 IFN$(I)<>N$(J) THEN 810
780 PRINT"SOMEONE ELSE ALREADY HAS THIS NAME SO PLEASE CHOOSE ANOTHER."
```

Lost & Forgotten Island

```
 790 PRINT
 800 GOTO 730
 810 NEXT J
 820 NEXT I
 830 FORU3=1TO3
 840 FOR U4=1TO9
 850 T2(U3,U4)=1
 860 T2(U3,U4)=T2(U3,U4)*(-10)
 870 NEXT U4
 880 NEXT U3
 890 REM
 900 FOR I=1TO5
 910 T3(1,I)=1
 920 NEXT I
 930 T3(1,6)=2
 940 T3(2,7)=1
 950 T3(2,8)=1
 960 T3(2,9)=2
 970 E=6-N1
 980 FOR I=1TON1
 990 FOR J=1TOE
1000 R1=INT(RND(1)*9+1)
1010 T2(I,J)=R1
1020 V1(I,J)=T3(1,R1)
1030 V2(I,J)=T3(2,R1)
1040 NEXT J
1050 C1(I)=INT(RND(1)*11+2)
1060 NEXT I
1070 GOSUB 1110
1080 DATA"AXE","CHISEL","HAMMER","NAILS AND SCREWS","SAW"
1090 DATA"LUMBER","SHOVEL","PICKAXE","EXPLOSIVES"
1100 STOP
1110 REM SUBROUTINE LAFIS21
1120 REM THIS IS LAFIS 21
1130 REM TRADING TOOLS
1140 IF N1=1 THEN 1240
1150 IF N1=3 THEN 1170
1160 N$(3)="STORAGE"
1170 J$(1)="A"
1180 J$(2)="ANOTHER"
1190 FOR I=3 TO 9
1200 J$(I)=J$(I-1)
1210 NEXT I
1220 I$(1)="WHO (ONE NAME ONLY PLEASE) WISHES TO TRADE"
1230 I$(2)="WHO ELSE WISHES TO TRADE"
1240 S=4
1250 FOR M=1TO5
1260 REM WHICH DAY?
1270 PRINT"THIS IS DAY ";M
1280 PRINT
1290 GOSUB 3990
1300 PRINT
1310 PRINT
1320 IFS=1THEN 3970
1330 IFS>3THEN1390
1340 S=S-1
1350 PRINT"THE STORM IS ABOUT TO HIT"
1360 PRINT
1370 IF N1=1THEN2910
1380 GOTO1430
1390 IFM=3THEN1420
1400 X=INT(RND(1)*4+1)
1410 IFX<>4THEN1430
1420 S=3
1430 IF N1=1THEN2910
1440 PRINT"DO ANY OF YOU WISH TO TRADE TOOLS";
1450 INPUTA$
1460 PRINT
1470 IF A$="YES"THEN1520
1480 IFA$="NO"THEN2910
1490 PRINT"PLEASE TRY AGAIN. YOU MUST ANSWER YES OR NO."
1500 PRINT
1510 GOTO 1430
1520 FOR I=1TO3
1530 FOR J=1TO9
1540 T3(I,J)=T2(I,J)
1550 V3(I,J)=V1(I,J)
1560 V4(I,J)=V2(I,J)
```

```
1570 NEXT J
1580 G2(I)=G1(I)
1590 NEXT I
1600 FORJ=1TO2
1610 N3(J)=1
1620 NEXT J
1630 FOR I=1TO2
1640 PRINTI$(I);
1650 INPUTB$(I)
1660 PRINT
1670 IFB$(I)=N$(1)THEN1760
1680 IFB$(I)=N$(2)THEN1750
1690 IFB$(I)=N$(3)THEN1740
1700 PRINT"YOU MUST ANSWER WITH '";N$(1);"', OR '";N$(3)
1710 PRINT"        PLEASE TRY AGAIN
1720 PRINT
1730 GOTO 1640
1740 N3(I)=N3(I)+1
1750 N3(I)=N3(I)+1
1760 NEXT I
1770 FOR I=1TO2
1780 N4=1
1790 PRINTB$(I);", ARE YOU GIVING ANY GOLD IN THIS TRADE";
1800 INPUTC$
1810 PRINT
1820 IFC$="X"THEN2830
1830 IFC$="NO"THEN 2080
1840 IFC$="YES"THEN1950
1850 IFC$="T"THEN 1910
1860 PRINT"PLEASE TRY AGAIN. YOU MUST ANSWER YES, NO,"
1870 PRINT"X (TO CALL OFF THE TRADE), OR T (TO SEE THE LIST OF"
1880 PRINT"TOOLS WHICH EVERYONE HAD BEFORE THE START OF THIS TRADE)."
1890 PRINT
1900 GOTO 1790
1910 PRINT"YOUR SITUATION AT THIS TIME
1920 PRINT
1930 GOSUB 4040
1940 GOTO 1790
1950 PRINTB$(I);", HOW MUCH GOLD (IN DOLLARS) ARE YOU GOING TO GIVE";
1960 INPUTA7
1970 PRINT
1980 IF G1(N3(I))>A7 THEN 2050
1990 PRINT"YOU MAY NOT GIVE MORE THAN YOU HAVE (";G1(N3(I));") DOLLARS"
2000 PRINT
2010 GOTO 1950
2020 IFA7>=0THEN2060
2030 PRINT"YOU MAY NOT INPUT A NEGATIVE NUMBER. TRY AGAIN."
2040 PRINT
2050 GOTO 1950
2060 G2(N3(I))=G1(N3(I))-A7
2070 G2(N3(3-I))=G1(N3(3-I))+A7
2080 PRINTB$(I);", ARE YOU GIVING A(NY) TOOL(S) IN THIS TRADE";
2090 INPUTD$
2100 PRINT
2110 IFD$="X"THEN 2830
2120 IFD$="NO"THEN 2680
2130 IFD$="YES"THEN2220
2140 IFD$="T"THEN2180
2150 PRINT"TRY AGAIN. ANSWER YES, NO, X OR T"
2160 PRINT
2170 GOTO 2080
2180 PRINT"YOUR SITUATION AT THIS TIME"
2190 PRINT
2200 GOSUB 4040
2210 GOTO2080
2220 PRINTB$(I);", HOW MANY TOOLS ARE YOU GIVING";
2230 INPUT N5
2240 PRINT
2250 FOR J=1TON5
2260 PRINTB$(I);", WHAT IS THE NAME OF ";J$(J);" TOOL THAT ";
2270 PRINT"YOU ARE GIVING IN TRADE";
2280 INPUT E$
2290 PRINT
2300 IFE$="X"THEN2830
2310 IFE$="B"THEN2680
2320 IFE$="T"THEN2530
2330 FORR=1TO9
2340 IFT$(R)=E$THEN2430
```

```
2350 NEXT R
2360 PRINT"PLEASE USE THE NAME OF THE TOOL, USE B IF YOU WANT TO"
2370 PRINT"GO AHEAD WITH THE TRADE WITHOUT GIVING MORE TOOLS,"
2380 PRINT"USE T IF YOU WANT TO SEE THE LIST OF TOOLS EVERYONE"
2390 PRINT"HAD BEFORE THIS TRADE STARTED,"
2400 PRINT"OR USE X IF YOU WANT TO CALL OFF THE TRADE."
2410 PRINT
2420 GOTO2260
2430 FORK=1TO9
2440 IFT2(N3(I),K)=R THEN 2570
2450 NEXT K
2460 PRINTB$(I);", YOU DO NOT HAVE THIS TOOL. PLEASE TRY AGAIN."
2470 PRINT"YOU MUST USE THE NAME OF A TOOL YOU HAVE, USE B TO GO"
2480 PRINT"AHEAD WITH THE TRADE WITHOUT GIVING MORE TOOLS, USE X"
2490 PRINT"TO CALL OFF THE TRADE, OR USE T TO SEE THE LIST OF TOOLS WHICH "
2500 PRINT"EVERYONE HAD BEFORE THE START OF THIS TRADE."
2510 PRINT
2520 GOTO 2260
2530 PRINT"YOUR SITUATION AT THIS TIME"
2540 PRINT
2550 GOSUB 4040
2560 GOTO 2260
2570 T3(N3(I),K)=-10
2580 V3(N3(I),K)=0
2590 V4(N3(I),K)=0
2600 FOR L=N4TO9
2610 IF T3(N3(3-I),L)=-10THEN2630
2620 NEXT L
2630 T3(N3(3-I),L)=R
2640 V3(N3(3-I),L)=V1(N3(I),K)
2650 V4(N3(3-I),L)=V2(N3(I),K)
2660 N4=L+1
2670 NEXT J
2680 NEXT I
2690 PRINT"THIS IS YOUR LAST CHANCE TO CALL OFF THE TRADE. IF YOU"
2700 PRINT"WANT TO CALL IT OFF TYPE X. OTHERWISE TYPE ANY OTHER LETTER AFTER"
2710 PRINT"THE QUESTION MARK."
2720 INPUTG$
2730 PRINT
2740 IF G$="X"THEN2830
2750 FOR I=1TO3
2760 FOR J=1TO9
2770 T2(I,J)=T3(I,J)
2780 V1(I,J)=V3(I,J)
2790 V2(I,J)=V4(I,J)
2800 NEXT J
2810 G1(I)=G2(I)
2820 NEXT I
2830 PRINT"DO ANY TWO OF YOU WISH TO TRADE NOW";
2840 INPUT H$
2850 PRINT
2860 IFH$="YES"THEN 1520
2870 IFH$="NO"THEN2910
2880 PRINT"PLEASE TRY AGAIN. YOU MUST ANSWER YES OR NO.
2890 PRINT
2900 GOTO 2830
2910 FOR I=1TON1
2920 IFC3(I)=1THEN3940
2930 P1=C1(I)
2940 REM WHAT TYPE OF WORK TODAY?
2950 PRINTN$(I);", WHAT ARE YOU GOING TO WORK ON TODAY";
2960 INPUT A$
2970 PRINT
2980 IFA$="BOAT"THEN3370
2990 IFA$="GOLD"THEN3050
3000 PRINT"PLEASE ANSWER BOAT IF YOU WANT TO WORK ON THE BOAT"
3010 PRINT"OR GOLD IF YOU WANT TO MINE GOLD."
3020 PRINT
3030 GOTO 2950
3040 REM WORKING ON SOME GOLD
3050 FOR J=1TO9
3060 IFT2(I,J)<>1THEN3220
3070 PRINTN$(I);", DO YOU WISH TO USE THE AXE TO MINE GOLD?"
3080 PRINT"REMEMBER THAT THE AXE DROPS GREATLY IN VALUE"
3090 PRINT"IF IT IS USED TO MINE GOLD."
3100 INPUTC$
3110 PRINT
3120 IFC$="NO"THEN 3220
```

```
3130 IFC$="YES"THEN 3170
3140 PRINT"PLEASE TRY AGAIN. YOU MUST USE YES OR NO."
3150 PRINT
3160 GOTO3070
3170 V2(I,J)=V1(I,J)
3180 P1=P1+V2(I,J)*C1(I)
3190 V1(I,J)=(INT((V1(I,J)/2)*10+.5))/10
3200 V2(I,J)=0
3210 GOTO 3230
3220 P1=P1+V2(I,J)*C1(I)
3230 NEXTJ
3240 Z8=RND(1)*2+1
3250 K=I
3260 IFC3(K)=1THEN3340
3270 C4=0
3280 IFK<>1THEN3300
3290 C4=.25
3300 C4=C4+.25
3310 Z9=C4*Z8*200*P1
3320 PRINTN$(K);" HAS JUST MADE ";INT(Z9);" DOLLARS MORE GOLD."
3330 G1(K)=G1(K)+Z9
3350 PRINT
3360 GOTO 3530
3370 REM WORKING ON THE BOAT
3380 B(I)=1
3390 FOR J=1TO9
3400 IFT2(I,J)<>2THEN3460
3410 FOR K=1TO9
3420 IFT2(I,K)<>3THEN3450
3430 P1=P1+2*V1(I,J)*C1(I)
3440 GOTO 3470
3450 NEXT K
3460 P1=P1+V1(I,J)*C1(I)
3470 NEXT J
3480 Z8=P1/12
3490 PRINTN$(I);" HAS EARNED ";INT(Z8);" MORE WORK POINTS."
3500 PRINT
3510 W(I)=W(I)+Z8
3520 C2=C2+Z8
3530 Y=INT(RND(1)*(9+C1(I))+1)
3540 FOR J=1TO9
3550 IF T2(I,J)=1THEN3580
3560 IFT2(I,J)=3THEN3580
3570 IFT2(I,J)<>8THEN 3640
3580 IFY<>T2(I,J)THEN3930
3590 PRINTN$(I);" HAS BEEN INJURED BY THE ";T$(T2(I,J));". HIS/HER"
3600 PRINT"TOOL PROFICIENCY WILL NOW BE CUT IN HALF."
3610 PRINT
3620 C1(I)=INT((C1(I)/2)+.5)
3630 J=9
3640 IFT2(I,J)<>9THEN3930
3650 IF Y<>T2(I,J)THEN3930
3660 PRINTN$(I);" HAS BEEN KILLED IN THE ACCIENTAL"
3670 PRINT"DISCHARGE OF SOME OF THE EXPLOSIVES. PLEASE"
3680 PRINT"NOTIFY HIS/HER FRIENDS AND RELATIVES IF YOU MAKE IT BACK."
3690 PRINT
3700 C3(I)=1
3710 IFD7=1THEN3740
3720 N$(I)="STORAGE"
3730 D7=1
3740 G1(I)=0
3750 G2(I)=0
3760 IFN1=1THEN3970
3770 FOR K=1TO9
3780 IFT2(I,K)=-10THEN3910
3790 R3=INT(RND(1)*N1+1)
3800 IFR3=ITHEN3850
3810 FOR L=1TO9
3820 IF T2(R3,L)<>-10THEN3900
3830 T2(R3,L)=T2(I,K)
3840 V1(R3,L)=V1(I,K)
3850 V2(R3,L)=V2(I,K)
3860 T2(I,K)=-10
3870 V1(I,K)=0
3880 V2(I,K)=0
3890 L=9
3900 NEXTL
3910 NEXTK
```

```
3920 J=9
3930 NEXT J
3940 NEXT I
3950 NEXT M
3960 GOSUB 3990
3970 GOSUB 4360
3980 REM THE FOLLOWING IS THE SUBROUTINE STATE
3990 FOR I=1TO3
4000 FOR J=1TO9
4010 T3(I,J)=T2(I,J)
4020 NEXT J
4030 NEXT I
4040 C4=C2
4050 FOR H=1TON1
4060 PRINT
4070 PRINT
4080 IFC3(H)=1THEN4270
4090 IFC2<>0THEN4110
4100 C2=1
4110 E=INT((W(H)/C2)*100+.5)
4120 PRINTN$(H);" HAS ";INT(G1(H));" DOLLARS WORTH OF GOLD, A TOOL"
4130 PRINT"PROFICIENCY OF ";C1(H);", ";INT(W(H));" WORK POINTS, WHICH"
4140 PRINT"IS ";E;" PERCENT OF THE TOTAL, AND THE FOLLOWING TOOLS:"
4150 PRINT
4160 FORJ2=1TO9
4170 K$=" "
4180 IFT2(H,J2)=-10THEN4220
4190 IFT2(H,J2)=T3(H,J2)THEN4210
4200 K$="*"
4210 PRINTTAB(6);K$;T$(T2(H,J2))
4220 NEXT J2
4230 PRINT
4240 PRINT"JUST HIT RETURN WHEN YOU ARE READY TO GO ON.";
4250 INPUT F$
4260 PRINT
4270 NEXT H
4280 PRINT
4290 PRINT"THE SUM OF EVERYONE'S WORK POINTS IS ";INT(C4);"."
4300 PRINT
4310 C2=C4
4320 RETURN
4330 DATA"AXE","CHISEL","HAMMER","NAILS AND SCREWS","SAW"
4340 DATA"LUMBER","SHOVEL","PICKAXE","EXPLOSIVES"
4350 RETURN
4360 REM SUBROUTINE LAFIS 31
4370 DEF FNE(Z7)=2.718^Z7
4380 DEF FNC(Z8)=FNE(Z8)+FNE(-Z8)
4390 DEF FNS(Z9)=FNE(Z9)-FNE(-Z9)
4400 C4=C2
4410 IFC2<>0THEN4430
4420 C2=1
4430 IF Z1=3THEN4500
4440 C4=0
4450 FOR I=1TON1
4460 IF C3(I)=1THEN4480
4470 IFW(I)/C2<.25 THEN 4490
4480 C4=C4+W(I)
4490 NEXT I
4500 FOR I=1TO N1
4510 IF C3(I)=1THEN4920
4520 PRINT
4530 PRINT
4540 REM THE RESULTS
4550 PRINT
4560 PRINT"THE RESULTS FOR ";N$(I);":"
4570 PRINT
4580 PRINT
4590 IFW(I)/C32<.25THEN4610
4600 W(I)=C4
4610 Z1=INT(60*2.718^((-W(I))/6))
4620 Z2=INT(50*(1+((FNS((7-W(I))/8.5))/FNC((7-W(I))/8.5))))
4630 Z3=INT(50*(1+(FNS((14-W(I))/5)/FNC((14-W(I))/5))))
4640 R5=INT(RND(1)*101)
4650 IFB(I)<>1THEN4850
4660 IFR5>Z1THEN4820
4670 PRINT"PROPER CONDOLENCES WILL BE SENT TO THE FRIENDS"
4680 PRINT"AND RELATIVES OF"; N$(I);" WHO DROWNED DURING"
4690 PRINT"TYPHOON URSULA."
```

```
4500 FOR I=1TO N1
4510 IF C3(I)=1THEN4920
4520 PRINT
4530 PRINT
4540 REM THE RESULTS
4550 PRINT
4560 PRINT"THE RESULTS FOR ";N$(I);":"
4570 PRINT
4580 PRINT
4590 IFW(I)/C32<.25THEN4610
4600 W(I)=C4
4610 Z1=INT(60*2.718^((-W(I))/6))
4620 Z2=INT(50*(1+((FNS((7-W(I))/8.5))/FNC((7-W(I))/8.5))))
4630 Z3=INT(50*(1+((FNS((14-W(I))/5))/FNC((14-W(I))/5))))
4640 R5=INT(RND(1)*101)
4650 IFB(I)<>1THEN4850
4660 IFR5>Z1THEN4820
4670 PRINT"PROPER CONDOLENCES WILL BE SENT TO THE FRIENDS"
4680 PRINT"AND RELATIVES OF"; N$(I);" WHO DROWNED DURING"
4690 PRINT"TYPHOON URSULA."
4700 GOTO 4920
4710 IFR5>Z2THEN4860
4720 PRINTN$(I);", YOU HAME IT BACK TO HONOLULU BUT A"
4730 PRINT"LARGE WAVE WASHED YOUR GOLD OVERBOARD. SORRY."
4740 GOTO 4920
4750 IFR5>Z3THEN4920
4760 PRINTN$(I);", YOU MADE IT BACK BUT THE BOAT NEARLY SWAPED."
4770 PRINT"SO, HALF OF YOUR GOLD WAS THROWN OVERBOARD."
4780 PRINT"THIS MEANS YOU HAVE";INT(G1(I)/2);
4790 PRINT" DOLLARS WORTH OF GOLD LEFT."
4800 GOTO 4920
4810 PRINTN$(I);", CONGRATULATIONS !"
4820 PRINT"YOU MADE IT WITH ALL YOUR GOLD,";INT(G1(1));
4830 PRINT" DOLLARS WORTH."
4840 GOTO 4920
4850 IFR5>=97THEN4890
4860 PRINTN$(I);", DID NOT GET OFF THE ISLAND AND WAS"
4870 PRINT"KILLED BY TYPHOON URSULA."
4880 GOTO 4920
4890 PRINTN$(I);", YOU SURVIVED TYPHOON URSULA, BUT LOST ALL YOUR GOLD"
4900 PRINT"AND HAD BETTER START MAKING SMOKE SIGNALS BECAUSE YOU WERE"
4910 PRINT"LEFT BEHIND."
4920 NEXT I
4930 PRINT
4940 PRINT"DO YOU WISH TO PLAY ANOTHER GAME";
4950 INPUT C$
4960 PRINT
4970 PRINT
4980 PRINT
4990 PRINT
5000 PRINT"************************"
5010 PRINT
5020 IFC$="NO"THEN5080
5030 IFC$="YES"THEN80
5040 PRINT"YOU MUST ANSWER YES OR NO. PLEASE TRY AGAIN."
5050 PRINT
5060 GOTO 4940
5070 RETURN
5080 END
```

```
WELCOME TO THE LOST AND FORGOTTEN ISLAND.
WOULD YOU LIKE SOME INSTRUCTIONS? YES
LOST AND FORGOTTEN ISLAND IS A SURVIVAL GAME BASED ON
COOPERATION. IT CONTAINS A MIXTURE OF LIFE'S VALUES.
IMAGINE:
        YOU HAVE BEEN SHIPWRECKED ON A REMOTE ISLAND.
YOU HAVE THE CHOICE OF DIGGING FOR GOLD AND/OR BUILDING
A SHIP TO SURVIVE THE APPROACHING HURRICANE.
CAN YOU SURVIVE?  IF SO, WITH HOW MUCH GOLD?

        GOOD LUCK


HOW MANY PEOPLE (1/2/3) ARE PLAYING? 2

PLAYER  1 WHAT NAME ARE YOU USING? OWEN

PLAYER  2 WHAT NAME ARE YOU USING? RUSS
```

```
THIS IS DAY  1


OWEN HAS  0  DOLLARS WORTH OF GOLD, A TOOL
PROFICIENCY OF 13 , 0  WORK POINTS, WHICH
IS  0  PERCENT OF THE TOTAL, AND THE FOLLOWING TOOLS:


JUST HIT RETURN WHEN YOU ARE READY TO GO ON.?


RUSS HAS  0  DOLLARS WORTH OF GOLD, A TOOL
PROFICIENCY OF  13 ,  0  WORK POINTS, WHICH
IS  0  PERCENT OF THE TOTAL, AND THE FOLLOWING TOOLS:
```

Lost & Forgotten Island

JUST HIT RETURN WHEN YOU ARE READY TO GO ON.?

THE SUM OF EVERYONE'S WORK POINTS IS 0 .

DO ANY OF YOU WISH TO TRADE TOOLS? NO

OWEN, WHAT ARE YOU GOING TO WORK ON TODAY? GOLD

OWEN HAS JUST MADE 3900 DOLLARS MORE GOLD.

RUSS, WHAT ARE YOU GOING TO WORK ON TODAY? BOAT

RUSS HAS EARNED 1 MORE WORK POINTS.

THIS IS DAY 2

OWEN HAS 3900 DOLLARS WORTH OF GOLD, A TOOL
PROFICIENCY OF 13 , 0 WORK POINTS, WHICH
IS 0 PERCENT OF THE TOTAL, AND THE FOLLOWING TOOLS:

JUST HIT RETURN WHEN YOU ARE READY TO GO ON.?

RUSS HAS 0 DOLLARS WORTH OF GOLD, A TOOL
PROFICIENCY OF 13 , 1 WORK POINTS, WHICH
IS 100 PERCENT OF THE TOTAL, AND THE FOLLOWING TOOLS:

JUST HIT RETURN WHEN YOU ARE READY TO GO ON.?

THE SUM OF EVERYONE'S WORK POINTS IS 1 .

DO ANY OF YOU WISH TO TRADE TOOLS? YES

WHO (ONE NAME ONLY PLEASE) WISHES TO TRADE? OWEN

WHO ELSE WISHES TO TRADE? RUSS

OWEN, ARE YOU GIVING ANY GOLD IN THIS TRADE? NO

OWEN, ARE YOU GIVING A(NY) TOOL(S) IN THIS TRADE? YES

OWEN, HOW MANY TOOLS ARE YOU GIVING? 1

OWEN, WHAT IS THE NAME OF A TOOL THAT YOU ARE GIVING IN TRADE? AXE

OWEN, YOU DO NOT HAVE THIS TOOL. PLEASE TRY AGAIN.
YOU MUST USE THE NAME OF A TOOL YOU HAVE, USE B TO GO
AHEAD WITH THE TRADE WITHOUT GIVING MORE TOOLS, USE X
TO CALL OFF THE TRADE, OR USE T TO SEE THE LIST OF TOOLS WHICH
EVERYONE HAD BEFORE THE START OF THIS TRADE.

OWEN, WHAT IS THE NAME OF A TOOL THAT YOU ARE GIVING IN TRADE? X

DO ANY TWO OF YOU WISH TO TRADE NOW? NO

OWEN, WHAT ARE YOU GOING TO WORK ON TODAY? GOLD

OWEN HAS JUST MADE 3900 DOLLARS MORE GOLD.

RUSS, WHAT ARE YOU GOING TO WORK ON TODAY? BOAT

RUSS HAS EARNED 1 MORE WORK POINTS.

THIS IS DAY 3

OWEN HAS 7800 DOLLARS WORTH OF GOLD, A TOOL
PROFICIENCY OF 13 , 0 WORK POINTS, WHICH
IS 0 PERCENT OF THE TOTAL, AND THE FOLLOWING TOOLS:

JUST HIT RETURN WHEN YOU ARE READY TO GO ON.?

RUSS HAS 0 DOLLARS WORTH OF GOLD, A TOOL
PROFICIENCY OF 13 , 2 WORK POINTS, WHICH
IS 100 PERCENT OF THE TOTAL, AND THE FOLLOWING TOOLS:

JUST HIT RETURN WHEN YOU ARE READY TO GO ON.?

THE SUM OF EVERYONE'S WORK POINTS IS 2 .

DO ANY OF YOU WISH TO TRADE TOOLS?

Monster Combat

Monster Combat was written by Lee J. Chapel and originally appeared in *Creative Computing*, February 1981.

Monster Combat is a game in which you wander around a forest and encounter various monsters. Your objective is to win as much treasure from each encounter as possible and, of course, not get killed in the process.

Play of the Game

When you play the game you will be randomly placed in a forest ten by ten squares in size. Only one of these squares (the one you are in) is displayed, thus allowing you to see only a small part of the forest at a time. The sector you are in is again divided into ten by ten squares. Each of these, too, is divided up to ten by ten; but you can see these hundred smallest squares. Each of these little squares is shown by a single character. It covers an area of forest ten by ten yards, making the fuller square that is displayed a hundred by a hundred yards and the entire forest a thousand by a thousand yards. T's are trees, -'s are paths, I's are

walls, ∧'s are inns, and M's are enchanted castles. The "0" is you.

Also displayed with the portion of forest you are in is your combat strength, treasure total, and the various magic spells you have. Your combat strength is used to fight the various monsters you meet, each monster having a combat strength of his own; these range from five (for a goblin) to a hundred (for a basilisk). Your combat strength is also used in movement, the amount used depending upon how far you go, how much treasure you're lugging around, and the type of terrain you end up on after you move.

At the inns you are allowed to regain the strength you began with and all the magic you had at the start. Don't worry when you find yourself displayed in the square below the inn when you stop there; that is the way the program is set up. Of course, the innkeeper takes some of your treasure for providing you with his services. However, sometimes he has information which he passes on to you at no additional cost—like where the forest edge is, or where an enchanted castle might be found.

There may be up to fifteen enchanted castles in the forest. These usually contain items of great value to treasure hunters, as you will see. (However, they tend to vanish if you make the wrong move, such as falling into a pit when you land on the castle square.)

Most of the time you will not be visiting inns and castles. You will be hacking your way through thick underbrush or trotting along forest paths in search of treasure. And you will find it, usually guarded by some sort of monster. Upon encountering one or more of these creatures you are given a choice of fighting them, running away, bribing them, or casting a spell on them.

To fight you must hit a "1"; then, when it asks you to, you enter however much of your combat strength you wish to use against the monster. If you choose to use strength equal to the monster's strength you then have a fifty-fifty chance of winning. The more strength you use the greater the odds are of winning, the less you use the smaller your odds of winning. Also affecting what you use to fight the monster is your treasure total. The more treasure you have the more strength you must use.

Sample Run

The first and third parts of the sample run give examples of fighting a monster or monsters. In the first case there are three cyclopses. Cyclopses have a combat strength of 20, which means that three of them have a total strength of 60. I used 121 of my combat strength to fight them, over twice the cyclopses' strength, which gave me over a 95% chance of winning. And, as can be seen in the example, I did beat him.

In the third part of the sample run I am fighting 19 goblins. Since goblins have a combat strength of 5, 19 have a combined strength of 95. I used only 60 combat points that time, giving me around a 30% chance of winning. And, as can be seen in the example, I did get myself killed.

Playing Strategy

If you do not wish to fight the monster you can always run. However, the higher the strength of the monster the less likely you will get away and the more likely that you will be forced to fight. Whether or not you do get away is based upon a random number and the strength of the monster. If you do get away you are randomly placed in an adjacent square and get to find out what is there. Once in a while, when you attempt to run, the monster catches you and kills you.

If you don't care to run or fight, you can try to bribe the monster. Few people like to do this since it means handing over some of your hard-earned treasure. Whether your bribe is accepted or not depends upon how much treasure the monster is guarding, his strength, and a random number. The greater the value of the treasure the monster has, the more you'll have to pay him if you don't care to fight. Usually if the monster doesn't care for your bribe you have to fight him. Sometimes, though, he just kills you anyway.

Finally, if you don't care for any of the previous choices, you may cast a spell. There are three types of spells: sleep, charms, and invisibility. Sleep spells tend to be the least effective and invisibility the most effective, with charms somewhere in the middle. Spells, no matter what kind they are, don't always work too well, sometimes not working at all, thus causing you to have to fight the monster.

In addtion to the various monsters, there are other things you will occasionally run into; some are good and some bad, as you will see when you run the program. Everything is determined randomly and thus you can go back to a spot where you were previously and find something different there.

You have thirty days to hunt for treasure in the forest. Each little square you move through takes a tenth of a day to cross, meaning it takes an entire day to cross the entire displayed square. To move, you enter the direction you wish to go (N meaning North, which is upwards, S meaning South, E meaning East, which is to the right, and W meaning West). Then you enter the distance, each little square being one. For example, in the first part of the sample run, I enter S (south) for the direction and then 3 for the distance. This places me on top of the arrow, which is an inn, and thus I am shown in the square below the inn when the next map of the area is drawn. In moving from the inn I again go south, this time a distance of 7, which causes me to end up in the next large square.

When you leave the forest, intentionally or accidentally, you can obtain a listing of the number of monsters you've killed, bribed, and run from, plus the amount of treasure you have won so far. If you decide not to return to the forest or your thirty days are up, you are offered several choices: you may go to a new forest with the same strength and magic (the treasure total going back to zero); you may go to a new forest with new strength and magic; or you can stop playing the game. If you should wish to use the strength and magic left over from the game you just played, you can obtain a listing of these at the very end of the game and then write them down or store them, however you wish. Then, the next time you play the game, you just answer the initial question with a "Y" and then enter the various things you are asked for.

As of this writing, the record treasure total is 7562, set by the author. Most of the time the scores run between 1000 and 2000, with many lower and a few higher. If you get above 2,000 you're doing well.

The following is a description of each monster, giving its combat strength and telling something about the tales and myths surrounding it.

Goblin (5)—A mischievous little sprite only about a yard in height. Rather ugly, uses coarse and uncouth language, is generally evil and malicious; all in all, a rather unpleasant little fellow. Even though they're little they can be very vicious, and more than one warrior has has been killed underestimating them.

Minotaur (10)—From Greek mythology, a monster with the head of a bull and the body of a man. Minos, king of Crete, received a bull from Poseidon, god of the sea, which he refused to sacrifice to the god. Poseidon inspired an unnatural love for the bull in Pasiphae, Minos' wife, and the minotaur resulted from the union. Minos enclosed the creature in a labyrinth constructed in the city of Knossos, and fed it seven young men and women (whom Athens had to pay as tribute to Crete) every few years. The original minotaur was eventually slain by the Athenian hero Theseus.

Cyclops (20)—Also from Greek mythology, a member of a race of one-eyed giants. According to Homer, the cyclopses were shepherds living on an island in the western area. The best known of these was Polyphemus, who had his eye poked out by the hero, Odysseus. According to Hesiod, the cyclopses were three of the children of Uranus and Gaea. They forged the thunderbolt for Zeus, king of the gods, and became the assistants of Hephaestus, god of the forge.

Zombie (30)—From legends in the West Indies, a corpse which has been reanimated. A rather unpleasant person to meet, he generally smells of rot and decay. He often has rotting pieces of himself falling off his body, yet never seems to fall apart completely. He is difficult to kill, since he is already dead. A person has to chop him into tiny pieces and then get away before the monster can pull himself back together.

Giant (40)—Appears in the mythology of almost all nations, huge beings of terrible aspect. In the Greek myths the giants are said to live in volcanic regions where they were banished after an unsuccessful war against the gods. Some giants are peaceful, but others, like the ones in the forest, would think nothing of having you or anyone else for a snack.

Harpy (50)—From Greek mythology, disgusting women with the wings and lower body of a bird, generally a bird of prey. They stole and befouled the food of blind Phineus as punishment from the gods. Phineus nearly died before Jason and the Argonauts arrived while sailing in search of the Golden Fleece. Two of the Argonauts, Zetes and Calais drove the harpies away and were then told by one of the gods that the harpies would bother Phineus no more. The harpies continued their disgusting practices elsewhere.

Griffin (60)—From Eastern mythology, a creature usually represented as having the head, beak, and wings of an eagle, and the body and legs of a lion. It builds its nest of gold, making it very tempting to hunters and forcing the griffin to keep vigilant guard. It instinctively knows where buried treasure is hidden and does its best to keep any plunderers at a distance.

Chimera (70)—From Greek mythology, a monster with the foreparts of a lion, the rearparts of a goat with a goat's head in the middle of its back, and with a serpent for a tail. The original chimera was slain by Bellerophon, who was riding on Pegasus, the winged horse. Ironically, Pegasus was a distant relative of the chimera.

Dragon (80)—Found in may of the world's mythologies, a reptilic monster resembling a giant lizard and usually represented as having wings, huge claws, and a fiery breath. In some places the dragon is considered to be a peaceful creature, notably in Japan and China, where it is regarded as a symbol of good fortune. However, the dragons in the forest are of the other sort; they will kill and eat you if you let them, and they take very unkindly to anyone trying to steal their treasure.

Wyvern (90)—A distant relative of the dragon, this is a fabulous two-legged creature, with wings and head of a dragon on a basilisk's body. Although he cannot kill you with one glance like the basilisk, he is still a very unpleasant creature to meet.

Basilisk (100)—The worst of all eleven monsters, his deadly glare kills anyone who gazes upon his face. From Greek mythology, the basilisk was called the king of serpents, being endowed with a scaly crest upon his head like a crown. This monster was supposedly produced from the egg of a cock hatched under toads or serpents. The weasel, the only animal which can withstand the basilisk's glare, often fought it to the death. Humans must use a mirror if they wish to be assured of victory over a basilisk, for the mirror will reflect the creature's gaze back upon it and kill it. This monster is not to be confused with the basilisk of South America, a harmless lizard with the ability to run across water.

Monster Combat

```
10 RANDOMIZE
20 REM "GIANT MONSTER ATTACK"
30 REM BY LEE J. CHAPEL 5/1/1980
40 REM MICROSOFT VERSION BY CHRIS VOGELI
50 PRINT "*** GIANT MONSTER ATTACK"
60 DIM E(10,10),B(10,10),M(11),M$(11),N(11),T$(11),P(11),G$(3)
70 DIM C(15),D(15)
80 FOR I=1 TO 11 : READ M$(I),T$(I),M(I),P(I) : NEXT I
90 V=INT(RND(1)*3)
100 C=INT(RND(1)*1501+500) : S=INT(RND(1)*6) : R=INT(RND(1)*4)
110 G$(1)="SLEEP SPELL" : G$(2)="CHARM" : G$(3)="INVISIBILITY SPELL"
120 PRINT:PRINT "DO YOU WISH TO USE THE STRENGTH AND MAGIC FROM A"
130 INPUT "PREVIOUS GAME (Y OR N)";X$ : IF X$="Y" THEN 3210
140 D=C : V1=V : S1=S : R1=R : PRINT"PLEASE WAIT"
150 FOR I=1 TO 10 : FOR J=1 TO 10
160 T=INT(RND(1)*10) : IF T<>1 OR CS=15 THEN T=0
170 H=INT(RND(1)*2) : W=INT(RND(1)*10) : P=INT(RND(1)*51)
180 A(I,J)=10000*T+100*P+10*W+H
190 IF T=1 THEN CS=CS+1 : C(CS)=I : D(CS)=J
200 NEXT J : NEXT I : T=0
210 X1=INT(RND(1)*8)+2 : Y1=INT(RND(1)*8)+2
220 X=INT(RND(1)*10)+1 : Y=INT(RND(1)*10)+1
230 IF X1<1 OR X1>10 OR Y1<1 OR Y1>10 THEN 2330
240 FOR I=1 TO 10 : FOR J=1 TO 10 : B(I,J)=0 : NEXT J : NEXT I
250 CA=INT(A(X1,Y1)/10000) : P=INT(((A(X1,Y1)-(10000*CA))/100))
260 W=INT((A(X1,Y1)-(10000*CA)-(100*P))/10)
270 H=A(X1,Y1)-10000*CA-100*P-10*W : I=0 : J=0
280 IF CA=1 THEN I=INT(RND(1)*10+1) : J=INT(RND(1)*10+1) : B(I,J)=7
290 IF CA=1 AND I=X AND Y=J THEN B(I,J)=0 : GOTO 280
300 IF H=1 THEN I=INT(RND(1)*10+1) : J=INT(RND(1)*9+1)
310 IF H=1 AND B(I,J)<>0 THEN 300
320 IF H=1 THEN B(I,J)=3
330 B(X,Y)=5 : IF W=0 THEN 380
340 FOR I=1 TO W
350 J=INT(RND(1)*10)+1 : K=INT(RND(1)*10)+1
360 IF B(J,K)<>0 THEN 350
370 B(J,K)=2 : NEXT I
380 IF P=0 THEN 430
390 FOR I=1 TO P
400 J=INT(RND(1)*10)+1 : K=INT(RND(1)*10)+1
410 IF B(J,K)<>0 THEN 400
420 B(J,K)=1 : NEXT I
430 FOR I=1 TO 10 :  FOR J=1 TO 10
440 IF B(J,I)=0 THEN PRINT "T";
450 IF B(J,I)=1 THEN PRINT "-";
460 IF B(J,I)=2 THEN PRINT "I";
470 IF B(J,I)=3 THEN PRINT "^";
480 IF B(J,I)=5 THEN PRINT "O";
490 IF B(J,I)=7 THEN PRINT "M";
500 NEXT J: PRINT TAB( 18);
510 IF I=2 THEN PRINT "COMBAT STRENGTH-"; : PRINT TAB( 40);C
520 IF I=3 THEN PRINT "TREASURE TOTAL -"; : PRINT TAB( 40);Q
530 IF I=4 THEN PRINT "MAGIC:"
540 IF I=5 THEN PRINT " SLEEP SPELLS";    : PRINT TAB( 40);S
550 IF I=6 THEN PRINT " CHARMS-"; : PRINT TAB( 40);R
560 IF I=7 THEN PRINT " INVISIBILITY-";   : PRINT TAB( 40);V
570 IF I=9 THEN PRINT "DAYS IN FOREST-";  : PRINT TAB( 40);D1
580 IF I=1 OR I=8 OR I=10 THEN PRINT
590 NEXT I: PRINT : IF T=1 THEN RETURN
600 IF T=2 THEN 1270
610 I=INT(RND(1)*5) : IF I=2 THEN GOSUB 2800
620 IF I=1 AND T<>9 THEN PRINT "THERE WAS NOTHING THERE" : GOTO 1270
630 IF I=1 AND T=9 THEN 1260
640 I=INT(RND(1)*16+1) : N=I : IF I=12 THEN 2040
650 IF I=13 THEN 2080
660 IF I=14 THEN 2120
670 IF I>14 THEN J=100 : GOTO 720
680 J=INT(RND(1)*100/M(I)) : N1=J : IF J=0 THEN J=1 : N1=J
690 IF J=1 THEN M$=M$(I) : PRINT "A ";M$;" IS GUARDING ";
700 IF J<>1 THEN M$=M$(I)+"S" : PRINT J;" ";M$;" ARE GUARDING ";
710 M=M(I)*J : I=INT(RND(1)*14+1)
720 IF I>11 AND J=100 THEN 610
730 IF I<12 AND J=100 THEN PRINT "NOTHING IS GUARDING ";
740 IF I>11 THEN 2230
750 IF I>11 THEN PRINT "NOTHING" : P=0 : GOTO 770
760 PRINT T$(I) : P=P(I)
770 IF M$=M$(11) AND M1=7 THEN 2030
780 IF J=100 THEN PRINT "YOU GET THE TREASURE FREE" : GOTO 1190
```

Monster Combat

```
790 PRINT "DO YOU WISH TO (1)FIGHT, (2)RUN, (3)BRIBE, OR (4)";
800 INPUT "CAST A SPELL";K
810 IF K<1 OR K>4 THEN 790
820 ON K GOTO 830,940,1080,1660
830 INPUT "HOW MANY COMBAT POINTS DO YOU WISH TO USE";K
840 IF K>C THEN PRINT "YOU ONLY HAVE";C; "COMBAT POINTS" : GOTO 830
850 I=INT(RND(1)*1001) : L=2 : C=C-K : K=K-.01*Q
860 FOR H=1000 TO 0 STEP -50
870 IF L*M<=K AND H>=I THEN 1170
880 L=L-.1 : NEXT H
890 PRINT "THE ";M$;" KILLED YOU. ";
900 PRINT "YOU LOSE EVERYTHING!"
910 INPUT "WISH TO TRY AGAIN (Y OR N)";X$ : PRINT
920 IF X$="Y" THEN RUN
930 PRINT : PRINT "SO LONG... BETTER LUCK NEXT TIME" : END
940 I=INT(RND(1)*12) : IF I=11 THEN 890
950 FOR H=0 TO 10 : IF H*10>=M AND H<=I THEN 970
960 NEXT H: GOTO 1150
970 A=X : B=Y : K=0 : T=0 : C=C-INT((RND(1)*21)+.001*Q)-5
980 X=A+INT(RND(1)*3)-1 : Y=B+INT(RND(1)*3)-1
990 IF X=A AND Y=B THEN 980
1000 D1=D1+.1 : IF X>10 THEN X=1 : X1=X1+1 : K=1
1010 IF Y>10 THEN Y=1 : Y1=Y1+1 : K=1
1020 IF X<1    THEN X=10: X1=X1-1 : K=1
1030 IF Y<1    THEN Y=10 : Y1=Y1-1 : K=1
1040 IF B(X,Y)>1 AND K=0 THEN 980
1050 B(A,B)=INT(RND(1)*3) : B(X,Y)=5 : IF I<>11 THEN Z=Z+1
1060 IF K=1 THEN 230
1070 GOTO 610
1080 INPUT "HOW MUCH DO YOU WISH TO PAY";K
1090 IF K>Q THEN PRINT "YOU ONLY HAVE";Q;"TREASURE POINTS." : GOTO 1080
1100 I=INT(RND(1)*22) : L=0 : IF I=21 OR (I>15 AND K<2) THEN 890
1110 J=(P+(M*.1))*N1 : IF K<2 THEN 1140
1120 FOR H=0 TO 20 : IF K<=J*L AND I>=H THEN 1140
1130 L=L+.1 : NEXT H: GOTO 1160
1140 PRINT "YOUR BRIBE WAS NOT ACCEPTED.";
1150 PRINT "YOU MUST FIGHT" : GOTO 830
1160 P=0 : Q=Q-K : BR=BR+1 : T=0 :  PRINT "YOUR BRIBE WAS ACCEPTED.";  : GOTO 1240
1170 N(N)=N(N)+N1
1180 PRINT "YOU BEAT THE ";M$
1190 IF N<12   THEN I=INT(RND(1)*7) : IF I=3 THEN 2150
1200 IF J=100 THEN I=INT(RND(1)*5) :IF I=3 THEN 2210
1210 Q=Q+P
1220 IF P=25 THEN 1900
1230 IF T>5 AND T<>9 THEN Q=Q-P : GOTO 2250
1240 PRINT "YOU NOW HAVE";Q;"TREASURE POINTS."
1250 IF P=200 THEN 1950
1260 IF T=9 THEN GOSUB 2530
1270 INPUT "WHICH DIRECTION (PRESS 1 FOR THE MAP)";X$
1280 IF X$="1" THEN T=2 : GOTO 430
1290 T=0 : INPUT "WHAT DISTANCE";K : IF K<>INT(K) THEN 1270
1300 GOTO 2500
1310 A1=X1 : B1=Y1 : A=X : B=Y : C=C-INT(7.5*K*RND(1))
1320 IF   LEFT$(X$,1)="N" THEN Y=Y-K
1330 IF   LEFT$(X$,1)="S" THEN Y=Y+K
1340 IF RIGHT$(X$,1)="E" THEN X=X+K
1350 IF RIGHT$(X$,1)="W" THEN X=X-K
1360 IF X>10 THEN X=X-10 : X1=X1+1 : IF X>10 THEN 1360
1370 IF X<1  THEN X=X+10 : X1=X1-1 : IF X<1 THEN 1370
1380 IF Y>10 THEN Y=Y-10 : Y1=Y1+1 : IF Y>10 THEN 1380
1390 IF Y<1  THEN Y=Y+10 : Y1=Y1-1 : IF Y<1 THEN 1390
1400 IF B(X,Y)=1 THEN C=C-5
1410 IF B(X,Y)=0 THEN C=C-10
1420 IF C<=0 THEN PRINT "YOU DIED FROM LACK OF STRENGTH.";  : GOTO 900
1430 IF X1<>A1 OR Y1<>B1 THEN 230
1440 IF B(X,Y)=7 THEN T=9
1450 IF B(X,Y)=2 THEN 1480
1460 IF B(X,Y)=3 THEN 1500
1470 B(A,B)=INT(RND(1)*3) : B(X,Y)=5 : GOTO 430
1480 PRINT "YOU TRIED TO GO THROUGH A WALL"
1490 C=C-INT(RND(1)*Q*.005)-25 : X=A : Y=B : GOTO 1270
1500 Y=Y+1 : C=D : B(A,B)=INT(RND(1)*3) : B(X,Y)=5 : T=1 : V=V1
1510 R=R1 : S=S1 : GOSUB 430
1520 PRINT "YOU STOPPED AT AN INN AND REGAINED YOUR STRENGTH"
1530 I=INT(RND(1)*Q*.75) : IF I<5 AND Q>5 THEN I=5
1540 IF I<5 AND Q<=5 THEN I=0
1550 PRINT "YOU PAID";I;"TREASURE POINTS TO SAY THERE" : Q=Q-I
1560 PRINT "YOU NOW HAVE";Q;"TREASURE POINTS"
```

Monster Combat

```
1570 I=INT(RND(1)*3) : IF I=2 THEN 1270
1580 IF I=1 THEN GOSUB 2670 : GOTO 1270
1590 I=INT(RND(1)*4+1)
1600 PRINT "THE INNKEEPER TOLD YOU THAT THE FOREST EDGE IS LESS THAN"
1610 ON I GOTO 1620,1630,1640,1650
1620 PRINT Y1*100;"YARDS TO THE NORTH" : GOTO 1270
1630 PRINT (11-Y1)*100;"YARDS TO THE SOUTH" : GOTO 1270
1640 PRINT X1*100;"YARDS TO THE WEST" : GOTO 1270
1650 PRINT (11-X1)*100;"YARDS TO THE EAST" : GOTO 1270
1660 IF T>5 THEN PRINT "YOU CAN'T USE MAGIC TO GET MAGIC" : GOTO 790
1670 IF S+V+R=0 THEN PRINT "YOU HAVE NO MAGIC" : GOTO 790
1680 PRINT "WHAT TYPE OF SPELL-(1)SLEEP, (2)CHARM, OR (3)INVISIBILITY";
1690 INPUT K : PRINT : IF K<1 OR K>3 THEN 1660
1700 ON K GOTO 1710,1790,1850
1710 IF S=0 THEN PRINT "YOU HAVE NO SLEEP SPELLS."; : GOTO 1150
1720 IF N=4 THEN PRINT "YOU CAN'T PUT ";M$(4);"S TO SLEEP."; : S=S-1 : GOTO 1150
1730 I=INT(RND(1)*10) : S=S-1
1740 IF I<3 THEN PRINT "YOUR SPELL WAS UNSUCCESSFUL."; : GOTO 1150
1750 IF I<8 THEN PRINT "YOU GOT THE TREASURE SAFELY" : GOTO 1190
1760 PRINT "THE ";M$;" WOKE TOO SOON"
1770 P=INT(RND(1)*P) : Q=Q+P
1780 PRINT "YOU GOT AWAY WITH";P;"TREASURE POINTS" : GOTO 1270
1790 IF R=0 THEN PRINT "YOU HAVE NO CHARMS."; : GOTO 1150
1800 I=INT(RND(1)*10) : R=R-1
1810 IF M<60 AND I>6 THEN PRINT "YOUR CHARM DIDN'T WORK."; : GOTO 1150
1820 IF M>50 AND I<2 THEN PRINT "YOUR CHARM DIDN'T WORK."; : GOTO 1150
1830 IF I=3 THEN PRINT "THE CHARM WORE OFF TOO SOON." : GOTO 1770
1840 I=3 : GOTO 1750
1850 IF V=0 THEN PRINT "YOU HAVE NO INVISIBILITY SPELLS."; : GOTO 1150
1860 I=INT(RND(1)*10) : V=V-1
1870 IF N>50 AND I>8 THEN PRINT "THE ";M$;" SMELLED YOU!" : GOTO 1770
1880 IF M<60 AND I=0 THEN PRINT "YOUR INVISIBILITY WORE OFF TOO SOON" : GOTO 1770
1890 GOTO 1840
1900 I=INT(RND(1)*2)+1 : ON I GOTO 1910,1930
1910 C=2*C : PRINT "YOU WON AN ENCHANTED SWORD. YOUR COMBAT STRENGTH "
1920 PRINT "IS DOUBLED AND IS NOW";C : GOTO 1240
1930 PRINT "YOU WON AN ORDINARY SWORD. YOUR COMBAT STRENGTH IS NOT"
1940 PRINT "DOUBLED AND REMAINS AT";C : GOTO 1240
1950 J=INT(RND(1)*10) : I=INT(RND(1)*10)
1960 IF J=7 AND M1<>7 THEN M1=7 : GOTO 1990
1970 IF I=1 THEN 2010
1980 GOTO 1260
1990 PRINT "THERE WAS A MIRROR IN THE CHEST. IT WILL PROTECT YOU"
2000 PRINT "AGAINST ANY ";M$(11);"S YOU MAY MEET" : M1=7 : GOTO 1270
2010 PRINT "THE TREASURE CHEST WAS A TRAP. YOU WERE KILLED WHEN ";
2020 PRINT "YOU OPENED IT" : GOTO 900
2030 PRINT "YOUR MIRROR KILLED THE ";M$ : N(11)=N(11)+1 : M=0 : GOTO 1190
2040 PRINT "A GIANT BAT GRABBED YOU AND CARRIED YOU TO A NEW SPOT"
2050 A=X : B=Y : T=0 : D1=D1+.1
2060 X=INT(RND(1)*10)+1 : Y=INT(RND(1)*10+1) : IF B(X,Y)>1 THEN 2060
2070 B(A,B)=INT(RND(1)*3) : B(X,Y)=5 : GOTO 610
2080 PRINT "YOU FELL INTO A PIT."; : I=INT((RND(1)*21)+.001*Q) : C=C-I
2090 IF C<=0 THEN PRINT "YOU DIED TRYING TO GET OUT" : GOTO 900
2100 PRINT "YOU USED";I;"COMBAT POINTS TRYING TO GET OUT" : I=11
2110 FOR J=1 TO 750 : NEXT J : GOTO 970
2120 J=0 : FOR I=1 TO 11 : J=J+N(I) : NEXT I : IF J<11 THEN 610
2130 PRINT "A GIANT NEIL CARRIED YOU TO SAFETY.";
2140 FOR I=1 TO 1000 : NEXT I: T=0 : GOTO 2340
2150 I=INT(RND(1)*11)+1 : M=M(I) : M$=M$(I) : N=I
2160 PRINT "A ";M$;" HEARD THE NOISE OF THE BATTLE AND CAME WANDERING BY"
2170 IF I=11 AND M1=7 THEN 2030
2180 INPUT "DO YOU WISH TO (1)FIGHT, (2)RUN, (3)CAST A SPELL";K
2190 IF K<1 OR K>3 THEN 2180
2200 ON K GOTO 830,940,1660
2210 I=INT(RND(1)*11)+1 : M=M(I) : M$=M$(I) : N=I
2220 PRINT "A ";M$;" CAME WANDERING BY" : GOTO 2170
2230 IF I<>14 THEN 750
2240 I=INT(RND(1)*3+1) : T=I+5 : PRINT "A ";G$(I) : P=INT(RND(1)*11) : GOTO 770
2250 I=INT(RND(1)*10)
2260 IF I=5 THEN PRINT "YOU WERE UNABLE TO MASTER THE SPELL.";
2270 IF I=5 THEN PRINT "YOU GAIN NO ";G$(T-5);"S" : GOTO 1270
2280 IF T=6 THEN S=S+1 : S1=S1+1
2290 IF T=7 THEN R=R+1 : R1=R1+1
2300 IF T=8 THEN V=V+1 : V1=V1+1
2310 PRINT "YOU WON THE ";G$(T-5) : T=0 : IF S1/5+R1/3+V1/2>6 THEN GOSUB 3280
2320 GOTO 1270
2330 FOR A=1 TO 750 : NEXT A
2340 PRINT "YOU SURVIVED THE FOREST" : FOR I=1 TO 1000 : NEXT I
```

Monster Combat

```
2350 PRINT "DO YOU WISH TO SEE THE # OF MONSTERS YOU KILLED, RAN FROM,"
2360 INPUT "AND BRIBED (Y OR N)";X$ : IF X$="N" THEN PRINT : GOTO 2420
2370 PRINT "MONSTER";TAB( 11)"# SLAIN";TAB( 32)"MONSTER";TAB( 43)"# SLAIN"
2380 FOR I=1 TO 5 : PRINT M$(I);TAB( 14);N(I);TAB( 32);M$(I+5);
2390 PRINT TAB( 46);N(I+5)
2400 NEXT I : PRINT TAB( 32); M$(11), TAB( 46); N(11)
2410 PRINT : PRINT "BRIBED-";BR; TAB( 32) "RAN FROM";Z
2420 PRINT TAB( 10)"TREASURE TOTAL-";Q
2430 IF Q1<>0 THEN GOSUB 3250
2440 PRINT "CONGRATULATIONS"; : IF Q1<>0 AND Q1>Q THEN PRINT " ANYWAY" : PRINT
2450 PRINT : X$=""
2460 IF D1<30 THEN INPUT "DO YOU WISH TO RETURN TO THE FOREST";X$
2470 REM
2480 S=S1 : V=V1 : R=R1 : C=D : IF X$<>"Y" THEN 3080
2490 GOTO 210
2500 D1=D1+K/10 : IF D1<30 THEN 1310
2510 PRINT "YOUR TIME IS UP. 30 DAYS HAVE PASSED"
2520 FOR I=1 TO 1000 : NEXT I : GOTO 2130
2530 FOR I=1 TO 2500 : NEXT I : T=0
2540 PRINT "YOU MADE IT INTO THE ENCHANTED CASTLE"
2550 I=INT(RND(1)*21)*100 : J=INT(RND(1*9) : A(X1,Y1)=A(X1,Y1)-10000
2560 GOSUB 2790 : PRINT "YOU FOUND ";I;"TREASURE POINTS THERE" : Q=Q+I
2570 IF J<>7 OR M1=7 THEN 2600
2580 PRINT "YOU ALSO FOUND A MIRROR WHICH WILL KILL ANY ";
2590 PRINT M$(11);"S" YOU MEET" : M1=7
2600 J=INT(RND(1)*20) : IF J=2 THEN C=2*C
2610 IF J=2 THEN PRINT "YOU ALSO FOUND AN ENCHANTED SWORD WHICH DOUBLES ";
2620 IF J=2 THEN PRINT "YOUR STRENGTH"
2630 FOR I=1 TO CS-1 : IF C(I)<>X1 THEN 2650
2640 FOR J=I TO CS-1 : C(J)=C(J+1) : D(J)=D(J+1) : NEXT J
2650 NEXT I : CS=CS-1 : IF CS=0 THEN PRINT "YOU FOUND THE LAST OF THE CASTLES"
2660 RETURN
2670 IF CS=0 THEN RETURN
2680 I=INT(RND(1)*CS+1)
2690 PRINT "THE INKEEPER TOLD YOU OF A LEGEND OF A CASTLE.";
2700 IF C(I)=X1 AND D(I)=Y1 THEN PRINT "VERY CLOSE BY" : RETURN
```

```
2710 J=X1-C(I) : I=Y1-D(I)
2720 IF ABS(I)=ABS(J) THEN PRINT "DIRECTLY TO THE "; : GOTO 2740
2730 PRINT "SOMEWHERE TO THE ";
2740 IF I<0 THEN PRINT "SOUTH";
2750 IF I>0 THEN PRINT "NORTH";
2760 IF J>0 THEN PRINT "WEST";
2770 IF J<0 THEN PRINT "EAST";
2780 PRINT : RETURN
2790 REM
2800 I=INT(RND(1)*11+1)
2810 ON I GOTO 2820, 2860, 2840, 2890, 2920, 2950, 2970, 2990, 3010, 3020, 3050
2820 PRINT "YOU STEPPED INTO A TIME WARP AND LOST SEVEN DAYS"
2830 D1=D1+7 : RETURN
2840 I=INT(RND(1)*10+1) : J=D1 : D1=D1-I : IF D1<.1 THEN D1=.1 : I=J-D1
2850 PRINT "YOU STEPPED INTO A TIME WARP AND GAINED";I;"DAYS" : RETURN
2860 IF C>=D THEN RETURN
2870 PRINT "YOU MET AN ELF WITH A MAGIC DRINK THAT GAVE"
2880 PRINT "YOUR COMBAT STRENGTH BACK" : C=D : RETURN
2890 IF V+R+S=V1+R1+S1 THEN RETURN
2900 PRINT "YOU RAN INTO A WIZARD WHO GAVE YOU A POTION THAT"
2910 PRINT "RESTORED ALL YOUR MAGIC" : V=V1 : R=R1 : S=S1 : RETURN
2920 IF Q<2 THEN RETURN
2930 PRINT "YOU FELL INTO SOME QUICKSAND. YOU LOST HALF OF YOUR"
2940 PRINT "TREASURE" : Q=INT(Q/2) : RETURN
2950 PRINT "YOU RAN INTO SOME THICK UNDERBRUSH AND USED UP HALF"
2960 PRINT "YOUR STRENGTH" : C=INT(C/2) : RETURN
2970 I=INT(RND(1)*50+1) : PRINT "YOU FOUND";I;"COINS LYING ON THE";
2980 PRINT " GROUND AND PICKED THEM UP" : Q=Q+I : RETURN
2990 IF M1<>7 THEN RETURN
3000 PRINT "YOU TRIPPED OVER SOME ROOTS AND LOST YOUR MIRROR" : M1=0 : RETURN
3010 PRINT "A HERMIT TOLD YOU THAT THERE ARE";CS;"CASTLES LEFT" : RETURN
3020 IF V+S+R=0 THEN RETURN
3030 PRINT "YOU WANDERED INTO AN AREA WERE MAGIC DOESN'T WORK"
3040 PRINT "YOU LOSE ALL YOUR PRESENT MAGIC" : V=0 : S=0 : R=0 : RETURN
3050 IF CS=0 THEN RETURN
3060 PRINT "YOU MET A HUNTER WHO TOLD YOU OF THE LEGEND OF A"
3070 PRINT "CASTLE "; : I=INT(RND(1)*CS)+1 : GOSUB 2700 : RETURN
3080 FOR I=1 TO 2000 : NEXT : PRINT
3090 PRINT "DO YOU WISH TO GO TO A NEW FOREST WITH THE SAME STRENGTH ";
3100 INPUT "AND MAGIC";X$ : IF X$="Y" THEN 3190
3110 PRINT "DO YOU WISH TO GO TO A NEW FOREST WITH A NEW STRENGTH AND ";
3120 INPUT " MAGIC";X$ : IF X$="Y" THEN RUN
3130 PRINT "DO YOU PLAN ON USING THE SAME STRENGTH AND MAGIC AGAIN"
3140 INPUT "SOME OTHER TIME (Y OR N)";X$ : IF X$="Y" THEN GOTO 3350
3150 PRINT : PRINT "ONCE AGAIN, YOU TREASURE TOTAL WAS";Q
3160 IF Q>Q1 THEN Q1=Q
3170 IF Q1<>0 THEN PRINT "THE LARGEST TREASURE TOTAL YOU GOT WITH THIS";
3180 PRINT "STRENGTH AND MAGIC WAS";Q1 : PRINT : PRINT " BYE NOW" : END
3190 BR=0 : Z=0 : D1=0 : FOR I=1 TO 11 : N(I)=0 : NEXT I: IF Q1<Q THEN Q1=Q
3200 Q=0 : GOTO 140
3210 INPUT "COMBAT STRENGTH";C
3220 IF C<500 OR C>2000 THEN 3210
3230 INPUT "SLEEP SPELLS";S : INPUT "CHARMS";R : INPUT "INVISIBILITY";V
3240 INPUT "PREVIOUS LARGEST TREASURE TOTAL";Q1 : GOTO 140
3250 IF Q1<Q THEN PRINT "YOU WON MORE TREASURE THIS TIME THAN BEFORE"
3260 IF Q1>Q THEN PRINT "YOU DIDN'T OBTAIN AS MUCH TREASURE THIS TIME"
3270 RETURN
3280 PRINT "YOUR MAGIC TOTAL IS RATHER LARGE. DO YOU WISH TO CONVERT IT TO"
3290 INPUT "COMBAT POINTS";X$ : IF X$="N" THEN RETURN
3300 S1=S1-5 : R1=R1-3 : V1=V1-2 : IF S1<=0 THEN S1=1
3310 IF R1<=0 THEN R1=1
3320 IF V1<=0 THEN V1=1
3330 S=S1 : R=R1 : V=V1 : C=C+100 : D=D+100 : PRINT "YOUR COMBAT STRENGTH IS";
3340 PRINT "PERMENANTLY INCREASED BY 100" : RETURN
3350 PRINT "COMBAT STRENGTH-";D : PRINT "SLEEP SPELLS-";S1 : PRINT "CHARMS-";R1
3360 PRINT "INVISIBILITY-";V1 : PRINT : RETURN
3370 DATA GOBLIN, 10 SILVER SPOONS (10 POINTS), 5, 10, MINOTAUR
3380 DATA A SWORD WHICH MIGHT BE ENCHANTED (25 POINTS), 10, 25
3390 DATA CYCLOPS, 50 SILVER COINS (50 POINTS), 20, 50, ZOMBIE
3400 DATA 100 GOLD PIECES (100 POINTS), 30, 100, GIANT
3410 DATA AN ENCHANTED BRACELET (50 POINTS), 40, 50, HARPY
3420 DATA A TREASURE CHEST (200 POINTS), 50, 200, GRIFFIN
3430 DATA A PEARL NECKLACE (50 POINTS),60, 50, CHIMERA
3440 DATA A JEWELED SWORD (30 POINTS), 70, 30, DRAGON
3450 DATA A JAR OF RUBIES (75 POINTS), 80, 75, WYVERN
3460 DATA A BOX OF JEWELS (100 POINTS), 90, 100, BASILISK
3470 DATA A GOLD GOBLET (50 POINTS), 100, 50
3480 END
```

Monster Combat

```
   -TTTTTTTTT
   T-T-TTTTTT      COMBAT STRENGTH-      1914
   TTT-0TTTTT      TREASURE TOTAL-       0
   TTTTTTTTTIT     MAGIC:
   TTTTTTTTT-T       SLEEP SPELLS-       2
   T-IT↑TTITI       CHARMS-             1
   -TTTTTTTTT        INVISIBILITY-       1
   TTTTTTTTTT
   TTTTTTTTT-      DAYS IN FOREST-       1.5
   TTT-TTT-TT

   3 CYCLOPSS ARE GUARDING 100 GOLD PIECES (100 POINTS)
DO YOU WISH TO (1)FIGHT,(2)RUN,(3)BRIBE,OR (4)CAST A SPELL?
1HOW MANY COMBAT POINTS DO YOU WISH TO USE? 121
YOU BEAT THE CYCLOPSS
YOU NOW HAVE 100 TREASURE POINTS
WHICH DIRECTION (PRESS 1 FOR THE MAP)? S
WHAT DISTANCE? 3

   -TTTTTTTTT
   T-T-TTTTTT      COMBAT STRENGTH-      1992
   TTT--TTTTT      TREASURE TOTAL-       100
   TTTTTTTTTIT     MAGIC:
   TTTTTTTTT-T       SLEEP SPELLS-       2
   T-IT↑TTITI       CHARMS-             1
   -TTT0TTTTT        INVISIBILITY-       1
   TTTTTTTTTT
   TTTTTTTTT-      DAYS IN FOREST-       1.8
   TTT-TTT-TT

YOU STOPPED AT AN INN AND REGAINED YOUR STRENGTH
YOU PAID 5 TREASURE POINTS TO STAY THERE
YOU NOW HAVE 95 TREASURE POINTS
WHICH DIRECTION (PRESS 1 FOR THE MAP)? S
WHAT DISTANCE? 7

   -TTTTT-T-T
   T----TTT--      COMBAT STRENGTH-      1936
   -T-T-TTT--      TREASURE TOTAL-       95
   -T-T0-I-TT      MAGIC:
   -T--TT--T         SLEEP SPELLS-       2
   T----TTTT-       CHARMS-             1
   ----TT-T-T        INVISIBILITY-       1
   --TTT---TT
   -T↑T--TTT-      DAYS IN FOREST-       2.5
   T----TTTT-

   19 GOBLINS ARE GUARDING A JEWELED SWORD (30 POINTS)
DO YOU WISH TO (1)FIGHT,(2)RUN,(3)BRIBE,OR (4)CAST A SPELL?
1HOW MANY COMBAT POINTS DO YOU WISH TO USE? 60
THE GOBLINS KILLED YOU. YOU LOSE EVERYTHING
DO YOU WISH TO TRY AGAIN?N

SO LONG.BETTER LUCK NEXT TIME
```

Mu-Torere

> **Mu-Torere** was written by Sandy Greenfarb and originally appeared in *Creative Computing*, August 1982.

I can't tell you how to pronounce it or what it means, but I know that Mu-Torere was played as late as 1912 by the Ngati-Porou tribe of the Maoris of the East Cape district of New Zealand. How's that for exotic origin! There appears to be some mystery about it. The fact that it was limited to one small corner of New Zealand suggests that it couldn't have been there very long, and that it must have been introduced by Europeans or by Polynesian seafarers. However, (according to an article in *Datalink*) no one has traced the game anywhere else.

The layout for Mu-Torere is a nine-pointed star (See Figure 1). The center circle is known as the *putahi*. The first player has four white stones which are initially placed at the ends of four adjacent arms of the star. The second player places four black stones at the ends of four adjacent arms. Players take alternate moves, playing one stone per move.

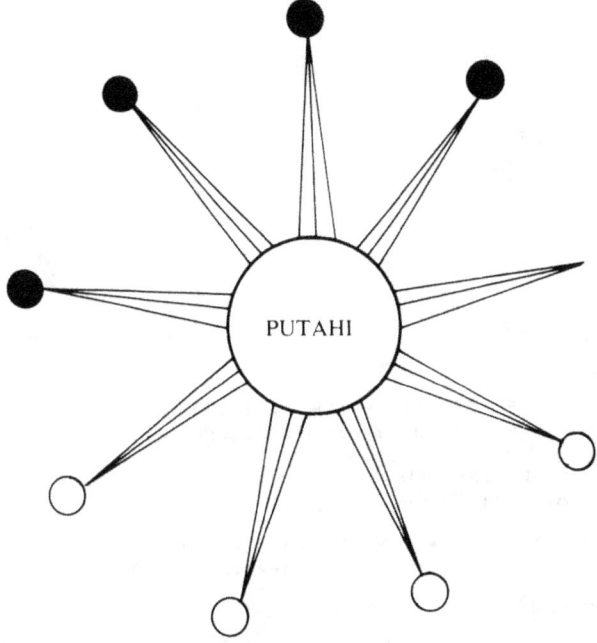

Figure 1. Normal Mu-Torere setup.

At any point in the game, there are three possible types of move:

1. Move sideways to the next arm if that point is vacant.

2. Move into the *putahi* if it is empty.

3. Move from the *putahi* to any unoccupied arm.

The game is won when an opponent is so placed that it is impossible to move any pieces. Despite the apparent simplicity, the game has a degree of subtlety that requires thinking ahead several moves in order to force the opponent into an unplayable position. One virtue of the game is its utter simplicity to create. It can be drawn on paper, sand, or almost anywhere.

Due to the ease of setup, I felt that a two-player version would be too simple and decided on a solitaire version. Also, since it is boring to lose everytime, I did not program the computer to play perfectly. Several situational strategies are built into the program. The program will also recognize one-move forced wins and avoid certain forced-loss situations. If none of the specific strategies applies, the program will select an arbitrary move, in some cases good and in others bad. In other words, it plays like most humans.

In order to keep the program adaptable for most micros, the star was converted to a linear arrangement of numbered squares (See Figure 2). The *putahi* became the zero square and the nine points of the star became the numbered squares, one through nine. The parallel to the original rules is as follows:

1. Move sideways to the next adjacent number if vacant. (One should be considered adjacent to two and nine.)

2. Any number can move into zero, the *putahi,* if it is empty.

3. Zero can move into any unoccupied number.

The human plays "X" and the computer plays "O". You have the choice of moving first or second. Good luck.

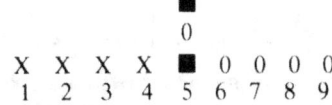

Figure 2. Video screen setup for Mu-Torere

Mu-Torere

```
10 REM ******************************
20 REM *          MU-TORERE          *
30 REM *      in Microsoft BASIC      *
40 REM ******************************
50 DEF FN P(X)=X-9*(-1*(X>9))
60 DEF FN A(X)=A(FN P(X))
70 DEF FN R(X)=INT(1+X*RND(1))
80 GOTO 1030
90 REM *** Player's Move ***
100 PRINT:PRINT:PRINT "Your move: ";
110 A$=INKEY$:IF A$="" THEN 110
120 PRINT A$;",";:X=VAL(A$)
130 A$=INKEY$:IF A$="" THEN 130
140 PRINT A$:Y=VAL(A$):PRINT
150 IF A(X)<>1 OR A(Y)<>0 THEN 170
160 IF X=0 OR Y=0 OR ABS(X-Y)=1 OR ABS(X-Y)=8 THEN 180
170 PRINT "Invalid move.  Try again: ";:GOTO 110
180 A(X)=0:A(Y)=1
190 ZR=Y
200 GOSUB 1250
210 P=1:GOSUB 770:P=-1
220 GOSUB 290
230 IF ZR=Y THEN GOSUB 550
240 A(X)=0:A(Y)=-1
250 CLS:PRINT "  My move: ";:PRINT USING"#";X;:PRINT ",";:PRINT USING"#";Y:PF=1:GOSUB 1150:GOSUB 950:
GOSUB 770
260 GOSUB 1250
270 GOTO 100
280 REM *** Computer's  Move ***
290 IF H(1)<>0 THEN H=H(1):GOSUB 660
300 IF SW=1 THEN SW=0:RETURN
310 IF H(2)<>0 THEN H=H(2):GOSUB 660
320 ON (A(0)+2) GOTO 590,340,510
330 REM *** If 0 Square is Empty ***
340 IF FN A(H(2)+8)<>-1 OR FN A(H(2)+1)<>-1 THEN 370
350 IF FN A(H(2)+7)=-1 THEN X=FN P(H(2)+8):Y=0:RETURN
360 IF FN A(H(2)+2)=-1 THEN X=FN P(H(2)+1):Y=0:RETURN
370 H(2)=H:IF FN A(H+7)=1 AND FN A(H+8)=-1 AND FN A(H+1)=1 THEN X=FN P(H+8):Y=-X
380 IF FN A(H+2)=1 AND FN A(H+3)=1 AND Y=-X THEN 430
390 IF Y=-X THEN Y=0:RETURN
400 IF FN A(H+2)=1 AND FN A(H+1)=-1 AND FN A(H+8)=1 THEN X=FN P(H+1):Y=-X
410 IF FN A(H+7)=1 AND FN A(H+6)=1 AND Y=-X THEN 430
420 IF Y=-X THEN Y=0:RETURN
430 I=0
440 I=I+1:IF I>9 THEN I=1
450 IF A(I)<>-1 OR FN R(4)<3 THEN 440
460 IF FN A(I+8)=0 AND FN R(4)<3 THEN X=I:Y=FN P(I+8):RETURN
470 IF FN A(I+1)=0 AND FN R(4)<3 THEN X=I:Y=FN P(I+1):RETURN
480 IF Y<>-I AND FN R(4)<3 THEN X=I:Y=0:RETURN
490 GOTO 440
500 REM *** If 0 Square Contains an X
510 H=H(1):GOSUB 690:IF SW=1 THEN SW=0:RETURN
520 H=H(2):GOSUB 690:IF SW=1 THEN SW=0:RETURN
530 IF FN A(H+1)=-1 AND FN R(4)<3 THEN X=FN P(H+1):Y=H:RETURN
540 IF FN A(H+8)=-1 AND FN R(4)<3 THEN X=FN P(H+8):Y=H:RETURN
550 IF A(0)=-1 AND FN R(4)<3 THEN X=0:Y=H(FN R(2)):RETURN
560 IF H=H(2) THEN H=H(1):GOTO 530
570 H=H(2):GOTO 530
580 REM *** IF 0 Square Contains an 0
590 H=H(1):GOSUB 720:IF SW=1 THEN SW=0:RETURN
600 H=H(2):GOSUB 720:IF SW=1 THEN SW=0:RETURN
610 H=H(1):GOSUB 750:IF SW=1 THEN SW=0:RETURN
620 H=H(2):GOSUB 750:IF SW=1 THEN SW=0:RETURN
630 H=H(1):GOSUB 690:IF SW=1 THEN SW=0:RETURN
640 H=H(2):GOSUB 690:IF SW=1 THEN SW=0:RETURN
650 GOTO 530
660 IF FN A(H+8)=1 AND FN A(H+1)=-1 AND FN A(H+2)=-1 THEN X=FN P(H+1):Y=H:SW=1:RETURN
670 IF FN A(H+1)=1 AND FN A(H+8)=-1 AND FN A(H+7)=-1 THEN X=FN P(H+8):Y=H:SW=1:RETURN
680 RETURN
690 IF FN A(H+1)=-1 AND FN A(H+2)=-1 THEN X=FN P(H+1):Y=H:SW=1:RETURN
700 IF FN A(H+8)=-1 AND FN A(H+7)=-1 THEN X=FN P(H+8):Y=H:SW=1:RETURN
710 RETURN
720 IF FN A(H+8)=-1 AND FN A(H+1)=-1 AND FN A(H+2)=0 THEN X=FN P(H+1):Y=FN P(H+2):SW=1:RETURN
730 IF FN A(H+1)=-1 AND FN A(H+8)=-1 AND FN A(H+7)=0 THEN X=FN P(H+8):Y=FN P(H+7):SW=1:RETURN
740 RETURN
750 IF FN A(H+8)=1 AND FN A(H+1)=1 THEN X=0:Y=H:SW=1:RETURN
760 RETURN
770 IF A(0)=0 OR A(0)=-P THEN RETURN
```

Mu-Torere

```
780 H=H(1):GOSUB 880:IF Q THEN RETURN
790 H=H(2):GOSUB 880:IF Q THEN RETURN
800 PRINT:PRINT:PRINT
810 BEEP:BEEP:BEEP
820 IF P=1 THEN PRINT "YOU WIN!"
830 IF P=-1 THEN PRINT "THE COMPUTER WINS!"
840 PRINT:PRINT "Care to play again (Y or N) ?";
850 A$=INKEY$:IF A$="" THEN 850
860 IF A$="N" OR A$="n" THEN:CLS:END
870 RUN
880 Q=0
890 IF A(0)=-P THEN Q=1:RETURN
900 IF H>1 THEN IF A(H-1)=-P THEN Q=1:RETURN
910 IF H<8 THEN IF A(H+1)=-P THEN Q=1:RETURN
920 IF H=1 THEN IF A(9)=-P THEN Q=1:RETURN
930 IF H=9 THEN IF A(1)=-P THEN Q=1:RETURN
940 RETURN
950 H(1)=-1:PRINT
960 FOR I=1 TO 9
970 PRINT TAB(4*I-3);
980 IF A(I)=1 THEN PRINT "X";
990 IF A(I)=-1 THEN PRINT "O";
1000 IF A(I)=0 THEN PRINT "I";
1010 IF GP=1 THEN RETURN
1020 NEXT I:RETURN
1030 DIM H(2),A(9)
1040 CLS:PRINT TAB(16)"MU-TORERE":PRINT
1050 PRINT "    The object of the game is to make it"::PRINT "impossible for your opponent to move.":PRINT
1060 PRINT "    There are 3 types of legal moves:":PRINT:PRINT "    1.  Sideways to the next adjacent":
PRINT "        square (1 and 9 are adjacent)"
1070 PRINT "    2.  To 0 if it is empty":PRINT "    3.  From 0 to any unoccupied number"
1080 PRINT:PRINT "    You and the computer take":PRINT "alternating moves until the game ends."
1090 PRINT:PRINT "    To move, just press the number you":PRINT "moving from and the number you are":
PRINT "moving to."
1100 PRINT:PRINT "    You play 'X' and the computer":PRINT "plays 'O'."
1110 PRINT "    Press any key to begin.";
1120 A$=INKEY$:IF A$="" THEN 1120
1130 CLS:FOR I=1 TO 4:A(I)=1:A(I+5)=-1:NEXT I
1140 A(0)=0:A(5)=0
1150 PRINT TAB(173)"O":PRINT TAB(17);:GP=1:I=0:GOSUB 980:GP=0:PRINT:PRINT:FOR I=1 TO 9:PRINT I;" ";;
NEXT I
1160 IF PF=1 THEN PF=0:RETURN
1170 GOSUB 950:GOSUB 1250
1180 REM
1190 PRINT:PRINT:PRINT "Do you want to go first (Y or N) ?";
1200 A$=INKEY$:IF A$="" THEN 1200
1210 PRINT:IF A$<>"N" AND A$<>"n" THEN 100
1220 P=-1
1230 IF FN R(3)<3 THEN A(6)=0:A(5)=-1:X=6:Y=5:GOTO 250
1240 X=FN R(4)+5:Y=0:A(X)=0:A(0)=-1:GOTO 250
1250 D=1:FOR I=0 TO 9:IF A(I)=0 THEN H(D)=I:D=D+1
1260 NEXT I:RETURN
```

Mu-Torere

```
            MU-TORERE
    The object of the game is to make it
impossible for your opponent to move.

    There are 3 types of legal moves:

    1.   Sideways to the next adjacent
         square (1 and 9 are adjacent)
    2.   To 0 if it is empty
    3.   From 0 to any unoccupied number

    You and the computer take
alternating moves until the game ends.

    To move, just press the number you
moving from and the number you are
moving to.

    You play 'X' and the computer
plays 'O'.
    Press any key to begin.■
```

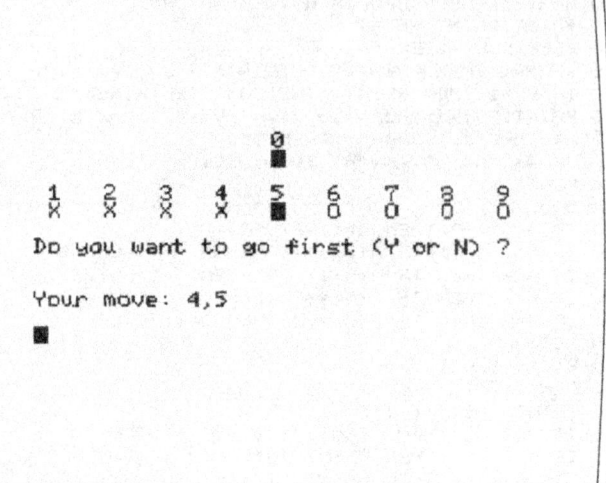

```
                    0
                    ■

   1   2   3   4   5   6   7   8   9
   X   X   X   X   ■   O   O   O   O

Do you want to go first (Y or N) ?

Your move: 4,5
■
```

```
    My move: 8,0


                    0
                    O

   1   2   3   4   5   6   7   8   9
   X   X   X   ■   X   O   O   ■   O

Your move: 3,4
■
```

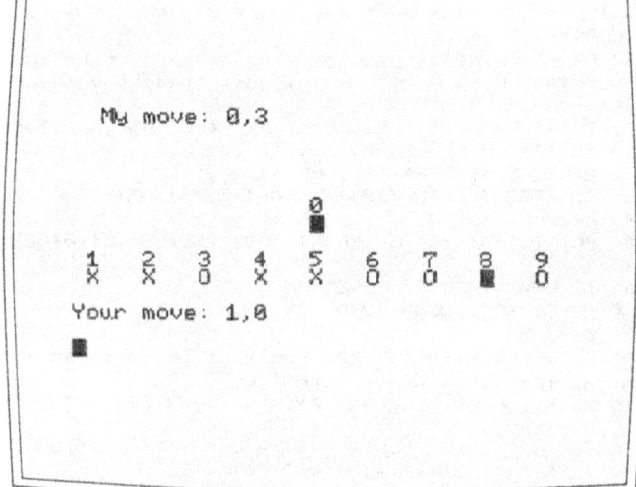

```
    My move: 0,3


                    0
                    ■

   1   2   3   4   5   6   7   8   9
   X   X   O   X   X   O   O   ■   O

Your move: 1,0
■
```

```
    My move: 7,8


                    0
                    X

   1   2   3   4   5   6   7   8   9
   ■   X   O   X   X   O   ■   O   O

Your move: 0,1
■
```

```
    My move: 8,0


                    0
                    O

   1   2   3   4   5   6   7   8   9
   X   X   O   X   X   O   ■   ■   O

THE COMPUTER WINS!

Care to play again (Y or N) ?■
```

Presidential Campaign

Presidential Campaign was written by Ralph G. White and orginally appeared in *Creative Computing*, October, 1980.

Presidential Campaign is a simulation of the nine month period leading up to a national presidential election. You must make decisions regarding issues, expenditures, travel, and other campaign activities. It is assumed that you are the chosen candidate of your party, and that there is no primary battle.

The country is divided into six regions:

The New England states

The upper midwest and middle Atlantic states

The southern states

The great plains states

The southwest states

The northwest and west coast states

Issue, party affiliation, campaign activities, etc. affect each group of states differently. Some actions have an equal effect on all states while others do not. Thus, some people will be more pleased than others with your approach to political issues whereas some of your decisions may be highly unpopular in some areas.

The incumbent initially gets a 10% edge. A routine to determine the popularity of the president then adjusts the figure accordingly. Party affiliation of the user also affects the initial conditions.

Not only do you get to choose whether to be the incumbent or challenger and whether to be a Democrat or Republican, but also to determine which of six different issues will be the most important issue to your campaign and which issue will be the least important. All of these decisions can influence the effectiveness fo your campaign. Which issues are chosen most important and least important do not affect initial conditions.

You have nine months in which to campaign. Status in an individual state can be improved by either campaigning in the state or spending campaign money in it. The influence you and your money have in each state varies. The major factor is the number of electoral votes. The number of days campaigning or the amount of money spent is also of importance. It costs $1100 per day to visit each state, however, some of the days you plan to be in a state can be designated for fund raising as well as campaigning. Fund raising does not help your popularity in a state, but it feeds the campaign treasury. Campaigning increases popularity, but depletes the treasury.

Aside from meeting campaign expenses, the money can be spent in each state to finance campaign committees. The maximum that can be spent in each state at one time is $50,000. You are allowed to visit as many states as time and money allow. You can spend as much money each month as you can afford.

At the end of each month, you will be given a report on the balance of the campaign treasury at the beginning of the month and at the end, the contributions and expenditures for the month, and the results of a political poll which will show your popularity status for a state chosen at random.

Before the beginning of the next month, a political event will happen. How the event affects you depends upon the conditions you set forth at the beginning of the program. Some of the events require you to make a decision and the course of actions taken influences your status. At the end of the campaign, the program calculates the results, state by state, of the popular vote, although only the electoral vote is shown.

Presidential Campaign

```
10 REM **************************
20 REM * THE PRESIDENTIAL CAMPAIGN *
30 REM *    in Microsoft BASIC    *
40 REM **************************
50 CLEAR 500:DIM ST(10,15)
60 M$(1)="February":M$(2)="March":M$(3)="April":M$(4)="May"
70 M$(5)="June":M$(6)="July":M$(7)="August":M$(8)="September":M$(9)="October"
80 A$="Your campaign fund has $###,###,###.##"
90 B$="$###,###,###.##    $###,###,###.##"
100 D$="Contributions = $$###,###.##          Expenditures = $$###,###.##"
110 FOR I=1 TO 6:ST(5,I)=50:ST(5,I)=50:NEXT I
120 FOR I=1 TO 13:ST(2,I)=50:ST(4,I)=50:NEXT I
130 FOR I=1 TO 7:ST(3,I)=50:ST(6,I)=50:NEXT I
140 F=0:A#=500000!
150 CLS:PRINT TAB(198)"*** THE PRESIDENTIAL CAMPAIGN ***"
160 PRINT:PRINT:INPUT "Please enter a number from 1 to 500";N
170 IF N<1 OR N>500 THEN 160
180 FOR I=1 TO N:R=RND(1):NEXT I
190 FOR I=1 TO 2000:NEXT I
200 GOSUB 2900
210 CLS
220 PRINT "Conditions":PRINT:PRINT
230 PRINT "Choose the conditions that you wish to":PRINT "be true."
240 PRINT "In what year to you wish the election":INPUT "to take place";EY:EY=ABS(EY):IF EY=0 THEN 240
250 IF EY/4=INT(EY/4) THEN 270
260 PRINT "That is not an election year.":GOTO 240
270 INPUT "Enter your name";N$
280 INPUT "Enter your opponent's name";O$
290 PRINT:PRINT"Do you wish to be 1) the incumbent or":INPUT"2) the challenger";P1
300 IF P1<0 OR P1>2 THEN 290
310 PRINT:PRINT "Do you wish to be 1) a Democrat or":INPUT "2) a Republican";P2
320 IF P2<1 OR P2>2 THEN 310
330 PR=INT(RND(1)*100)
340 IF PR<30 THEN PA=-8
350 IF PR>=30 AND PR<40 THEN PA=-5
360 IF PR>=40 AND PR<55 THEN PA=2
370 IF PR>=55 AND PR<65 THEN PA=6
380 IF PR>=65 THEN PA=10
390 IF P1=2 THEN PA=-PA
400 FOR I=1 TO 6:C(I)=PA:NEXT I
410 GOSUB 1380
420 C(1)=-8:C(2)=10:C(3)=-15:C(4)=12:C(5)=6:C(6)=-9
430 IF P2=1 THEN 450
440 FOR I=1 TO 6:C(I)=-C(I):NEXT I
450 GOSUB 1380
460 CLS:PRINT TAB(13);"I S S U E S":PRINT
470 PRINT "1) Unemployment  4) Social Adjustments"
480 PRINT "2) Inflation      5) Defense"
490 PRINT "3) Energy         6) Foreign Affairs"
500 PRINT:PRINT "Which is most important to your":INPUT "campaign";I1
510 IF I1<1 OR I1>6 OR INT(I1)<>I1 THEN 500
520 INPUT "Which is least important";I2
530 IF I2<1 OR I2>6 OR INT(I2)<>I2 THEN 520
540 FOR T=1 TO 9
550 CLS:PRINT "Date: ";M$(T):PRINT (10-T);"Months before election"
560 CM#=0:TS#=0
570 PRINT USING A$;A#:AB#=A#:MD=0:PRINT
580 INPUT "What state do you wish to visit";V$
590 PRINT "You have";(30-MD);"unscheduled days":PRINT "left this month."
600 PRINT "How many days to you wish to stay":INPUT "there";DV
610 IF MD+DV>30 THEN 600
620 MD=MD+DV
630 PRINT "How many of the";DV;"days will be":INPUT "for fund raising";DF
640 INPUT "How many days for campaigning";DC
650 IF DV<DC+DF THEN 630
660 RESTORE
670 READ ST$,EV,I,J
680 IF ST$<>"end" THEN 710
690 PRINT "You did not spell the state correctly."
700 MD=MD-DV:GOTO 580
710 IF ST$<>V$ THEN 670
720 CC#=INT(EV*1600*(DF/30)):CE=DV*1100:A#=A#+CC#-CE:CM#=CM#+CC#:TS#=TS#+CE
730 ST(I,J)=ST(I,J)+INT((100-ST(I,J))*DC/30)
740 IF MD>=30 THEN 780
750 PRINT "Do you wish to visit another":INPUT"state (yes/no)";C$
760 UY$=LEFT$(C$,1):IF UY$="Y" OR UY$="y" THEN 580
770 IF UY$<>"N" AND UY$<>"n" THEN 750
780 CLS
```

Presidential Campaign

```
790 PRINT "Spend campaign money in which":INPUT "state";SP$
800 PRINT USING A$;A#
810 PRINT:INPUT "How much do you wish to spend";AS
820 IF AS<=50000! THEN 840
830 PRINT "The most you can spend at a single":PRINT "time is $50,000.":GOTO 810
840 IF AS>50000! THEN 810
850 IF AS>A# THEN 800
860 A#=A#-AS:TS#=TS#+AS
870 RESTORE
880 READ ST$,EV,I,J
890 IF ST$<>"end" THEN 920
900 PRINT "You did not spell the state correctly."
910 A#=A#+AS:GOTO 790
920 IF ST$<>SP$ THEN 880
930 ST(I,J)=ST(I,J)+INT((100-ST(I,J))*AS/1000000##*(1/EV))
940 IF A#<=0 THEN 980
950 PRINT "Do you wish to spend money in another":INPUT "state (yes/no)";C$
960 YU$=LEFT$(C$,1):IF YU$="Y" OR YU$="y" THEN 790
970 IF YU$<>"N" AND YU$<>"n" THEN 950
980 CLS:PRINT "Monthly Report to the Election":PRINT "Committee:":PRINT
990 PRINT "Beginning of Month          End"
1000 PRINT USING B$;AB#;A#:PRINT
1010 PRINT USING D$;CM#,TS#
1020 PL=INT((RND(1)/2)*100):IF PL=0 THEN 1020
1030 RESTORE:FOR Z=1 TO PL:READ ST$,EV,I,J:NEXT Z
1040 IF ST(I,J)>50 THEN 1080
1050 IF ST(I,J)<50 THEN 1100
1060 PRINT:PRINT "Polls show you are even with";O$
1070 PRINT "in ";ST$;".":GOTO 1120
1080 PRINT:PRINT "Polls show you are ahead of ";O$
1090 PRINT "in ";ST$;:PRINT ".   You have";ST(I,J);"% of the vote.":GOTO 1120
1100 PRINT:PRINT "Polls show ";O$;" ahead of you in"
1110 PRINT ST$;".":PRINT "He has";(100-ST(I,J));"% of the vote."
1120 PRINT:INPUT "Press <ENTER> to begin next month";Z$
1130 CLS:GOSUB 1420
1140 FOR Y=1 TO 6:ST(1,Y)=ST(1,Y)-2:ST(5,Y)=ST(5,Y)-2:NEXT Y
1150 FOR Y=1 TO 13:ST(2,Y)=ST(2,Y)-2:ST(4,Y)=ST(4,Y)-2:NEXT Y
1160 FOR Y=1 TO 7:ST(3,Y)=ST(3,Y)-2:ST(6,Y)=ST(6,Y)-2:NEXT Y
1170 INPUT "Press <ENTER>";Z$
1180 NEXT T
1190 CLS:PRINT TAB(9);"Election Night Results"
1200 PRINT TAB(13);"Electoral Votes":PRINT:PRINT TAB(25);"Your";TAB(31);"Opponent";
1210 PRINT "State";TAB(15);"You";TAB(20)"Opp.";:PRINT
1220 PRINT TAB(25);"Total";TAB(31);"Total"
1230 RESTORE
1240 FOR K=1 TO 51
1250 READ ST$,EV,I,J
1260 IF ST(I,J)>50 THEN 1280
1270 OT=OT+EV:X=20:GOTO 1290
1280 YT=YT+EV:X=15
1290 PRINT ST$;TAB(X);EV;TAB(25);YT;TAB(31);OT
1300 FOR TM=1 TO 750:NEXT TM
1310 NEXT
1320 IF YT>OT THEN 1340
1330 W$=O$:L$=N$:WT=OT:GOTO 1350
1340 W$=N$:L$=O$:WT=YT
1350 PRINT:PRINT W$;" is the winner of the";EY:PRINT "presidential election."
1360 PRINT W$;" has";WT;"electoral votes, more":PRINT "than his opponent, ";L$;"."
1370 END
1380 FOR I=1 TO 6:ST(1,I)=ST(1,I)+C(1):ST(5,I)=ST(5,I)+C(5):NEXT I
1390 FOR I=1 TO 13:ST(2,I)=ST(2,I)+C(2):ST(4,I)=ST(4,I)+C(4):NEXT I
1400 FOR I=1 TO 7:ST(3,I)=ST(3,I)+C(3):ST(6,I)=ST(6,I)+C(6):NEXT I
1410 RETURN
1420 PE=INT(RND(1)*10):IF PE>8 THEN 1420
1430 IF PE>1 THEN 1530
1440 PRINT "The U.S. is the target of":PRINT "demonstrations in several middle east"
1450 PRINT "countries.  Several European countries":PRINT "have also been critical of":PRINT "our foreign
     policy.":C=0
1460 IF P1=1 THEN C=C-1
1470 IF P1=2 THEN C=C+1
1480 IF I1=6 THEN C=C+1
1490 IF I2=2 THEN C=C-1
1500 FOR Y=1 TO 6:C(Y)=C:NEXT Y
1510 GOSUB 1380
1520 GOTO 2370
1530 IF PE>2 THEN 1670
1540 IN=1:IF INT(RND(1)*10)>5 THEN IN=2
1550 PRINT "The rate of inflation has ";
```

49

Presidential Campaign

```
1560 IF IN=1 THEN IN$="dropped.":GOTO 1580
1570 IN$="risen."
1580 PRINT IN$:C=0
1590 IF P1=1 THEN 1630
1600 IF I1=1 THEN C=C+1
1610 IF I2=1 THEN C=C+1
1620 IF IN=1 THEN C=C+1
1630 IF IN=1 THEN C=C+1
1640 IF IN=2 THEN C=C-1
1650 FOR Y=1 TO 6:C(Y)=6:NEXT Y
1660 GOTO 2370
1670 IF PE>3 THEN 1760
1680 PRINT "There is a shortage of all petroleum":PRINT "products, especially gasoline.  The"
1690 PRINT "reasons for the shortage are unclear":PRINT "at this time.":C=1
1700 IF I1=3 THEN C=C+1
1710 IF I2=3 THEN C=C-1
1720 IF P1=1 THEN C=-C
1730 FOR Y=1 TO 6:C(Y)=C:NEXT Y
1740 GOSUB 1380
1750 GOTO 2370
1760 IF PE>4 THEN 1850
1770 PB=INT(RND(1)*1000)+1000
1780 PRINT "A political boss promises to":PRINT "contribute";PB;"dollars to your":PRINT "campaign if you
     will appoint some of"
1790 PRINT "his friends to powerful positions if":PRINT "you win.  This contribution is not":
     PRINT "legal."
1800 INPUT "Will you accept (yes/no)";C$
1810 YU$=LEFT$(C$,1):IF YU$="N" OR YU$="n" THEN 2370
1820 IF YU$<>"Y" AND YU$<>"y" THEN 1800
1830 F=F+1:A#=A#+PB
1840 GOTO 2370
1850 IF PE>5 THEN 1960
1860 PRINT "Allegations have been made that you":PRINT "have accepted illegal campaign funds.":
     PRINT "You are presently under investigation."
1870 IF F=0 THEN 1950
1880 IF F>5 THEN 1900
1890 PRINT "You have been found guilty and you":PRINT "lose";INT(100/(G-F));"% of your support":
     PRINT "in each state.":GOTO 1910
1900 PRINT "You have been found guilty and thrown":PRINT "in the federal penetentary at":PRINT "Leaven
     worth, Kansas for twenty years.":END
1910 FOR Y=1 TO 6:ST(1,Y)=INT((1/(G-F))*ST(1,Y)):ST(5,Y)=INT((1/(G-F))*ST(5,Y)):NEXT Y
1920 FOR Y=1 TO 13:ST(2,Y)=INT((1/(G-F))*ST(5,Y)):ST(4,Y)=INT((1/(G-F))*ST(4,Y)):NEXT Y
1930 FOR Y=1 TO 7:ST(3,Y)=INT((1/(G-F))*ST(3,Y)):ST(6,Y)=INT((1/(G-F))*ST(6,Y)):NEXT Y
1940 GOTO 2370
1950 PRINT "You have been found innocent.":GOTO 2370
1960 IF PE>6 THEN 2190
1970 PRINT "You and ";O$;" agree to a televised":PRINT "debate."
1980 IF I1>1 THEN 2000
1990 FOR Y=1 TO 12:ST(2,Y)=ST(2,Y)+INT(.07*(100-ST(2,Y)))
2000 IF I1<>5 THEN 2020
2010 FOR Y=1 TO 13:ST(4,Y)=ST(4,Y)+INT(.06*(100-ST(4,Y)))
2020 IF I2>1 THEN 2040
2030 FOR Y=1 TO 12:ST(2,Y)=ST(2,Y)-INT(.05*ST(2,Y))
2040 IF I2<>5 THEN 2060
2050 FOR Y=1 TO 13:ST(4,Y)=ST(4,Y)-INT(.02*ST(2,Y))
2060 DB=INT(RND(1)/3*10):IF DB=0 THEN 2060
2070 IF DB=2 THEN 2160
2080 IF DB=1 THEN 2120
2090 FOR Y=1 TO 6:ST(1,Y)=ST(1,Y)+INT(.02*(100-ST(1,Y))):ST(5,Y)=ST(5,Y)+INT(.02*(100-ST(5,Y))):NEXT Y
2100 FOR Y=1 TO 7:ST(3,Y)=ST(3,Y)+INT(.01*(100-ST(3,Y))):ST(6,Y)=ST(6,Y)+INT(.01*(100-ST(6,Y))):NEXT Y
2110 GOTO 2150
2120 FOR Y=1 TO 6:ST(1,Y)=ST(1,Y)-INT(.02*ST(1,Y)):ST(5,Y)=ST(5,Y)-INT(.02*ST(5,Y)):NEXT Y
2130 FOR Y=1 TO 13:ST(2,Y)=ST(2,Y)-INT(.01*ST(2,Y)):ST(4,Y)=ST(4,Y)-INT(.01*ST(4,Y)):NEXT Y
2140 FOR Y=1 TO 7:ST(3,Y)=ST(3,Y)-INT(.01*ST(3,Y)):ST(6,Y)=ST(6,Y)-INT(.01*ST(6,Y)):NEXT Y
2150 IF DB=1 THEN PRINT "You lost the debate."
2160 IF DB=2 THEN PRINT "The debate was a draw."
2170 IF DB=3 THEN PRINT "You won the debate."
2180 GOTO 2370
2190 IF PE>7 THEN 2290
2200 PRINT "The president of a large union promises":PRINT "the support of the union's members if"
2210 PRINT "you make some pro-union campaign":PRINT "speeches."
2220 INPUT "Will you accept his help (yes/no)";C$
2230 YU$=LEFT$(C$,1):IF YU$="Y" OR YU$="y" THEN 2250
2240 IF YU$<>"N" AND YU$<>"n" THEN 2220
2250 C(1)=0:C(2)=2:C(3)=-2:C(4)=-1:C(5)=1:C(6)=-1:GOSUB 1380
2260 GOTO 2370
2270 C(1)=0:C(2)=-2:C(3)=3:C(4)=1:C(5)=0:C(6)=0:GOSUB 1380
2280 GOTO 2370
```

Presidential Campaign

```
2290 PRINT "Farmers and ranchers want you to":PRINT "capaign that they should receive":PRINT "higher
     prices for their products."
2300 PRINT "Keep in mind that consumers will not":PRINT "like this.":C=0
2310 PRINT "Will you support the farmers and":INPUT "ranchers (yes/no)";C$
2320 YU$=LEFT$(C$,1):IF YU$="Y" OR YU$="y" THEN 2340
2330 IF YU$<>"N" AND YU$<>"n" THEN 2310
2340 C(1)=-1:C(2)=-1:C(3)=3:C(4)=2:C(5)=-1:C(6)=2:GOTO 2360
2350 C(1)=2:C(2)=3:C(4)=-2:C(5)=1:C(6)=-2
2360 GOSUB 1380
2370 RETURN
2380 DATA Alabama,9,4,9
2390 DATA Alaska,3,5,4
2400 DATA Arizona,6,6,4
2410 DATA Arkansas,6,4,12
2420 DATA California,45,5,6
2430 DATA Colorado,7,6,7
2440 DATA Connecticut,8,1,5
2450 DATA Delaware,3,2,3
2460 DATA D.C.,3,2,12
2470 DATA Florida,17,4,7
2480 DATA Georgia,12,4,8
2490 DATA Hawaii,4,5,5
2500 DATA Idaho,4,5,1
2510 DATA Illinois,26,2,9
2520 DATA Indiana,13,2,8
2530 DATA Iowa,8,3,2
2540 DATA Kansas,7,3,5
2550 DATA Kentucky,9,4,3
2560 DATA Louisiana,10,4,11
2570 DATA Maine,4,1,1
2580 DATA Maryland,10,2,5
2590 DATA Massachusetts,14,1,5
2600 DATA Michigan,21,2,7
2610 DATA Minnesota,10,2,11
2620 DATA Mississippi,7,4,10
2630 DATA Missouri,12,4,13
2640 DATA Montana,4,3,6
2650 DATA Nebraska,5,3,4
2660 DATA Nevada,3,6,5
2670 DATA New Hampshire,4,1,2
2680 DATA New Jersey,17,2,4
2690 DATA New Mexico,4,6,3
2700 DATA New York,41,2,1
2710 DATA North Carolina,13,4,5
2720 DATA North Dakota,4,3,1
2730 DATA Ohio,25,2,6
2740 DATA Oklahoma,8,6,2
2750 DATA Oregon,6,5,3
2760 DATA Pennsylvania,27,2,2
2770 DATA Rhode Island,4,1,6
2780 DATA South Carolina,8,4,6
2790 DATA South Dakota,4,3,3
2800 DATA Tennessee,10,4,4
2810 DATA Texas,26,6,1
2820 DATA Utah,4,6,6
2830 DATA Vermont,3,1,3
2840 DATA Virginia,12,4,2
2850 DATA Washington,8,5,2
2860 DATA West Virginia,6,4,1
2870 DATA Wisconsin,11,2,10
2880 DATA Wyoming,3,3,7
2890 DATA end,0,0,0
2900 CLS:PRINT TAB(11);"S C E N A R I O":PRINT
2910 PRINT "     You have decided to run for":PRINT "president and have obtained nomination"
2920 PRINT "from your party.  The campaign begins"
2930 PRINT "nine months before the election.  You"
2940 PRINT "have the options of deciding which"
2950 PRINT "states to visit each month, how many":PRINT "days you wish to spend in the states"
2960 PRINT "you visit, and whether the visit is":PRINT "for campaigning (which wins popular"
2970 PRINT "votes) or fund raising (which wins":PRINT "no popular votes but brings in"
2980 PRINT "contributions to meet expenses and":PRINT "finance campaign activities in other"
2990 PRINT "states).  The money that is in the":PRINT "campaign treasury can bespent as you":PRINT "wish
     in any state."
3000 PRINT:INPUT "Press <ENTER> to continue";Z$:CLS
3010 PRINT "     At the beginning of the campaign,"
3020 PRINT "you are allowed to make some political"
3030 PRINT "decisions.  These will affect the":PRINT "initial attitudes of the voters with"
3040 PRINT "respect to you and your opponent."
```

Presidential Campaign

```
3050 PRINT "Throughout the campaign, you will have":PRINT "to make additional political decisions"
3060 PRINT "that will influence voter opinion.  As"
3070 PRINT "with all political decisions, whatever":PRINT "you decide will not please everyone."
3080 PRINT "In addition, some of your decisions":PRINT "will be compared to those made earlier":
PRINT "to determine your sincerity."
3090 PRINT "Therefore, try to weigh the conditions":PRINT "of each decision carefully.  In some"
3100 PRINT "cases, changing position during  a":PRINT "campaign can be the best strategy,"
3110 PRINT "while at other times, it may be":PRINT "disastrous."
3120 PRINT:INPUT "Press <ENTER> to continue";Z$:CLS
3130 PRINT "    At the end of each month, you":PRINT "will receive a report of the finances"
3140 PRINT "of the treasury.  You will be shown":PRINT "the balance at the beginning of the"
3150 PRINT "month, the balance at the end of the":PRINT "month, total contributions during the":
PRINT "month, and total expenditures during"
3160 PRINT "the month.":PRINT "    Campaigning is expensive not only"
3170 PRINT "because of advertising in states but":PRINT "also for your actual visits.  It is"
3180 PRINT "helpful to spend time fund raising."
3190 PRINT:INPUT "Press <ENTER> to continue";Z$:CLS
3200 PRINT "    There are a few campaign laws to":PRINT "consider:"
3210 PRINT "  1) You can not put the campaign":PRINT "treasury into debt."
3220 PRINT "  2) A $50,000 maximum is placed on":PRINT "each transaction."
3230 PRINT "  3) Unreported campaign contributions":PRINT "are illegal.  You may be tempted to"
3240 PRINT "accept some, but you may get caught.":PRINT "It may cost you the election or merely"
3250 PRINT "a few votes.":PRINT "  4) You may campaign as many days per":PRINT"month as you wish and
    visit as many"
3260 PRINT "states as you wish.  Each month is":PRINT "considered to have thirty days."
3270 PRINT:INPUT "Press <ENTER> to continue";Z$:CLS
3280 PRINT "    At the end of each month, you":PRINT "will be shown your status in one state"
3290 PRINT "as of the end of the month.  This is":PRINT "the only indication that you will"
3300 PRINT "receive on your progress."
3310 PRINT "    At the end of the campaign, the":PRINT "election is held and you will be shown"
3320 PRINT "the number of electoral college votes":PRINT "awarded by each state, to whom they":
PRINT "were awarded, and the totals of"
3330 PRINT "votes that you and your opponent":PRINT "received."
3340 PRINT:INPUT "Press <ENTER> to continue";Z$:CLS
3350 PRINT "    Be sure to spell each state":PRINT "correctly.  Do not use a dollar sign"
3360 PRINT "when entering amounts of money and do":PRINT "not use commas between number digits."
3370 PRINT:INPUT "Press <ENTER> to begin the campaign";Z$:CLS
3380 RETURN
```

Presidential Campaign

You have decided to run for president and have obtained nomination from your party. The campaign begins nine months before the election. You have the options of deciding which states to visit each month, how many days you wish to spend in the states you visit, and whether the visit is for campaigning (which wins popular votes) or fund raising (which wins no popular votes but brings in contributions to meet expenses and finance campaign activities in other states). The money that is in the campaign treasury can be spent as you wish in any state.

Press <ENTER> to continue? ▇

At the beginning of the campaign, you are allowed to make some political decisions. These will affect the initial attitudes of the voters with respect to you and your opponent. Throughout the campaign, you will have to make additional political decisions that will influence voter opinion. As with all political decisions, whatever you decide will not please everyone. In addition, some of your decisions will be compared to those made earlier to determine your sincerity. Therefore, try to weigh the conditions of each decision carefully. In some cases, changing position during a campaign can be the best strategy, while at other times, it may be disastrous.

Press <ENTER> to continue? ▇

At the end of each month, you will receive a report of the finances of the treasury. You will be shown the balance at the beginning of the month, the balance at the end of the month, total contributions during the month, and total expenditures during the month.
Campaigning is expensive not only because of advertising in states but also for your actual visits. It is helpful to spend time fund raising.

Press <ENTER> to continue? ▇

There are a few campaign laws to consider:
1) You can not put the campaign treasury into debt.
2) A $50,000 maximum is placed on each transaction.
3) Unreported campaign contributions are illegal. You may be tempted to accept some, but you may get caught. It may cost you the election or merely a few votes.
4) You may campaign as many days per month as you wish and visit as many states as you wish. Each month is considered to have thirty days.

Press <ENTER> to continue? ▇

At the end of each month, you will be shown your status in one state as of the end of the month. This is the only indication that you will receive on your progress.
At the end of the campaign, the election is held and you will be shown the number of electoral college votes awarded by each state, to whom they were awarded, and the totals of votes that you and your opponent received.

Press <ENTER> to continue? ▇

Be sure to spell each state correctly. Do not use a dollar sign when entering amounts of money and do not use commas between number digits.

Press <ENTER> to begin the campaign? ▇

Conditions

Choose the conditions that you wish to be true.
In what year to you wish the election to take place? 1984
Enter your name? Andrew Hurdidge
Enter your opponent's name? Steve Williams

Do you wish to be 1) the incumbent or 2) the challenger? 2

Do you wish to be 1) a Democrat or 2) a Republican? 2▇

I S S U E S

1) Unemployment   4) Social Adjustments
2) Inflation   5) Defense
3) Energy   6) Foreign Affairs

Which is most important to your campaign? 5
Which is least important? 4▇

Date: February
 9 Months before election
Your campaign fund has $ 500,000.00

What state do you wish to visit? New Jersey
You have 30 unscheduled days left this month.
How many days to you wish to stay there? 5
How many of the 5 days will be for fund raising? 2
How many days for campaigning? 3
Do you wish to visit another state (yes/no)? no▇

Spend campaign money in which state? New Jersey
Your campaign fund has $ 496,313.00

How much do you wish to spend? 6000.00
Do you wish to spend money in another state (yes/no)? no▇

Monthly Report to the Election Committee:

Beginning of Month   End
$ 500,000.00 $ 490,313.00

Contributions = $1,813.00
 Expenditures = $11,500.00

Polls show Steve Williams ahead of you in
North Carolina.
He has 72 % of the vote.

Press <ENTER> to begin next month? ▇

The U.S. is the target of demonstrations in several middle east countries. Several European countries have also been critical of our foreign policy.
Press <ENTER>? ▇

Spend campaign money in which state? New York
Your campaign fund has $ 501,046.00

How much do you wish to spend? 50000.00

Do you wish to spend money in another state (yes/no)? no▇

Presidential Campaign

Monthly Report to the Election
Committee:

Beginning of Month   End
$ 490,313.00 $ 451,046.00

Contributions = $43,733.00
 Expenditures = $83,000.00

Polls show Steve Williams ahead of you
in
Connecticut.
He has 103 % of the vote.

Press <ENTER> to begin next month? ▮

The U.S. is the target of
demonstrations in several middle east
countries.   Several European countries
have also been critical of
our foreign policy.
Press <ENTER>? ▮

Date: April
 7 Months before election
Your campaign fund has $ 451,046.00

What state do you wish to visit? Florid
a
You have 30 unscheduled days
left this month.
How many days to you wish to stay
there? 20
How many of the 20 days will be
for fund raising? 5
How many days for campaigning? 10
Do you wish to visit another
state (yes/no)? no▮

Spend campaign money in which
state? Florida
Your campaign fund has $ 433,579.00

How much do you wish to spend? 30000.00

Do you wish to spend money in another
state (yes/no)? no▮

Monthly Report to the Election
Committee:

Beginning of Month   End
$ 451,046.00 $ 403,579.00

Contributions = $4,533.00
 Expenditures = $52,000.00

Polls show Steve Williams ahead of you
in
Arizona.
He has 53 % of the vote.

Press <ENTER> to begin next month? ▮

The U.S. is the target of
demonstrations in several middle east
countries.   Several European countries
have also been critical of
our foreign policy.
Press <ENTER>? ▮

Spend campaign money in which
state? Washington
Your campaign fund has $ 383,379.00

How much do you wish to spend? 3379.00
Do you wish to spend money in another
state (yes/no)? no▮

Monthly Report to the Election
Committee:

Beginning of Month   End
$ 403,579.00 $ 380,000.00

Contributions = $12,800.00
 Expenditures = $36,379.00

Polls show you are ahead of Steve Willi
ams
in Kansas.   You have 52 % of the vote.

Press <ENTER> to begin next month? ▮

Farmers and ranchers want you to
capaign that they should receive
higher prices for their products.
Keep in mind that consumers will not
like this.
Will you support the farmers and
ranchers (yes/no)? yes▮

Date: June
 5 Months before election
Your campaign fund has $ 380,000.00

What state do you wish to visit? Kansas

You have 30 unscheduled days
left this month.
How many days to you wish to stay
there? 20
How many of the 20 days will be
for fund raising? 15
How many days for campaigning? 5
Do you wish to visit another
state (yes/no)? yes
What state do you wish to visit? Ohio
You have 10 unscheduled days
left this month.
How many days to you wish to stay
there? 10
How many of the 10 days will be
for fund raising? 10
How many days for campaigning? 0▮

Spend campaign money in which
state? Kansas
Your campaign fund has $ 365,933.00

How much do you wish to spend? 20000.00

Do you wish to spend money in another
state (yes/no)? yes
Spend campaign money in which
state? Ohio
Your campaign fund has $ 345,933.00

How much do you wish to spend? 20000.00

Do you wish to spend money in another
state (yes/no)? no▮

Monthly Report to the Election
Committee:

Beginning of Month   End
$ 380,000.00 $ 325,933.00

Contributions = $18,933.00
 Expenditures = $73,000.00

Polls show you are ahead of Steve Willi
ams
in Nebraska.   You have 53 % of the vote
.

Press <ENTER> to begin next month? ▮

There is a shortage of all petroleum
products, especially gasoline. The
reasons for the shortage are unclear
at this time.
Press <ENTER>? ▮

Date: July
 4 Months before election
Your campaign fund has $ 325,933.00

What state do you wish to visit? Texas
You have 30 unscheduled days
left this month.
How many days to you wish to stay
there? 25
How many of the 25 days will be
for fund raising? 15
How many days for campaigning? 10
Do you wish to visit another
state (yes/no)? no▮

Presidential Campaign

Spend campaign money in which
state? Texas
Your campaign fund has $ 319,233.00

How much do you wish to spend? 19233.00

Do you wish to spend money in another
state (yes/no)? no

Monthly Report to the Election
Committee:

Beginning of Month   End
$ 325,933.00 $ 300,000.00

Contributions = $20,800.00
 Expenditures = $46,733.00

Polls show Steve Williams ahead of you
in
Florida.
He has 52 % of the vote.

Press <ENTER> to begin next month? █

A political boss promises to
contribute 1079 dollars to your
campaign if you will appoint some of
his friends to powerful positions if
you win.   This contribution is not
legal.
Will you accept (yes/no)? no
Press <ENTER>? █

Date: August
 3 Months before election
Your campaign fund has $ 300,000.00

What state do you wish to visit? Maine

You have 30 unscheduled days
left this month.
How many days to you wish to stay
there? 30
How many of the 30 days will be
for fund raising? 30
How many days for campaigning? 0█

Spend campaign money in which
state? Maine
Your campaign fund has $ 273,400.00

How much do you wish to spend? 10000.00

Do you wish to spend money in another
state (yes/no)? no█

Monthly Report to the Election
Committee:

Beginning of Month   End
$ 300,000.00 $ 263,400.00

Contributions = $6,400.00
 Expenditures = $43,000.00

Polls show Steve Williams ahead of you
in
Mississippi.
He has 78 % of the vote.

Press <ENTER> to begin next month? █

You and Steve Williams agree to a telev
ised
debate.
You won the debate.
Press <ENTER>? █

Date: September
 2 Months before election
Your campaign fund has $ 263,400.00

What state do you wish to visit? Califo
rnia
You have 30 unscheduled days
left this month.
How many days to you wish to stay
there? 20
How many of the 20 days will be
for fund raising? 15
How many days for campaigning? 5█

Date: September
 2 Months before election
Your campaign fund has $ 263,400.00

What state do you wish to visit? Califo
rnia
You have 30 unscheduled days
left this month.
How many days to you wish to stay
there? 20
How many of the 20 days will be
for fund raising? 15
How many days for campaigning? 5
Do you wish to visit another
state (yes/no)? no█

Your campaign fund has $ 277,400.00

How much do you wish to spend?
You did not spell the state correctly.
Spend campaign money in which
state?
Your campaign fund has $ 277,400.00

How much do you wish to spend?
You did not spell the state correctly.
Spend campaign money in which
state?
Your campaign fund has $ 277,400.00

How much do you wish to spend?
You did not spell the state correctly.
Spend campaign money in which
state? California
Your campaign fund has $ 277,400.00

How much do you wish to spend? 7000.00
Do you wish to spend money in another
state (yes/no)? no█

Monthly Report to the Election
Committee:

Beginning of Month   End
$ 263,400.00 $ 270,400.00

Contributions = $36,000.00
 Expenditures = $29,028.00

Polls show Steve Williams ahead of you
in
D.C..
He has 81 % of the vote.

Press <ENTER> to begin next month? █

Farmers and ranchers want you to
campaign that they should receive
higher prices for their products.
Keep in mind that consumers will not
like this.
Will you support the farmers and
ranchers (yes/no)? yes
Press <ENTER>? █

Spend campaign money in which
state? D.C.
Your campaign fund has $ 237,400.00

How much do you wish to spend? 50000.00

Do you wish to spend money in another
state (yes/no)? no█

Monthly Report to the Election
Committee:

Beginning of Month   End
$ 270,400.00 $ 187,400.00

Contributions = $0.00
 Expenditures = $83,000.00

Polls show Steve Williams ahead of you
in
North Carolina.
He has 80 % of the vote.

Press <ENTER> to begin next month? █

Presidential Campaign

The president of a large union promises
the support of the union's members if
you make some pro-union campaign
speeches.
Will you accept his help (yes/no)? yes
Press <ENTER>? ■

```
         Election Night Results
              Electoral Votes

                            Your   Opponent
State            You  Opp.  Total  Total
Alabama               9     0      9
Alaska                3     0      12
Arizona               6     0      18
Arkansas              6     0      24
California            45    0      69
Colorado              7     0      76
Connecticut           8     0      84
Delaware              7     0      69
D.C.                  8     0      76
Florida          3    3     0      84
Georgia                     0      87
Hawaii                17    3      87
Idaho                 12    3      104
Illinois              4     3      116
Indiana               4     3      120
Iowa                  26    3      124
Kansas                13    3      150
Kentucky         7    8     3      163
Louisiana                   3      171
Maine                 9     10     171
Maryland              10    10     180
Massachusetts         4     10     190
Michigan              10    10     194
Minnesota             14    10     204
Mississippi           21    10     218
Missouri              10    10     239
Montana               7     10     249
Nebraska              12    10     250
Nevada                4     10     265
New Hampshire         5     10     272
New Jersey            3     10     272
New Mexico            4     10     280
New York              17    10     284
North Carolina        4     10     301
North Dakota          41    10     305
Ohio                  13    10     346
Oklahoma              4     10     355
Oregon                6     10     402
Pennsylvania          27    10     429
Rhode Island          4     10     433
South Carolina        8     10     441
South Dakota          4     10     445
Tennessee             10    10     455
Texas            26         36     455
Utah                  4     36     459
Vermont               3     36     462
Virginia              12    36     474
Washington            8     36     482
West Virginia         6     36     488
Wisconsin             11    36     499
Wyoming               3     36     502
```

Steve Williams is the winner of the
 1984
presidential election.
Steve Williams has 502 electoral votes,
 more
than his opponent, Andrew Hurdidge.
Ok
■

Star Merchant

Star Merchant was written by Lloyd Johnson and originally appeared in *Creative Computing*, August 1981.

Introduction

Star Merchant is a futuristic trade simulation game. When this article first appeared in the August 1981 issue of *Creative Computing*, I was negligent in not giving the game "Traveller" proper credit as a source for cargo names and base prices. "Traveller" is a role playing system set in the far future. Its rules cover many facets of life in the 57th century and are constantly being expanded. "Traveller" is available from hobby stores or from Game Designers' Workshop, Box 1646, Bloomington, IL 61701.

Historical Background

Early in the 26th century the 50XFTL drive was developed. This drive, when properly installed on a spaceship, would cause a controlled warping of space enabling the spaceship to travel at fifty times faster than light (50XFTL). Massive colonization of the nearby stars took place in the following two centuries due to the crowded conditions on inhabitable planets of the solar system and the development of this drive.

By the mid-29th century, large orbiting space stations (starports) were constructed at the ten most populated star systems. These starports had facilities for docking and refueling starships as well as massive cargo storage capability. The construction of these starports was closely paralleled by a simplification of starship design. With the advent of the starports, it was no longer necessary for a starship to land on a planet. This eliminated the need for atmospheric streamlining, as well as the large reaction engines required to lift the starship from the planetary surface, while it substantially increased the cargo hold of starships.

The type of cargo which will be available for purchase at any particular starport is difficult to predict, since most of the cargos did not originate at that star system, but were brought there by other merchant starships. Coordination of trade routes to guarantee cargo availability at a starport had never occurred due to the independent nature of the star merchants and the slow communication between the star systems.

As trade developed between the starports, each starport was assigned a trade classification. Although the trade classification is useless in determining which cargos might be available for purchase, it is extremely useful in predicting the price of the cargo. As political and economic conditions change at a star system, the assigned trade classification may change slightly.

Game Description

The game has recently been modified from the original publication to include a two player option. When playing Star Merchant, the player or players will find themselves in command of a merchant starship. Their goal is to not only make enough money by trading cargos to stay in business and to regain the initial investment for the lease of the starship, but to make more money than the other player.

There are ten different starports where trade is conducted and thirty-six different types of cargos which may be traded. The different types of cargos range from agricultural produce and raw materials to industrially produced items, such as weapons and machinery. The price at which these cargos will be traded is dependent upon the trade classification of the starport where the item is being traded. For example, farm machinery might bring top dollar at a starport with an agricultural trade class, whereas the price of grain at this starport will probably be very low.

The starport distances and directions are all represented in two dimensions. This was done to simplify game play. Command 7, DISPLAY STARPORT MAP, will display the relative positions of these starports. This command is useful to the players when planning their trade routes.

Ship expenses must be paid every time a new starport is reached. If the player's account becomes negative after paying these expenses, he must sell enough cargo to make it positive before he can leave the starport. If he does not have enough cargo to do this, the game will end for the player. If two players are playing, the other player may continue the game as a one player game if desired.

The expenses which must be paid consist of a docking fee, fuel expenses, and crew salary. The docking fee will always be 50,000 credits. The fuel expenses are directly proportional to the distance traveled from the last starport. The cost of fuel per lightyear is 100,000 credits. The crew's salary is based on an annual salary of 500,000 credits and the amount of ship time that has passed since the crew was last paid. Ship time increases approximately .02 years (a week) for each lightyear traveled and approximately .003 years (a day) for each cargo transaction.

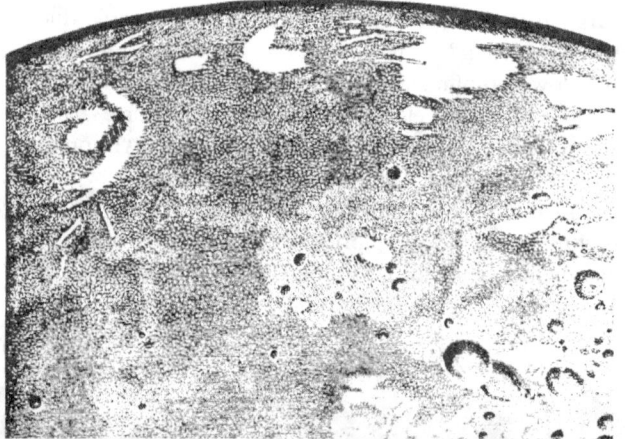

Before leaving a starport the player will be asked if he wants to purchase piracy insurance. This question is skipped if the player's account does not hold enough revenue to make this payment. The price of piracy insurance is ten percent of the total value of the cargo presently stored in the hold. If the cargo should be stolen by pirates, the player will be reimbursed for the last accessed value of his cargo. No reimbursement will take place if the player had not purchased piracy insurance.

The pirates are a highly technical organization which have found a loophole in the law of relativity. They utilize this loophole to empty a starship of cargo while it is in the warped space generated by the 50XFTL drive. With their ability to alter the rate of time, the pirates are able to rendezvous with a starship, board it and take its cargo, leave an insulting message, and disappear all within a time interval too short to be measured by the starship's chronometers.

The true origin of the pirates is still unknown, however investigations are being undertaken. Although a major breakthrough in this investigation had occurred when several lots of stolen cargo were identified at one of the starports, the player can still expect to have his cargo stolen from him approximately ten percent of the time.

As the player's fortune grows, the probability will increase that the crew will go on strike for a higher salary. When a strike occurs the crew presents their salary demands and the player is asked for a counter-offer. The probability that the counter offer will be accepted depends upon the amount that was offered and the number of counter-offers that have been rejected previously. Once the crew has rejected ten counter-offers, they will accept only their original salary demands or higher. For this reason an early strike settlement is desirable.

The lease on a player's ship will expire after two years of ship time. At this time, the player will be asked to renew his lease if he has enough money to do so. It will cost 2,000,000 credits for another two year lease. If the player does not renew his lease, the game will end for him and his final game results will be displayed. The other player will be allowed to continue playing until his lease expires.

Star Merchant

```
10 REM *****************************!
20 REM *        STAR MERCHANT        *
30 REM *     in Microsoft BASIC      *
40 REM *****************************!
50 REM Initialization
60 DIM A$(20),B$(8),A(5,4),D(10)
70 DIM H(20,4),P(14),S(6),T(10)
80 CLS:PRINT TAB(12)"STAR MERCHANT"
90 PRINT:PRINT "You have just spent 2 million credits"
100 PRINT "on a 2 year lease for a merchant"
110 PRINT "starship.  This leaves you with 2"
120 PRINT "million credits operating capital."
130 PRINT
140 PRINT "Your ship can hold a total of 20 cargos";
150 PRINT "with a total cargo weight of 200 tons."
160 PRINT "The fuel capacity of your ship is great";
170 PRINT "enough such that travel between any 2"
180 PRINT "starports is possible without"
190 PRINT "refueling."
200 PRINT
210 PRINT "You are presently traveling from Alpha"
220 PRINT "Centauri to Sol.  You are carrying no"
230 PRINT "cargo."
240 PRINT:PRINT "Press any key to continue.";
250 A$=INKEY$:IF A$="" THEN 250
260 CLS:PRINT "The starport trade classifacation"
270 PRINT "determines the cargo price but does not";
280 PRINT "determine which cargos are available."
290 PRINT
300 PRINT "Abbreviations used for trade class are"
310 PRINT "as follows:"
320 PRINT "    R-Rich; P-Poor; I-Indstrial;"
330 PRINT "    NI-Nonindstrial; A-Agricultural;"
340 PRINT "    NA-Nonagricultural"
350 PRINT
360 PRINT "Press any key to continue.";
370 A$=INKEY$:IF A$="" THEN 370
380 CLS:PRINT "Commands available are as follows:":PRINT
390 GOSUB 3420
400 R1=1
410 PRINT
420 PRINT "Enter a random number between 1"
430 INPUT "and 500 ";I
440 PRINT
450 FOR J=1 TO I
460 D9=RND(R1)
470 NEXT J
480 DEF FN A(R1)=INT(6*RND(R1))+1
490 DEF FN B(N2)=INT(N2*RND(R1))+1
500 DEF FN C(R1)=FN A(R1)+FN A(R1)
510 B2=2000000#
520 D(5)=4.3
530 S1=5
540 E1=50000!
550 E2=100000!
560 E3=500000!
570 N2=36
580 N3=10
590 W1=200
600 W2=W1
610 FOR I=1 TO 20
620 H(I,1)=0
630 NEXT I
640 GOSUB 3650
650 FOR I=1 TO 14
660 READ P(I)
670 NEXT I
680 T5=0
690 T6=0
700 T7=0
710 GOSUB 2310
720 REM Main Logic
730 IF RND(R1)>.01+5E-03*B2/E3 THEN 750
740 GOSUB 1120
750 PRINT
760 PRINT "   Account balance:";:PRINT USING"##,###,###";B2:PRINT " Empty cargo
space:      ";:PRINT USING"###";W2
770 PRINT TAB(9)"Ship time:";INT(T6*1000)/1000;"years"
```

Star Merchant

```
780 PRINT:INPUT "Enter command";C1:PRINT
790 IF C1>0 AND C1<7 AND C1=INT(ABS(C1)) THEN 820
800 GOSUB 3420
810 GOTO 720
820 ON C1 GOSUB 1310,1480,1650,1950,2090,2180
830 B3=B2+T1
840 IF B3<0 THEN 960
850 IF T6-2*T5<2 THEN 720
860 PRINT
870 PRINT "The lease has expired on your ship."
880 IF B3<2000000# THEN 960
890 PRINT "Another lease will cost 2 million"
900 PRINT "credits."
910 INPUT "Do you wish to renew your lease (Y/N)";A$
920 IF A$="N" OR A$="n" THEN 960
930 B2=B2-2000000#
940 T5=T5+1
950 GOTO 720
960 REM End Program
970 G1=(B3-4000000#)/T6
980 A$="loss"
990 IF G1<0 THEN 1010
1000 A$="gain"
1010 IF B3>0 THEN 1040
1020 PRINT
1030 PRINT "You no longer have sufficient funds to":PRINT"operate your ship."
1040 PRINT
1050 PRINT "You began with 4 million credits and"
1060 IF B2<0 THEN B2=0
1070 PRINT "now have";B2;"credits."
1080 PRINT "Cargo in the hold is worth";T1
1090 PRINT
1100 PRINT "This represents a ";A$;" of";ABS(INT(G1*1000)/1000):PRINT "credits per year."
1110 GOTO 4690
1120 REM Strike sub
1130 PRINT
1140 PRINT "The crew has gone on strike!  You are"
1150 PRINT "currently paying them";E3;"credits":PRINT "anually.  ";
1160 E5=E3+.5*RND(R1)*E3
1170 PRINT "They are asking for";E5;"credits."
1180 N4=0
1190 E6=E3+N4*(E5-E3)/10
1200 PRINT
1210 INPUT "Enter counter offer";E7
1220 IF E7>=E5 THEN 1280
1230 IF E7<E6 THEN 1250
1240 IF (E5-E7)/(E5-E6)<RND(R1) THEN 1280
1250 PRINT "Offer rejected - try again"
1260 N4=N4+1
1270 GOTO 1190
1280 PRINT "Offer accepted."
1290 E3=E7
1300 RETURN
1310 REM List Hold
1320 PRINT "Cargo stored in hold:"
1330 IF W2<W1 THEN 1360
1340 PRINT "All partitions are empty."
1350 RETURN
1360 PRINT "Pt Description        AMT     Price       %"
1370 FOR I=1 TO 20
1380 RESTORE
1390 IF H(I,1)=0 THEN 1460
1400 FOR J=1 TO 19+H(I,1)
1410 READ A$
1420 NEXT J
1430 READ A$
1440 PRINT USING"##";I;:PRINT TAB(3);A$;TAB(20);:PRINT USING"###";H(I,3);
1450 PRINT TAB(25);:PRINT USING"#######";H(I,2);:PRINT TAB(35);:PRINT USING"###";H(I,4)
1460 NEXT I
1470 RETURN
1480 REM List Cargo for Sale
1490 PRINT "Cargos available for purchase:"
1500 IF N1>0 THEN 1530
1510 PRINT "All available cargos have been bought."
1520 RETURN
1530 PRINT "No Description        AMT     Price       %"
1540 FOR I=1 TO 5
1550 RESTORE
```

Star Merchant

```
1560 IF A(I,1)=0 THEN 1630
1570 FOR J=1 TO 19+A(I,1)
1580 READ A$
1590 NEXT J
1600 READ A$
1610 PRINT USING"##";I;:PRINT TAB(3);A$;TAB(20);:PRINT USING"###";A(I,3);
1620 PRINT TAB(25);:PRINT USING"########";A(I,2);:PRINT TAB(35);:PRINT USING"###
";A(I,4)
1630 NEXT I
1640 RETURN
1650 REM Buy Cargo Sub
1660 PRINT "Enter the lot number of cargo that you":INPUT "want to purchase";K
1670 IF K=ABS(INT(K)) AND K>0 AND K<6 THEN 1700
1680 PRINT "Invalid lot number."
1690 RETURN
1700 IF A(K,1)>0 THEN 1730
1710 PRINT "Lot";K;"has already been purchased."
1720 RETURN
1730 IF A(K,2)<=B2 THEN 1760
1740 PRINT "You can not buy cargo on credit."
1750 RETURN
1760 IF A(K,3)<=W2 THEN 1790
1770 PRINT "You do not have sufficient cargo space.";
1780 RETURN
1790 FOR I=1 TO 20
1800 IF H(I,1)=0 THEN 1840
1810 NEXT I
1820 PRINT "All 20 cargo partitions are occupied."
1830 RETURN
1840 FOR J=1 TO 4
1850 H(I,J)=A(K,J)
1860 NEXT J
1870 A(K,1)=0
1880 W2=W2-H(I,3)
1890 B2=B2-H(I,2)
1900 T6=T6+3E-03
1910 N1=N1-1
1920 PRINT:PRINT "Transaction completed"
1930 PRINT "Cargo stored in partition";I
1940 RETURN
1950 REM Sell Cargo Sub
1960 INPUT"Enter partition of cargo to be sold";K
1970 IF K=ABS(INT(K)) AND K>0 AND K<21 THEN 2000
1980 PRINT "Invalid partition number"
1990 RETURN
2000 IF H(K,1)>0 THEN 2030
2010 PRINT "Cargo partition is empty."
2020 RETURN
2030 B2=B2+H(K,2)
2040 W2=W2+H(K,3)
2050 T6=T6+3E-03
2060 H(K,1)=0
2070 PRINT "Transaction completed"
2080 RETURN
2090 REM List Starports Sub
2100 PRINT "No.   Name              Trade Cl  Dist Dir"
2110 RESTORE
2120 FOR I=1 TO 10
2130 READ A$,B$
2140 PRINT USING"##";I;:PRINT TAB(5);A$;TAB(21);B$;
2150 PRINT TAB(29);:PRINT USING"##.##";D(I);:PRINT TAB(35);:PRINT USING"###";T(I)
2160 NEXT I
2170 RETURN
2180 REM Travel Sub
2190 IF B2>0 THEN 2220
2200 PRINT "You can not leave starport until all":PRINT "debts are cleared."
2210 RETURN
2220 PRINT "Enter destination star number";
2230 INPUT I
2240 IF I<>S1 THEN 2270
2250 PRINT "You are already at";I
2260 RETURN
2270 IF I=ABS(INT(I)) AND I>0 AND I<N3+1 THEN 2300
2280 PRINT "Invalid star number"
2290 RETURN
2300 S1=I
2310 REM Get Star Trade & Location Data
2320 GOSUB 3510
```

```
2330 IF S1=1 THEN 2370
2340 FOR I=1 TO (S1-1)*3
2350 READ D9
2360 NEXT I
2370 READ X3,Y3,M1
2380 FOR I=1 TO 6
2390 M2=2^(6-I)
2400 S(I)=INT(M1/M2)
2410 M1=M1-S(I)*M2
2420 NEXT I
2430 REM Appraise Cargo in Hold
2440 T1=0
2450 FOR I=1 TO 20
2460 IF H(I,1)=0 THEN 2660
2470 GOSUB 3580
2480 IF H(I,1)=1 THEN 2520
2490 FOR J=1 TO (H(I,1)-1)*8
2500 READ D9
2510 NEXT J
2520 D2=0
2530 FOR J=1 TO 6
2540 READ D3
2550 D2=D2+D3*S(J)
2560 NEXT J
2570 READ B1
2580 P2=FN C(R1)+D2-1
2590 IF P2>1 THEN 2610
2600 P2=1
2610 IF P2<14 THEN 2630
2620 P2=14
2630 H(I,4)=P(P2)*100
2640 H(I,2)=P(P2)*B1*H(I,3)
2650 T1=T1+H(I,2)
2660 NEXT I
2670 REM Get Cargos for Sale
2680 N1=5
2690 FOR I=1 TO 5
2700 D2=0
2710 T2=FN B(N2)
2720 A(I,1)=T2
2730 GOSUB 3580
2740 IF T2=1 THEN 2780
2750 FOR J=1 TO (T2-1)*8
2760 READ D9
2770 NEXT J
2780 FOR J=1 TO 6
2790 READ D3
2800 D2=D2+D3*S(J)
2810 NEXT J
2820 P2=FN C(R1)+D2-1
2830 IF P2>1 THEN 2850
2840 P2=1
2850 IF P2<14 THEN 2870
2860 P2=14
2870 A(I,4)=P(P2)*100
2880 READ B1,Q1
2890 Q2=1
2900 IF T2<17 THEN 2940
2910 Q2=5
2920 IF T2<32 THEN 2940
2930 Q2=10
2940 Q3=0
2950 FOR J=1 TO Q1
2960 Q3=FN A(R1)*Q2+Q3
2970 NEXT J
2980 IF Q3>200 THEN Q3=200
2990 A(I,3)=Q3
3000 A(I,2)=B1*Q3*P(P2)
3010 NEXT I
3020 REM Dist. and Direction of Stars
3030 D4=D(S1)
3040 GOSUB 3510
3050 FOR I=1 TO 10
3060 READ X1,Y1,D9
3070 X2=X1-X3
3080 Y2=Y1-Y3
3090 IF X2<>0 THEN 3150
3100 IF Y2<0 THEN 3130
```

```
3110 T(I)=90
3120 GOTO 3220
3130 T(I)=270
3140 GOTO 3220
3150 T(I)=ATN(Y2/X2)*180/3.14159
3160 IF X2>0 THEN 3180
3170 T(I)=T(I)+180
3180 IF T(I)<360 THEN 3200
3190 T(I)=T(I)-360
3200 IF T(I)>0 THEN 3220
3210 T(I)=T(I)+360
3220 D(I)=SQR(X2^2+Y2^2)
3230 NEXT I
3240 REM Arrival Expense and Star Name
3250 T6=T6+.02*D4+.02
3260 E4=(T6-T7)*E3
3270 T7=T6
3280 RESTORE
3290 IF S1=1 THEN 3330
3300 FOR I=1 TO S1-1
3310 READ A$,B$
3320 NEXT I
3330 READ A$,B$
3340 PRINT
3350 CLS:PRINT "You have arrived at ";A$;".":PRINT
3360 PRINT "Expenses have been deducted as follows:";
3370 PRINT TAB(7)"Docking fee:";:PRINT USING"##,###,###";E1
3380 PRINT TAB(14)"Fuel:";:PRINT USING"##,###,###";E2*D4
3390 PRINT TAB(7)"Crew salary:";:PRINT USING"##,###,###";E4
3400 B2=B2-(E1+E2*D4+E4)
3410 RETURN
3420 PRINT "Command";TAB(12);"Description"
3430 PRINT TAB(4)"1";TAB(12)"List cargo in hold"
3440 PRINT TAB(4)"2";TAB(12)"List cargo which":PRINT TAB(12)
"may be purchased"
3450 PRINT TAB(4)"3";TAB(12)"Buy cargo"
3460 PRINT TAB(4)"4";TAB(12)"Sell cargo"
3470 PRINT TAB(4)"5";TAB(12)"List starports"
3480 PRINT TAB(4)"6";TAB(12)"Travel to new star"
3490 PRINT "  Other";TAB(12)"List available commands"
3500 RETURN
3510 REM Restore to Star Data Sub
3520 RESTORE
3530 FOR L=1 TO (2*N3+N2)
3540 READ A$
3550 NEXT L
3560 IF KQ=1 THEN KQ=0:GOTO 3600
3570 RETURN
3580 REM Restore to Cargo Data Sub
3590 KQ=1:GOTO 3510
3600 FOR L=1 TO 3*N3
3610 READ D9
3620 NEXT L
3630 IF LQ=1 THEN LQ=0:GOTO 3670
3640 RETURN
3650 REM Restore to Price Data Sub
3660 LQ=1:GOTO 3590
3670 FOR L=1 TO 8*N2
3680 READ D9
3690 NEXT L
3700 RETURN
3710 REM Star Names
3720 DATA "Lalande 21185","NI,P"
3730 DATA "Alpha Centauri","NA,I"
3740 DATA "Sirius","A"
3750 DATA "Barnards Star","I,P"
3760 DATA "Sol","R"
3770 DATA "Ross 154","NI,NA"
3780 DATA "Epsilon Eridani","A,P"
3790 DATA "Luyten 726-8","NA"
3800 DATA "Luyten 789-6","A,NI,P"
3810 DATA "Ross 248","A,I"
3820 REM Cargo Names
3830 DATA "Crystals"
3840 DATA "Radioactives"
3850 DATA "Alloys"
3860 DATA "Medicine"
3870 DATA "Gems"
```

Star Merchant

```
3880 DATA "Aircraft"
3890 DATA "Grav sleds"
3900 DATA "Computers"
3910 DATA "ATV"
3920 DATA "AFV"
3930 DATA "Firearms"
3940 DATA "Ammunition"
3950 DATA "Plasma guns"
3960 DATA "Tools"
3970 DATA "Body armor"
3980 DATA "Farm machinery"
3990 DATA "Liquor"
4000 DATA "Silver"
4010 DATA "Spices"
4020 DATA "Electronics"
4030 DATA "Mechanical parts"
4040 DATA "Cybernetic parts"
4050 DATA "Computer parts"
4060 DATA "Machine tools"
4070 DATA "Space suits"
4080 DATA "Fruit"
4090 DATA "Textiles"
4100 DATA "Polymers"
4110 DATA "Meat"
4120 DATA "Petrochemicals"
4130 DATA "Grain"
4140 DATA "Wood"
4150 DATA "Copper"
4160 DATA "Tin"
4170 DATA "Steel"
4180 DATA "Aluminum"
4190 REM Star Data
4200 DATA 2.83,-7.36,20
4210 DATA -2.4,-3.56,9
4220 DATA 8.38,9.93,2
4230 DATA -6.1,0,24
4240 DATA 0,0,32
4250 DATA -8.87,2.05,5
4260 DATA 8.45,6.65,18
4270 DATA 2.99,7.42,1
4280 DATA -4.43,9.3,22
4290 DATA -.89,10.26,10
4300 REM Cargo Data
4310 DATA 3,-2,2,-2,0,-4,20000,1
4320 DATA 0,1,4,-3,0,-2,1000000,1
4330 DATA -2,0,-4,6,1,-2,200000,1
4340 DATA -1,4,-4,3,-2,0,100000,1
4350 DATA 4,-2,4,-4,-1,1,1000000,1
4360 DATA -2,4,-3,3,1,-1,1000000,1
4370 DATA 2,0,-1,1,0,0,6000000,1
4380 DATA 1,0,-2,0,0,0,10000000,1
4390 DATA -2,2,-2,1,1,0,300000,1
4400 DATA 0,2,-2,0,0,1,700000,1
4410 DATA -2,6,-4,1,0,0,30000,2
4420 DATA -1,6,-5,2,0,0,30000,2
4430 DATA -1,3,-2,0,0,0,200000,2
4440 DATA -4,7,-8,4,5,0,10000,2
4450 DATA -3,6,-4,1,0,0,50000,2
4460 DATA -2,2,-6,0,6,-4,150000,1
4470 DATA 3,3,-1,0,-3,0,10000,1
4480 DATA 3,-1,3,-1,0,-2,70000,1
4490 DATA 4,-2,3,-1,-5,2,6000,1
4500 DATA 0,0,-4,4,1,1,100000,1
4510 DATA 0,1,-3,3,2,1,75000,1
4520 DATA 1,0,-4,2,1,0,250000,1
4530 DATA -1,0,-2,3,0,0,150000,1
4540 DATA 1,0,-2,1,0,0,750000,1
4550 DATA -1,2,-3,2,2,0,400000,1
4560 DATA 1,2,3,3,-4,-6,1000,2
4570 DATA 3,0,-3,1,-5,-3,3000,3
4580 DATA -2,0,3,3,0,0,7000,4
4590 DATA 0,0,5,2,-5,5,1500,4
4600 DATA 2,0,4,-2,3,0,10000,6
4610 DATA 0,0,1,3,-5,6,300,8
4620 DATA 0,0,1,2,-7,3,1000,2
4630 DATA 2,2,3,-2,-1,-4,2000,2
4640 DATA 2,2,3,-4,-1,-2,9000,3
4650 DATA -1,2,6,0,0,0,500,4
4660 DATA -1,1,3,-2,0,-2,1000,5
4670 REM Price Data
4680 DATA .4,.5,.7,.8,.9,1,1.1,1.2,1.3,1.5,1.7,2,3,4
4690 END
```

```
                 STAR MERCHANT

You have just spent 2 million credits
on a 2 year lease for a merchant
starship.  This leaves you with 2
million credits operating capital.

Your ship can hold a total of 20 cargos
with a total cargo weight of 200 tons.
The fuel capacity of your ship is great
enough such that travel between any 2
starports is possible without
refueling.

You are presently traveling from Alpha
Centauri to Sol.  You are carrying no
cargo.

Press any key to continue.█




The starport trade classifacation
determines the cargo price but does not
determine which cargos are available.

Abbreviations used for trade class are
as follows:
    R-Rich; P-Poor; I-Indstrial;
    NI-Nonindstrial; A-Agricultural;
    NA-Nonagricultural

Press any key to continue.█
```

```
Commands available are as follows:

Command      Description
   1         List cargo in hold
   2         List cargo which
             may be purchased
   3         Buy cargo
   4         Sell cargo
   5         List starports
   6         Travel to new star
  Other      List available commands

Enter a random number between 1
and 500 ? 162█


You have arrived at Sol.

Expenses have been deducted as follows:
      Docking fee:     50,000
             Fuel:    430,000
      Crew salary:     53,000

   Account balance: 1,467,000
   Empty cargo space:     200
         Ship time: .106 years

Enter command? 1

Cargo stored in hold:
All partitions are empty.

   Account balance: 1,467,000
   Empty cargo space:     200
         Ship time: .106 years

Enter command? 2
```

Star Merchant

```
Cargos available for purchase:
No Description       AMT    Price      %
1 Mechanical parts   15   1125000    100
2 Steel             110     49500     90
3 Silver             15   1260000    120
4 Machine tools      25  22500000    120
5 Mechanical parts   15    562500     50

   Account balance: 1,467,000
   Empty cargo space:      200
        Ship time: .106 years

Enter command? 3

Enter the lot number of cargo that you
want to purchase? 5

Transaction completed
Cargo stored in partition 1

   Account balance:  904,500
   Empty cargo space:     185
        Ship time: .109 years

Enter command? 3

Enter the lot number of cargo that you
want to purchase? 2

Transaction completed
Cargo stored in partition 2

   Account balance:  855,000
   Empty cargo space:      75
        Ship time: .112 years

Enter command? 5

No.    Name            Trade Cl  Dist  Dir
1      Lalande 21185   NI,P      7.89  291
2      Alpha Centauri  NA,I      4.29  236
3      Sirius          A        12.99   50
4      Barnards Star   I,P       6.10  180
5      Sol             R         0.00   90
6      Ross 154        NI,NA     9.10  167
7      Epsilon Eridani A,P      10.75   38
8      Luyten 726-8    NA        8.00   68
9      Luyten 789-6    A,NI,P   10.30  115
10     Ross 248        A,I      10.30   95

   Account balance:  855,000
   Empty cargo space:      75
        Ship time: .112 years

Enter command? 6

Enter destination star number? 2▮

You have arrived at Alpha Centauri.

Expenses have been deducted as follows:
       Docking fee:     50,000
             Fuel:    429,344
       Crew salary:     55,934

   Account balance:  319,722
   Empty cargo space:      75
        Ship time: .217 years

Enter command? 1

Cargo stored in hold:
Pt Description      AMT    Price      %
1 Mechanical parts   15    787500     70
2 Steel             110    220000    400

   Account balance:  319,722
   Empty cargo space:      75
        Ship time: .217 years

Enter command? 2

Cargos available for purchase:
No Description      AMT    Price      %
1 Gems                1   1000000    100
2 Gems                4   8000000    200
3 Tin               100    810000     90
4 Spices             10    240000    400
5 Wood               70    210000    300

   Account balance:  319,722
   Empty cargo space:      75
        Ship time: .217 years

Enter command? 4

Enter partition of cargo to be sold? 2
Transaction completed
```

```
   Account balance:  539,722
   Empty cargo space:      185
        Ship time: .22 years

Enter command? 4

Enter partition of cargo to be sold? 1
Transaction completed

   Account balance: 1,327,222
   Empty cargo space:     200
        Ship time: .223 years

Enter command? 3

Enter the lot number of cargo that you
want to purchase? 3

Transaction completed
Cargo stored in partition 1

   Account balance:  517,222
   Empty cargo space:     100
        Ship time: .226 years

Enter command? 5

No.    Name            Trade Cl  Dist  Dir
1      Lalande 21185   NI,P      6.46  324
2      Alpha Centauri  NA,I      0.00   90
3      Sirius          A        17.27   51
4      Barnards Star   I,P       5.13  136
5      Sol             R         4.29   56
6      Ross 154        NI,NA     8.56  139
7      Epsilon Eridani A,P      14.90   43
8      Luyten 726-8    NA       12.23   64
9      Luyten 789-6    A,NI,P   13.02   99
10     Ross 248        A,I      13.90   84

   Account balance:  517,222
   Empty cargo space:     100
        Ship time: .226 years

Enter command? 6

Enter destination star number? 1▮

You have arrived at Lalande 21185.

Expenses have been deducted as follows:
       Docking fee:     50,000
             Fuel:    646,474
       Crew salary:     79,147

   Account balance:  -258,400
   Empty cargo space:     100
        Ship time: .376 years

Enter command? 1

Cargo stored in hold:
Pt Description      AMT    Price      %
1 Tin               100    630000     70

   Account balance:  -258,400
   Empty cargo space:     100
        Ship time: .376 years

Enter command? 4

Enter partition of cargo to be sold? 1
Transaction completed

   Account balance:  371,600
   Empty cargo space:     200
        Ship time: .379 years

Enter command? 2

Cargos available for purchase:
No Description      AMT    Price      %
1 Aluminum          150    120000     80
2 Grain             140     42000    100
3 Plasma guns         5   2000000    200
4 Textiles           85    280500    110
5 Tools              11    440000    400

   Account balance:  371,600
   Empty cargo space:     200
        Ship time: .379 years

Enter command? 3

Enter the lot number of cargo that you
want to purchase? 1

Transaction completed
Cargo stored in partition 1
```

Star Merchant

```
    Account balance:    251,600
  Empty cargo space:        50
      Ship time: .382 years

Enter command? 5

No.   Name              Trade Cl   Dist  Dir
 1    Lalande 21185     NI,P       0.00   90
 2    Alpha Centauri    NA,I       6.46  144
 3    Sirius            A         18.16   72
 4    Barnards Star     I,P       11.57  141
 5    Sol               R          7.89  111
 6    Ross 154          NI,NA     15.01  141
 7    Epsilon Eridani   A,P       15.10   68
 8    Luyten 726-8      NA        14.78   89
 9    Luyten 789-6      A,NI,P    18.17  114
10    Ross 248          A,I       18.01  102

    Account balance:    251,600
  Empty cargo space:        50
      Ship time: .382 years
```

```
Enter command? 6

Enter destination star number? 2

You have arrived at Alpha Centauri.

Expenses have been deducted as follows:
     Docking fee:      50,000
            Fuel:     646,474
    Crew salary:      77,647

You no longer have sufficient funds to
operate your ship.

You began with 4 million credits and
now have 0 credits.
Cargo in the hold is worth 135000

This represents a loss of 8255624.637
credits per year.
Ok
```

Streets of the City

Streets of the City was written by Kenneth R. Murray and originally appeared in the April 1981 issue of *Creative Computing*.

Congratulations! You have been named Transportation Director of River City, Michigan. River City is a central city with a declining population which is now at 185,000 persons. Budget problems over the past decade have resulted in a severely deteriorated road system and inadequate bus service.

Prior to your being hired, the City Commission approved a ten-year transportation improvement plan that will now be your responsibility to complete. In the Street Fund, the plan calls for reconstructing 44 miles of main streets, called primaries, and 16 miles of interstate. At the same time, you have to significantly improve the overall street conditions and traffic safety. For the Transit Authority, an aging bus fleet needs to be expanded and modernized, and ridership must be expanded.

Your success wil be measured in two ways. The first is how well you progress each year in meeting the overall goal. Second is your ability to maintain a majority vote of the City Commission. Each influences the other.

Goals to be Achieved

In the initialization of the simulation, the initial conditions are randomly set. This includes the first budgets, street mileage and conditions, the traffic safety index, fleet size and age, and transit performance. The goals that you must achieve are as follows:

Goals	Standard
Primary Street Reconstruction	Reconstruct 44 Miles
Interstate Highway Construction	Build 16 Miles
Street Condition Index	Reduce 60 Percent
Traffic Safety Index	Reduce 60 Percent
Bus Fleet Age	Reduce 60 Percent
Bus Ridership	Increase 4 Times
Fleet Downtime Index	Reduce 60 Percent
On-Schedule Performance Index	Reduce 60 Percent

Highway Construction: The costs are initially set at random. Each year, costs will increase because of inflation. An inadequate maintenance program will also cause the construction costs to rise.

Street Conditions: A street condition index is randomly set; the higher the index, the worse the con-

dition. Each year the index is adjusted according to street mileage (total streets will be added in relation to inflationary pressures on development) and how well you budget for street maintenance. Your maintenance costs are determined by street mileage, street conditions, labor negotiations, and inflation.

Traffic Safety: A traffic safety index is also set randomly; again, the higher the index, the worse the traffic accident rate. This index is adjusted each year according to changes in the street conditions and how well you meet your maintenance and safety budget. The safety needs are determined by street mileage, the traffic safety index, labor negotiations, and inflation.

Age of Bus Fleet: The size and age of the fleet are randomly set and are incremented each year according to your sale and acquisition of buses. Sale is assumed on the basis of the oldest buses being sold first. Sale and purchase prices are influenced by inflation.

Ridership: Ridership is initially determined randomly. It is then affected by decisions on the number of routes, the hours of service, the days of service, and bus fare. The performance measures of downtime and on-schedule performance (referred to as service delay) and strikes will also affect ridership.

Fleet Downtime: This is measured by an index; the higher the index, the greater the downtime. The index is adjusted according to the age of the fleet and how well you meet your maintenance budget. The maintenance needs are determined by the size and age of the fleet, the level of service, labor negotiations, and inflation.

Service Delay: The higher the service delay index, the poorer your on-schedule performance. This index is determined by the size of the fleet relative to the number of routes, downtime, and meeting your operational budget. Operating needs are affected by the number of routes, hours and days of operation, labor negotiations, and inflation. You should not let the average number of buses per route drop below three.

Transit Authority Service Decisions

In this phase you determine the level of transit service you will have for the year. Your decisions and ranges are as follows:

Service	Initial Value	Range of Options
Routes	6	6 to 25
Hours of Operation Per Day	12	12, 17, or 24
Days of Operation	6	6 or 7
Fare	$.35	$.25 to $1.00

Bonding

In years 3 and 7, you will have the option of seeking authority to borrow money (in the form of bonds) for street construction. In year 3, the bond limit is $1.5 million, and in year 7, it is $2.0 million, each per year. You do not have to request the entire amount. The City Commission will decide what size of a bond issue to put to a vote of the citizens. The Commission decision will depend upon the size of the bond requested and your support among the Commission members. Once the issue is submitted to a vote, you will be asked to make certain pledges to the Coalition of Neighborhood Associations. Making the pledges will improve the chance of passage; however, if you fail to keep your pledges, you will be penalized severely.

Property Taxes

In this phase you will ask the City Commission to levy up to ten mils of property tax for street and transit operation. The amount that is approved will depend upon your support of the Commission and the size of the levy requested. The tax that is approved must then be divided between streets and transit. If you are too greedy, the chances that the Commission will approve a less-than-adequate property tax increase.

The amount of the property tax base is set at the start of the simulation. Each year it changes according to inflation, street improvements, and bus ridership. The theory is that with streets and more bus riders, property values will increase. Conversely, with poorer streets and fewer riders, property values will decrease.

Street Fund Budget

Once the tax levy is determined, you must decide how much to spend from the Street Fund on maintenance, safety, and construction. You will be able to transfer money from the operating account to the capital account and vice versa. The percentage that you can shift will change according to the amount of bonds you have issued. Your operating revenue, which includes funds left over from the previous year, gasoline taxes, and tax levy, is automatically adjusted to delete bond payments. Gasoline tax revenue is initially calculated at the start of the simulation based on street mileage and vehicle miles, then adjusted according to mileage changes and inflation. It is not a variable over which you have control. The construction budget, exclusive of bonds, is similarly set.

In making your maintenance and safety decisions, you should remember that the needs shown are the minimum amounts necessary to keep the maintenance and safety indexes approximately the same. Reducing the indexes requires more than the minimum appropriation.

Transit Budget

You have a similar set of decisions to make on the Transit Authority budget. Operating revenues include rider fare (ridership times fare), a federal subsidy which is automatically set at half of the operating and maintenance needs for the year and tax revenues. The capital budget consists of revenues from the sale of buses and from occasional federal grants. You may transfer up to 25% of the operating revenues to acquisition, but you may not use the capital fund for operations. By random determination, you may receive a federal grant for fees acquisition. In those years you cannot transfer funds from the operating account. Your decision whether to buy and/or sell buses depends upon your fleet needs. Remember that buses add to maintenance costs, whether you need them or not. A rule of thumb is that three buses are needed per route. Again, the operating and maintenance needs are minimums necessary to hold the indexes about the same.

Labor Negotiations

The final phase of decision making is labor negotiations for the next year. The outcome of the negotiations directly affects your operating and maintenance budget for streets and the Transit Authority.

There will be between two and six rounds of negotiations, with the Union making the first offer. Subsequent union offers will depend upon how willing you are to bargain in good faith. If you reach settlement, excellent. If you do not reach settlement, you risk a strike. The possibility of a strike depends upon the beginning and ending positions of the two parties and how much each has changed its position. A strike negatively affects your performance for the year in which it occurs, so you should not risk one lightly.

Performance Review

Once you have completed the decision process, you will be given a comparision of the effects of your decisions this year against the past year and against the fiscal plan. You will also be shown a graphic display of the status of your street construction. Your general performance will be evaluated and you will be told the strengths and weaknesses of your performance. Depending on your performance, you can gain or lose support among the Commissioners. You begin the game with the unanimous support of all eleven Commissioners.

End of the Game

The game can end in one of three ways. The most desirable, and the one requiring the most political acumen, is for you to satisfactorily complete the transportation plan. The second way is to serve out the ten years but not complete the plan, which results in a demotion for you. The third ending is that you will be asked to resign. This will happen if you fail to keep the support of at least six Commissioners. And, it's easier to lose votes than it is to gain them.

Good luck on your new job!

Streets of the City

```
1 CLEAR 1500:DEFSTR F:DIM T$(6),T(6,11),TB(9,10),A(8,2),BF(100)
2 DIM B(2,10),S(5,11),U(10),M(10):C$=CHR$(207):D$=CHR$(212):E$=CHR$(255)
3 CLS:PRINT @ 214,"Streets of the City"
4 PRINT @ 471,"Creative Computing"
5 PRINT @ 278,"by Kenneth R Murray"
56 FOR X=1 TO 1500:NEXT
100 CLS:PRINT"CONGRATULATIONS! YOU HAVE BEEN NAMED TRANSPORTATION"
105 PRINT"DIRECTOR OF RIVER CITY, MICHIGAN, A CENTRAL CITY WITH"
110 PRINT"A DECLINING POPULATION AND WHICH HAS SUFFERED DETERIORATION"
115 PRINT"OF ITS TRANSPORTATION SERVICES OVER THE LAST SEVERAL YEARS.":PRINT
120 PRINT"PRIOR TO YOUR BEING HIRED, THE CITY COMMISSION ADOPTED"
125 PRINT"A TEN-TEAR TRANSPORTATION PLAN TO RESTORE SERVICES FOR"
130 PRINT"BOTH STREETS AND BUSES TO AN ADEQUATE LEVEL. IT WILL BE"
135 PRINT"YOUR RESPONSIBILITY TO CARRY OUT THIS PLAN.":PRINT
140 PRINT"FOR THE STREET FUND, YOU WILL NEED TO CONSTRUCT SEVERAL"
145 PRINT"MILES OF INTERSTATE HIGHWAYS AND RECONSTRUCT MAJOR LOCAL"
150 PRINT"STREETS (CALLED PRIMARIES). YOU WILL ALSO NEED TO IMPROVE"
155 PRINT"STREET CONDITIONS AND TRAFFIC SAFETY.":PRINT
814 S$(1)="RIDERSHIP":S$(2)="FLEET AGE":S$(3)="DOWNTIME":S$(4)="SERVICE DELAY"
815 S$(5)="FLEET SIZE"
850 T$(2)="PRIMARY ST. MILEAGE":T$(3)="INTERSTATE MILEAGE"
860 T$(4)="STREET CONDITION INDEX":T$(5)="TRAFFIC SAFETY INDEX"
865 T$(1)="LOCAL ST. MILEAGE":T$(6)="VEHICLE MILES"
1000 FA="$$#####,###.":FB="######,###":FC="$$##.##"
1002 FOR R=1 TO 8
1003 FOR C=1 TO 2
1004 READ A(R,C)
1005 NEXT C
1006 NEXT R
1007 DATA 128,191,384,431,640,687,704,767,896,959
1008 DATA 15,975,31,991,47,1007
1029 YR=0:CV=11:G1=0:G3=0:B=50:P1=140000:P2=75000:M9=RND(150)*1000
1030 CI=(((RND(250)+250)*1000)+1000000)/2
1040 MI=RND(5000)+35000
1050 T(1,YR)=450+RND(100):T(2,YR)=85+RND(25):T(3,YR)=0
1060 T(4,YR)=RND(50)*.1+6:T(5,YR)=RND(50)*.1+6
1065 XX=3000+RND(3000):XY=7000+RND(3000):XZ=20000+RND(8000)
1070 T(6,YR)=(XX*T(1,YR))+(XY*T(2,YR))
1080 TB(1,YR)=T(6,YR)/1.6:PT=TB(1,YR)*((30+RND(20))*.01):TB(8,YR)=TB(1,YR)+PT
1081 TB(2,YR)=1
1090 TB(3,YR)=(RND(500)*1000)+1600000:TB(9,YR)=TB(3,YR)
2000 MN=(T(1,YR)*MI*.16*(T(4,YR)*.1))+(T(2,YR)*MI*.5*(T(4,YR)*.1))+(T(3,YR)*MI)
2010 SN=MN*.04*T(5,YR):TB(6,YR)=MN:TB(7,YR)=SN
2011 S(1,YR)=RND(350)*1000+550000
2012 S(5,YR)=INT(RND(10)+15)
2013 M1=INT(RND(3000)+5000)
2015 FOR X=1 TO S(5,YR)
2016 BF(X)=INT(RND(12)+3)
2017 NEXT X:GOTO 6596
2018 S=(RND(300)+500)*.01:S1=6:S2=12:S3=6:M5=(S1*S2*S3*312*S)+M9
2021 S4=.35:B(1,YR)=(RND(500)*1000)+200000
2022 S(3,YR)=INT(S(2,YR)/3)+6+(RND(50)*.1):S(4,YR)=INT(S(3,YR)/3)+6+(RND(50)*.1)
2023 S(1,YR)=S(1,YR)-(((S(3,YR)+S(4,YR))*.01)*S(1,YR)):BE=M5:M2=M2+(M5*.1):BD=M2
2030 T(4,11)=INT(T(4,YR)*.4):T(5,11)=INT(T(5,YR)*.4):S(1,11)=S(1,YR)*4
2031 S(2,11)=INT(S(2,YR)*.4):S(3,11)=INT(S(3,YR)*.4):S(4,11)=INT(S(4,YR)*.4)
2032 T(2,11)=44+T(2,YR):T(3,11)=16
2040 INPUT"PRESS ENTER";Z:CLS:PRINT"FOR THE TRANSIT AUTHORITY, YOU MUST REPLACE A"
2041 PRINT"DELAPIDATED BUS FLEET, INCREASE RIDERSHIP, REDUCE THE"
2042 PRINT"MAINTENANCE DOWNTIME, AND IMPROVE ON-SCHEDULE PERFORMANCE"
2043 PRINT"(ALSO REFERRED TO AS SERVICE DELAY).":PRINT
2044 PRINT"FOR ALL INDICES USED, THE HIGHER THE INDEX VALUE THE"
2045 PRINT"WORSE THE CONDITION INDICATED.  THE BUDGET NEEDS LISTED"
2046 PRINT"ARE THE MINIMUMS NEEDED TO MAINTAIN THE INDEX AT ITS "
2047 PRINT"PRESENT LEVEL; IMPROVING THE LEVEL REQUIRES BUDGETS THAT"
2048 PRINT"ARE HIGHER THAN THE MINIMUM NEEDS.":PRINT@960,"PRESS ENTER";:INPUT Z
2049 CLS:PRINT:PRINT"YOUR GOALS FOR THE PLAN ARE AS FOLLOWS:":PRINT
2050 PRINT"STANDARD";TAB(30)"PRESENT";TAB(45)"GOAL"
2051 PRINT
2052 FOR X=2 TO 5:PRINT T$(X);TAB(30)T(X,YR);TAB(45)T(X,11):NEXT X
2053 PRINT
2054 FOR X=1 TO 4
2055 IF X=1 THEN 2058
2056 PRINT S$(X);TAB(30)S(X,YR);TAB(45)S(X,11):NEXT X
2057 GOTO 2060
2058 PRINT S$(X);TAB(30);:PRINT USING FB;S(X,YR);:PRINT TAB(45);
2059 PRINT USING FB;S(X,11):NEXT X
2060 PRINT:PRINT"GOOD LUCK!":PRINT@935,"PRESS ENTER";:INPUT Z
2990 YR=YR+1
```

```
2991 FOR X=1 TO 5
2992 S(X,YR)=S(X,YR-1)
2993 NEXT X
3010 FOR X=1 TO 6
3020 T(X,YR)=T(X,YR-1)
3030 NEXT X
3040 FOR X=1 TO 9
3050 TB(X,YR)=TB(X,YR-1)
3051 NEXT X
3052 B(1,YR)=B(1,YR-1):B(2,YR)=B(2,YR-1)
3053 IF RND(10)<5 THEN GG=(RND(4)*P1)-100000 ELSE GG=0
3054 B(2,YR)=B(2,YR)+GG+B1:IFB(2,YR)>P1*6 THEN B(2,YR)=P1*6
3065 IF YR=1 THEN 3241
3070 I=(RND(10)+5)*.01::P1=P1+(P1*I):P2=P2+(P2*I):M9=M9+(M9*I)
3080 MI=MI+(MI*I):CI=CI+(CI*I):TB(1,YR)=TB(1,YR)+(TB(1,YR)*I)
3081 IF YR>2 AND T(4,YR)>T(4,YR-2) THEN CI=CI*1.1:M2=M2+(M2*I)
3082 FORX=1TO100:IF BF(X)=0 THEN 3085
3083 IF BF(X)>1 THEN BF(X)=BF(X)+1
3084 IF BF(X)=.5 THEN BF(X)=1
3085 NEXT X
3100 IF I>.11 THEN T(1,YR)=T(1,YR)+RND(7)
3110 IF I<=.11 AND I>.08 THEN T(1,YR)=T(1,YR)+RND(15)
3120 IF I<=.08 THEN T(1,YR)=T(1,YR)+RND(22)
3190 T(6,YR)=T(6,YR)+(XX*(T(1,YR)-T(1,YR-1)))+(XY*(T(2,YR)-T(2,YR-2)))
3191 T(6,YR)=T(6,YR)+(XZ*T(3,YR)-T(3,YR-2)))
3200 TB(1,YR)=((T(6,YR))/1.6)+(TB(1,YR)*I)
3201 PT=PT+(PT*I+.02))+(PT*(((S(5,YR)-S(5,YR-1))/S(5,YR-1))/2))
3210 TB(3,YR)=TB(3,YR)+TB(3,YR)*(I1-.02)
3220 TB(9,YR)=TB(9,YR)+TB(3,YR):TB(8,YR)=TB(8,YR)+TB(1,YR)
3230 MN=(T(1,YR)*MI*.16*(T(4,YR)*.1))+(T(2,YR)*MI*.5*(T(4,YR)*.1))+T(3,YR)*MI
3235 MN=(MN*.6)+((MN*.4)*(1+U*.01))
3240 SN=MN*.04*T(5,YR):SN=(SN*.6)+((SN*.4)*(1+U*.01))
3241 CLS:PRINT"YOUR TRANSIT AUTHORITY SERVICE OPTIONS ARE:":PRINT
3242 PRINT TAB(5)"1.   ROUTES":PRINT TAB(5)"2.   HOURS OF OPERATION"
3243 PRINT TAB(5)"3.   DAYS OF SERVICE":PRINT TAB(5)"4.   FARE"
3244 PRINT TAB(5)"5.   TO CONTINUE"
3245 PRINT:INPUT"WHAT IS YOUR CHOICE";Z:IFINT(Z)<>Z AND Z<1 OR Z>5 THEN 3241
3247 ON Z GOTO 3248,3254,3262,3270,3286
3248 PRINT@640,"PRESENT NUMBER OF ROUTES=";S1
3249 PRINT@704,"NEW NUMBER OF ROUTES (MIN. OF 6, MAX. OF 25)";
3250 INPUT S1(1):PRINT@960,E$::IF INT(S1(1))<>S1(1) THEN 3280
3251 IF S1(1)<6 THEN 3281
3252 IF S1(1)>25 THEN 3281 ELSE 3241
3253 PRINT@640,"POSSIBLE HOURS OF OPERATION ARE LISTED BELOW":IFS2=12THENS2=1
3254 IFS2=17THENS2=2
3255 IFS2=24THENS2=3
3256 PRINT@704,"CURRENT OPTION=";S2:PRINT@768,"1. 6AM TO 6PM":IFS2=24THENS2=3
3257 PRINT@808,"2. 6AM TO 11PM":PRINT@832,"3. 24 HOURS":PRINT@872,"NEW HOURS";
3258 INPUT S2(1):PRINT@960,E$::IFINT(S2(1))<>S2(1)ORS2(1)<1ORS2(1)>3THEN3282
3259 IFS2(1)=1THENS2(1)=12:GOTO3241
3260 IFS2(1)=2THENS2(1)=17:GOTO3241
3261 IFS2(1)=3THENS2(1)=24:GOTO3241
3262 PRINT@640,"YOUR OPTIONS FOR DAYS OF SERVICE ARE AS FOLLOWS"
3263 IF S3=6 THEN S3=1 ELSE S3=2
3264 PRINT@704,"CURRENT OPTION=";S3:PRINT@768,"1. MONDAY THROUGH SATURDAY"
3265 PRINT@832,"2. MONDAY THROUGH SUNDAY"
3266 PRINT@872,"NEW DAYS =";:INPUT S3(1):PRINT@960,E$;
3267 IF INT(S3(1))=S3(1) AND S3(1)=1 OR S3(1)=2 THEN 3268 ELSE 3283
3268 IF S3(1)=1 THEN S3(1)=6 ELSE S3(1)=7
3269 GOTO 3241
3270 PRINT@640,"THE FARE MAY BE CHANGED IN NICKEL UNITS, WITH A"
3271 PRINT@704,"MINIMUM FARE OF $.25 AND A MAXIMUM OF $1.00"
3272 PRINT@768,"DO NOT ENTER DOLLAR SIGN"
3273 PRINT@832,"CURRENT FARE =";S4:PRINT@872,"NEW FARE =";
3274 INPUT S4(1):PRINT@960,E$;
3275 IF S4(1)<.25 OR S4(1)>1 THEN 3284
3276 S4$=STR$(S4(1)):IF RIGHT$(S4$,1)="0"ORRIGHT$(S4$,1)="5"THEN3277ELSE3285
3277 GOTO 3241
3278 GOSUB 10670
3279 GOTO 3286
3280 PRINT@960,"YOU MUST ENTER A WHOLE NUMBER";:PRINT@704,E$:GOTO 3249
3281 PRINT@960,"YOUR NUMBER IS OUTSIDE THE RANGES";:PRINT@704,E$:GOTO 3249
3282 PRINT@960,"YOUR OPTION MUST BE 1, 2, OR 3";:PRINT@832,E$:GOTO 3257
3283 PRINT@960,"YOUR OPTION MUST BE 1 OR 2";:PRINT@832,E$:GOTO 3265
3284 PRINT@960,"YOUR FARE IS OUTSIDE THE RANGE";:PRINT@832,E$:GOTO 3273
3285 PRINT@960,"THE FARE MUST BE IN NICKEL INCREMENTS";:PRINT@832,E$:GOTO 3273
3286 S6=0:IF S1(1)=0 AND S2(1)=0 AND S3(1)=0 AND S4(1)=0 THEN 3302
3287 IF S3(1)<>0 AND S3(1)-S3=5 THEN S6=S6+((RND(15000)+75000)*S1)
```

```
3288 IF S3(1)<>0  AND  S3(1)-S3=7 THEN S6=S6+((RND(25000)+90000)*S1)
3289 IF S3(1)<>0 AND  S3(1)-S3=12 THEN S6=S6+((RND(30000)+110000)*S1)
3291 IF  S3(1)<>0 AND  S3-S3(1)=5 THEN S6=S6-((RND(15000)+75000)*S1)
3292 IF S3(1)<>0 AND  S3-S3(1)=7 THEN S6=S6-((RND(25000)+90000)*S1)
3293 IF S3(1)<>0 AND  S3-S3(1)=12 THEN S6=S6-((RND(30000)+110000)*S1)
3294 IF S1(1)<>0 AND S1(1)>0 THEN S6=(RND(160)*500)*(S1(1)-S1)
3295 IF S2(1)<>0 AND S2(1)>0 THEN S6=S6+(RND(10000)+15000)*(S2(1)-S2)
3296 IF S4(1)<>0 AND S4(1)>S4 THEN S6=S6-(((S4(1)-S4)/5)*2000)
3297 IF S1(1)>0 THEN S1=S1(1)
3298 IF S2(1)>0 THEN S2=S2(1)
3299 IF S3(1)>0 THEN S3=S3(1)
3300 IF S4(1)>0 THEN S4=S4(1)
3302 S1(1)=0:S2(1)=0:S3(1)=0:S4(1)=0
3303 IF YR=3 OR YR=7 THEN 3304 ELSE 3680
3304 IF YR=3 THEN B1=1500000 ELSE B1=2000000
3309 CLS:PRINT TAB(15)"STREET FUND BOND PROPOSAL":PRINT
3310 PRINT"YOU MAY PROPOSE BONDING UP TO";:PRINT USING FA;B1;
3311 PRINT"SUBJECT TO"
3315 PRINT"APPROVAL OF THE CITY COMMISSION AND A VOTE OF THE"
3320 PRINT"CITIZENS.  HOW MUCH DO YOU WISH TO PROPOSE (IN"
3325 INPUT"THOUSANDS, TYPE '0' IF NONE)";Z
3326 IF Z=0 THEN 3675
3330 Z=Z*1000:IF Z<0 OR Z>B1 THEN 3300:B1=Z
3335 IF CV<8 THEN B1=B1-(RND(35)*10000)
3340 IF CV<10 THEN B1=B1-(RND(20)*10000)
3345 PRINT:PRINT"THE COMMISSION HAS APPROVED A BOND REFERENDUM"
3350 PRINT"FOR";
3355 PRINT USING FA;B1;
3356 PRINT"EACH YEAR.":PRINT:PRINT:INPUT"PRESS ENTER";Z
3360 CLS:PRINT:PRINT"THE COALITION OF NEIGHBORHOOD ASSOCIATIONS HAS ASKED"
3361 PRINT
3365 PRINT"YOU TO MAKE THE FOLLOWING PLEDGES FOR THE NEXt THREE"
3370 PRINT"YEARS.  WILL YOU MAKE ANY OF THEM (Y/N)?"
3375 IF T(4,YR)<T(4,0) THEN B2=T(4,YR)-2 ELSE B2=T(4,0)-2
3380 IF B2<1 THEN B2=1
3385 IF T(5,YR)<T(5,0) THEN B3=T(5,YR)-2 ELSE B2=T(5,0)-2
3390 IF B3<1 THEN B3=1
3395 IF G1>22 THEN B4=44-G1 ELSE B4=20
3400 IF G3>11 THEN B5=16-G3 ELSE B5=6
3405 PRINT TAB(5)"1.  IMPROVE STREET CONDITION INDEX TO";B2
3410 PRINT TAB(5)"2.  IMPROVE SAFETY INDEX TO";B3
3415 PRINT TAB(5)"3.  CONSTRUCT";B4;"MILES OF PRIMARIES";
3420 PRINT TAB(5)"4.  CONSTRUCT";B5;"MILES OF INTERSTATES";
3423 PRINT:PRINT@768,"PLEDGE 1";TAB(15)"PLEDGE 2";TAB(30)"PLEDGE 3";
3424 PRINT TAB(45)"PLEDGE 4":PRINT@832,C$
3425 PRINT@832,;
3426 INPUT Z$
3430 IF Z$<>"Y" AND Z$<>"N" THEN 3405
3435 IF Z$="N" THEN B2=0
3439 PRINT@847,C$
3440 PRINT@847,;
3441 INPUT Z$
3445 IF Z$<>"Y" AND Z$<>"N" THEN 3410
3450 IF Z$="N" THEN B3=0
3454 PRINT@862,C$
3455 PRINT@862,;:INPUT Z$
3460 IF Z$<>"Y" AND Z$<>"N" THEN 3415
3465 IF Z$="N" THEN B4=0
3469 PRINT@877,C$
3470 PRINT@877,;:INPUT Z$
3475 IF Z$<>"Y" AND Z$<>"N" THEN 3420
3480 IF Z$="N" THEN B5=0
3485 PRINT@960,"PRESS ENTER FOR ELECTION RESULTS";
3490 INPUT Z:CLS:PRINT TAB(18)"BOND ELECTION RESULTS"
3492 PRINT:PRINT"WARD";TAB(10)"YES";TAB(20)"NO";TAB(35)"TOT. YES";TAB(50)"TOT. NO
3495 PRINT:V5=0:V6=0
3500 IF CV>9 THEN V1=5000 ELSE V1=4000
3505 IF T(4,YR)<T(4,YR-1) AND T(4,YR)<T(4,0) THEN V1=V1+500
3510 IF T(5,YR)<T(5,YR-1) AND T(5,YR)<T(5,0) THEN V1=V1+500
3515 IF YR=7 THEN 3530
3520 IF B1<1100000 THEN V1=V1+500
3525 GOTO 3535
3530 IF B1<1600000 THEN V1=V1+500
3535 IF B2>0 THEN V1=V1+500
3540 IF B3>0 THEN V1=V1+500
3545 IF B4>0 THEN V1=V1+500
3550 IF B4>0 THEN V1=V1+500
3555 V2=RND(5)
```

```
3560 FOR X=1 TO 5
3565 IF X=V2 THEN 3580
3575 V3=V1+RND(11000)
3580 GOTO 3590
3585 V3=(V1/2)+RND(12000)
3586 IF V3<3000 THEN V3=4000
3590 V4=21000-V3:V5=V5+V3:V6=V6+V4
3595 PRINT TAB(2)X;TAB(9)V3;TAB(19)V4;TAB(35)V5;TAB(50)V6
3600 FOR Y=1 TO 500:NEXT Y
3605 NEXT X
3610 IF V5<=V6 THEN 3650
3615 PRINT:PRINT"CONGRATULATIONS.   THE BOND ISSUE WAS APPROVED BY"
3620 PRINT"THE VOTERS.   YOUR ANNUAL DEBT PAYMENT WILL BE";
3625 DS=DS+(PT*.4)
3630 PRINT USING FA;DS
3635 TB(9,YR)=TB(9,YR)+B1:B=B-10
3640 INPUT"PRESS ENTER";Z:GOTO 3680
3650 PRINT"THE REFERENDUM HAS FAILED."
3651 IF V6/(V5+V6)<(55+RND(15))*.01 THEN 3675
3652 PRINT"BECAUSE OF THE MARGIN OF DEFEAT, YOU HAVE LOST"
3653 PRINT"THE VOTE OF A COMMISSIONER.": CV=CV-1
3655 IF CV<6 THEN 6770
3660 B1=0:B2=0:B3=0:B4=0:B5=0
3675 PRINT:INPUT"PRESS ENTER";Z
3680 CLS:PRINT TAB(18)"PROPERTY TAX LEVY"
3681 M5=(S1*S2*S3*312*S)+M9:M2=M2+(M5*.1):B(1,YR)=B(1,YR)+(S4*S(1,YR))+((M2+M5)/2)
3685 PRINT TAB(30)"STREET FUND";TAB(45)"TRANSIT AUTHORITY"
3690 PRINT"OPERATING NEEDS";TAB(30);:PRINT USING FA;MN+SN+DS;:PRINT TAB(45);
3691 PRINT USING FA;M2+M5
3695 PRINT"NON-TAX REVENUE";TAB(30);:PRINT USING FA;TB(8,YR);:PRINT TAB(45);
3696 PRINT USING FA;B(1,YR)
3700 PRINT"PROPERTY TAX NEEDED (MILLS)";:PRINT TAB(30);
3701 PRINT USING FA;MN+SN+DS-TB(8,YR);:PRINT TAB(45);
3702 PRINT USING FA;M2+M5-B(1,YR)
3705 TN=INT(((MN+SN+DS+M2+M5-TB(8,YR)-B(1,YR))/PT)*10)*.1:PRINT
3706 PRINT"TOTAL PROPERTY TAX NEEDED (IN MILLS) =";TN
3710 PRINT@640,"WHAT PROPERTY TAX LEVY (0-10 MILLS) DO YOU PROPOSE";
3711 INPUT TB(2,YR):PRINT@960,E$;
3715 IF TB(2,YR)>=0 AND TB(2,YR)<=10 THEN 3725
3720 PRINT@960,"YOU CANNOT EXCEED THE LIMITS";:PRINT@640,E$:GOTO 3710
3725 IF TB(2,YR)<=TB(2,YR-1) THEN 3805
3770 X1=0:X2=0
3775 FOR X=1 TO 11
3780 IF CV>9 THEN 3783
3781 IF X<=CV THEN X3=RND(5) ELSE X3=RND(8)
3782 GOTO 3785
3783 IF X<=2 THEN X3=RND(4)
3784 IF X>2 AND X<=CV THEN X3=RND(5):IF X>CV THEN X3=RND(8)
3785 IF X3<=3 THEN X1=X1+1 ELSE X2=X2+1
3790 NEXT X
3795 IF X1>=6 THEN 3801
3800 IF TB(2,YR)<=TN THEN TB(2,YR)=TB(2,YR) ELSE TB(2,YR)=TB(2,YR)-(.1*(X2+1))
3801 IFX1>=6THEN3805:IFTB(2,YR)>=TN+2ANDX1<10 THEN TB(2,YR)=TB(2,YR)-(2*(X2+1))
3805 PRINT@704,"THE CITY COMMISSION HAS APPROVED A LEVY OF";TB(2,YR);"MILLS"
3810 PRINT@768,"HOW MANY MILLS ARE FOR THE STREET FUND";:INPUT T8:PRINT@960,E$;
3815 IF T8<=TB(2,YR) THEN 3825
3820 PRINT@960,"YOU CANNOT ALLOCATE MORE THAN YOU ARE AUTHORIZED";:PRINT@768,E$
3821 GOTO 3810
3825 TB(8,YR)=TB(8,YR)+(PT*T8)-DS:B(1,YR)=B(1,YR)+(PT*(TB(2,YR)-T8))
4000 CLS:C=0:GOTO 4020
4010 C=1
4020 CLS:PRINT TAB(10)"STREET FUND BUDGET DECISIONS FOR YEAR";YR
4030 PRINT"OPERATIONS:";TAB(33)"CONSTRUCTION:"
4040 PRINT TAB(5)"AVAILABLE:";
4041 PRINT USING FA;TB(8,YR);
4050 PRINT TAB(38)"AVAILABLE:";:PRINT USING FA;TB(9,YR)
4060 PRINT TAB(5)"MAINT. NEED=";:PRINT USING FA;MN;
4070 PRINT TAB(38)"COST PER HALF MILE UNIT:"
4080 PRINT TAB(5)"SAFETY NEED=";:PRINT USING FA;SN;
4090 PRINT TAB(38)"PRIMARY RDS.=";:PRINT USING FA;CI*.2
4100 PRINT TAB(38)"INTERSTATES=";:PRINT USING FA;CI
4110 PRINT:IF C=1 THEN 4260
4150 PRINT"YOU MAY TRANSFER UP TO ";B;"% FROM AN ACCOUNT"
4160 PRINT TAB(10)"1.   OPERATIONS TO CONSTRUCTION"
4170 PRINT TAB(10)"2.   CONSTRUCTION TO OPERATIONS"
4180 PRINT TAB(10)"3.   NO TRANSFER"
4190 INPUT Z:IF Z<>1 AND Z<>2 AND Z<>3 THEN 4020
4195 IF Z=3 THEN 4010 ELSE 4200
```

Streets of the City

```
4200 INPUT"HOW MUCH DO YOU WANT TO TRANSFER (IN THOUSANDS, WITHOUT $ SIGN)";T
4201 T=T*1000
4210 IF Z=1 AND T>TB(8,YR)/(B*.01) THEN 4200
4220 IF Z=2 AND T>TB(9,YR)/(B*.01) THEN 4200
4230 IF Z=2 THEN 4250
4240 TB(8,YR)=TB(8,YR)-T:TB(9,YR)=TB(9,YR)+T:GOTO 4010
4250 TB(8,YR)=TB(8,YR)+T:TB(9,YR)=TB(9,YR)-T:GOTO 4010
4260 PRINT"ENTER CONSTRUCTION BY THE NUMBER OF HALF MILE UNITS;"
4265 PRINT"ENTER MAINTENANCE AND SAFETY BY THOUSAND DOLLAR UNITS."
4270 PRINT"DO NOT USE COMMAS OR DOLLAR SIGNS"
4280 PRINT:PRINT TAB(10)"PRIMARIES";TAB(20);"INTERSTATES";TAB(36)"MAINTENANCE";
4282 PRINT TAB(53)"SAFETY"
4290 PRINT"LAST YR";TAB(13)PC;TAB(23)IC;
4300 PRINT TAB(35);
4301 PRINT USING FA;TB(6,YR-1);
4305 PRINT TAB(50);
4306 PRINT USING FA;TB(7,YR-1)
4310 PRINT"THIS YR";
4315 PRINT@844,;
4316 INPUT PC
4317 PRINT@960,E$;
4318 IF INT(PC)<>PC THEN 4390
4319 IF G1+(PC/2)>44 THEN 4392
4320 PRINT@854,;
4321 INPUT IC
4322 PRINT@960,E$;
4323 IF INT(IC)<>IC THEN 4393
4324 IF T(3,YR)+(IC/2)>16 THEN 4395
4325 IF (PC*(CI*.2))+(IC*CI)>TB(9,YR) THEN 4397
4326 PRINT@870,;:INPUT T1:T1=T1*1000
4327 PRINT@960,E$;:IFLEN(STR$(T1))>LEN(STR$(MN))+1ORT1<100000THENGOSUB4399ELSE4330
4328 IF Z$="Y" THEN 4330
4329 Z$="Y":PRINT@870,D$:GOTO 4326
4330 PRINT@885,;:INPUTT2:PRINT@960,E$;:T2=T2*1000
4332 IFLEN(STR$(T2))>LEN(STR$(SN))+1 OR T2<100000THEN GOSUB4399ELSE4334
4334 IFZ$="Y"THEN4336
4335 Z$="Y":PRINT@855,D$:GOTO4330
4336 IF T1+T2>TB(8,YR) THEN 4405
4337 GOTO 4440
4390 PRINT@960,"YOU MUST ENTER A WHOLE NUMBER.";
4391 PRINT@841,C$:GOTO 4315
4392 PRINT@960,"YOU CAN BUILD ONLY";(44-G1)/2;" MORE HALF MILE UNITS";:GOTO 4391
4393 PRINT@960,"YOU MUST ENTER A WHOLE NUMBER.";
4394 PRINT@851,C$:GOTO 4320
4395 PRINT@960,"YOU CAN BUILD ONLY";(16-T(3,YR))/2;"MORE HALF MILE UNITS.";
4396 GOTO4394
4397 PRINT@960,"YOUR CONSTRUCTION PROGRAM EXCEEDS YOUR BUDGET.";
4398 PRINT@841,C$:PRINT@851,C$:GOTO 4315
4399 PRINT@960,E$;:PRINT@960,"ARE YOU SURE (Y/N)";
4400 INPUT Z$:IF Z$<>"Y" AND Z$<>"N" THEN 4399
4401 RETURN:END
4402 PRINT@960,E$;:PRINT@960,"ARE YOU SURE (Y/N)";
4403 INPUT Z$:IF Z$<>"Y" AND Z$<>"N" THEN 4402:IF Z$="Y" THEN 4332
4404 PRINT@885,D$:GOTO 4330
4405 PRINT@960,"YOUR MAINTENANCE AND SAFETY BUDGET EXCEEDS YOUR FUNDS";
4406 PRINT@870,D$:PRINT@885,D$:GOTO 4326
4440 TB(6,YR)=T1:TB(7,YR)=T2
4445 T(2,YR)=T(2,YR)+PC/2:T(3,YR)=T(3,YR)+IC/2
4450 TB(8,YR)=TB(8,YR)-TB(6,YR)-TB(7,YR)
4460 TB(9,YR)=TB(9,YR)-(PC*CI*.2)-(IC*CI)
4470 PRINT@960,"PRESS ENTER";:INPUT Z
5200 T(4,YR)=T(4,YR)-(INT(((TB(6,YR)-MN)/MN)*18)*.1)
5210 IF T(4,YR)<1 THEN T(4,YR)=1
5240 T(5,YR)=T(5,YR)-(INT(((TB(7,YR)-SN)/SN)*18)*.1)
5249 IF T(4,YR)>T(4,YR-1) THEN T(5,YR)=T(5,YR)+.2
5250 IF T(5,YR)<1 THEN T(5,YR)=1
6000 CLS:C=0:GOTO 6020
6010 C=1
6020 CLS:PRINT TAB(15)"TRANSIT BUDGET FOR YEAR";YR
6030 PRINT"OPERATIONS";TAB(33)"BUS FLEET"
6040 PRINT TAB(5)"AVAILABLE";:PRINT USING FA;B(1,YR);:PRINT TAB(38)"AVAILABLE";
6041 PRINT USING FA;B(2,YR)
6080 PRINT TAB(5)"MAINT. NEED=";:PRINT USING FA;M2;:PRINT TAB(38)"(COST PER BUS):
6090 PRINT TAB(5)"OPERATIONS NEED=";:PRINT USING FA;M5;
6091 PRINT TAB(38)"ACQUISITION=";:PRINT USING FA;P1
6100 PRINT TAB(38)"SALE=";:PRINT USING FA;P2
6110 IF C=1 THEN 6340
6120 IF GG>0 THEN PRINT@640,"BECAUSE OF THE FEDERAL GRANT, YOU CAN'T TRANSFER FROM
```

```
6121 PRINT@704,"OPERATIONS TO THE BUS FLEET":FORX=1TO750:NEXT:GOTO6200
6140 PRINT@640,"YOU MAY TRANSFER UP TO 25% FROM OPERATIONS TO ACQUISITION"
6141 PRINT@960,E$;
6150 PRINT@704,"HOW MANY THOUSANDS DO YOU WANT TO TRANSFER (NO $ SIGN)";
6151 INPUT Z:Z=Z*10000:IFZ<0ORZ>B(1,YR)/4 THEN 6180 ELSE 6190
6180 PRINT@640,E$:PRINT@704,E$:GOTO 6140
6190 B(2,YR)=B(2,YR)+Z:B(1,YR)=B(1,YR)-Z
6200 PRINT@640,E$:PRINT@704,E$
6210 PRINT@640,"HOW MANY BUSES DO YOU WISH TO SELL";:INPUT NB
6211 IFNB>S(5,YR) OR NB<0 OR INT(NB)<>NB THEN 6230 ELSE 6240
6230 PRINT@640,E$:GOTO 6210
6240 IF NB=0 THEN 6010
6250 FOR X=1 TO NB:C1=0:C2=0
6270 FOR X1=1 TO 100:IF BF(X1)=0 THEN 6310
6280 IF BF(X1)<=C1 THEN 6310
6290 C1=BF(X1):C2=X1
6310 NEXT X1:BF(C2)=0:NEXT X
6330 S(5,YR)=S(5,YR)-NB
6331 B(2,YR)=B(2,YR)+(NB*P2):GOTO 6010
6340 PRINT:PRINT"ENTER BUDGETS IN THOUSAND DOLLAR UNITS. DO NOT"
6350 PRINT"USE COMMAS OR DOLLAR SIGNS"
6360 PRINT:PRINT TAB(22)"MAINTENANCE";TAB(36)"OPERATIONS";TAB(50)"NEW BUSES"
6370 PRINT"LAST YEAR";TAB(20);:PRINT USING FA;BD;:PRINT TAB(35);
6371 PRINT USING FA;BE;:PRINT TAB(53);BN
6375 PRINT"THIS YEAR";
6400 PRINT@793,;:INPUT BD:PRINT@960,E$;:BD=BD*1000
6401 IF BD<0 THEN GOSUB 6690
6402 IF BD<0 THEN 6400
6403 IF BD<100000 THEN GOSUB 4399 ELSE 6410
6404 IF Z$="Y" THEN 6410
6405 Z$="Y":PRINT@841,D$:GOTO 6400
6410 IF LEN(STR$(BD))>LEN(STR$(M2))+1 THEN 6600
6420 PRINT@806,;:INPUT BE:PRINT@960,E$;:BE=BE*1000
6421 IF BE<0 GOSUB 6690
6422 IF BE<0 THEN 6420
6423 IF BE<100000 GOSUB 4399 ELSE 6430
6424 IF Z$="Y" THEN 6430
6425 PRINT@841,D$:GOTO 6420
6430 IF LEN(STR$(BE))>LEN(STR$(M5))+1 THEN 6630
6440 IF BD+BE>B(1,YR) THEN 6660
6450 PRINT@820,;:INPUT BN:PRINT@960,E$;
6460 IF BN>100-S(5,YR) THEN 6680
6470 IF BN<0 THEN GOSUB 6690
6471 IF BN>=0 THEN 6480
6472 PRINT@820,C$:GOTO 6450
6475 IF INT(BN)<>BN THEN 6710
6480 IF BN*P1>B(2,YR) THEN 6700
6490 IF BN=0 THEN 6580 ELSE Y=0
6500 FOR X=1 TO BN
6510 FOR X1=1 TO 100
6520 IF BF(X1)<>0 THEN 6560
6530 BF(X)=.5
6540 X=X+1
6550 IF X=NB THEN 6580
6560 NEXT X1
6570 NEXT X
6580 B(2,YR)=B(2,YR)-(P1*BN):B(1,YR)=B(1,YR)-(BD+BE)
6595 S(5,YR)=S(5,YR)+BN
6596 BF=0:M2=0:FOR X=1 TO 100:IF BF(X)=0 THEN 6598
6597 M2=(M1+(2000*BF(X))/100)+M2:BF=BF+BF(X)
6598 NEXT X:S(2,YR)=INT((BF/S(5,YR))*10)*.1:IF YR=0 THEN 2018
6599 GOTO 6750
6600 PRINT@960,"ARE YOU SURE (Y/N)";:INPUT Z$
6610 IF Z$<>"Y" AND Z$<>"N" THEN 6600:IF Z$="Y" THEN 6420
6620 PRINT@792,D$:GOTO 6400
6630 PRINT@960,"ARE YOU SURE (Y/N)";:INPUT Z$
6640 IF Z$<>"Y" AND Z$<>"N" THEN 6630: IF Z$="Y" THEN 6440
6650 PRINT@806,D$:GOTO 6420
6660 PRINT@960,"YOUR OPERATING AND MAINTENANCE BUDGETS EXCEED YOUR FUNDS";
6670 PRINT@792,D$:PRINT@806,D$:GOTO6400
6680 PRINT@960,"YOU CAN PURCHASE ONLY";100-S(5,YR);"BUSES";:GOTO 6450
6690 PRINT@960,"YOU CANNOT ENTER A NEGATIVE NUMBER";:RETURN:END
6700 PRINT@960,"YOUR PROPOSED ACQUISITION EXCEEDS YOUR BUDGET";:PRINT@820,C$
6701 GOTO 6450
6710 PRINT@960,"YOU MUST ENTER A WHOLE NUMBER";:PRINT@820,C$:GOTO 6450
6750 S(3,YR)=S(3,YR)-(INT(((BD-M2)/M2)*18)*.1)
6751 IFS(2,YR)>S(2,YR-1)THENS(3,YR)=S(3,YR)+.2
6752 IFS(3,YR)<1 THEN S(3,YR)=1
```

```
6755 S(4,YR)=S(4,YR)-(INT(((BE-M5)/M5)*18)*.1)
6756 IFS(3,YR)>S(3,YR-1)THENS(3,YR)=S(3,YR)+.2
6757 IFS(5,YR)/S1<3 THEN S(4,YR)=S(4,YR)+.2
6758 IFS(4,YR)<1 THEN S(4,YR)=1
6760 S(1,YR)=(S(1,YR)+S6)-((S(3,YR)+S(4,YR)-S(3,YR-1)-S(4,YR-1))*S(1,YR)*.01)
10030 REM SALARY NEGOTIATIONS
10040 NR=RND(4)+2:I=I*100:IF I=0 THEN U(1)=INT(RND(8)+8) ELSE U(1)=INT(RND(I)+8)
10060 CLS:LS=0
10070 PRINT"YOUR PRESENT WAGE IS";S;"DOLLARS PER HOUR"
10110 PRINT"THE UNION'S INITIAL OFFER IS FOR A";U(1);"PERCENT INCREASE"
10120 INPUT"WHAT IS YOUR RESPONSE";M(1)
10130 CLS
10140 PRINT"PRESENT SALARY=$";S
10160 PRINT:PRINT"UNION","MANAGEMENT"
10170 PRINT"POSITION","POSITION"
10180 PRINT
10190 PRINT U(1),M(1)
10200 FOR X=2 TO NR
10210 IF X<>NR THEN 10240
10220 PRINT"THIS IS THE LAST ROUND OF NEGOTIATIONS.  FAILURE"
10230 PRINT"TO SETTLE COULD RESULT IN A STRIKE"
10240 UO=U(X-1)-M(X-1):IF UO=0 THEN 10250 ELSE 10270
10250 U(X)=M(X-1):U=U(X)
10260 GOTO 10440
10270 IF M(X-1)-M(X-2)>=5 THEN R3=1
10280 IF M(X-1)-M(X-2)<5 THEN R3=2
10290 IF M(X-1)-M(X-2)<3 THEN R3=3
10300 IF M(X-1)-M(X-2)<1 THEN R3=4
10310 IF UO>5 THEN U(X)=U(X-1)-((RND(40)*.1)/R3)
10320 IF UO>10 OR UO<5 THEN U(X)=U(X-1)-((RND(60)*.1)/R3)
10330 IF UO>15 THEN U(X)=U(X-1)-((RND(80)*.1)/R3)
10340 IF UO>20 THEN U(X)=U(X-1)-((RND(100)*.1)/R3)
10350 IF U(X)<=M(X-1) THEN U(X)=M(X-1)
10360 U(X)=INT(U(X)*100)*.01
10370 U=U(X)
10380 PRINT U(X),
10390 IF U(X)=M(X-1) THEN 10440
10400 INPUT M(X)
10410 IF M(X)=>U(X) THEN 10440
10420 NEXT X
10430 IF M(NR)<>U(NR) THEN 10490
10440 S=INT(S*(100+U))*.01
10450 PRINT"YOU HAVE REACHED AGREEMENT ON A ";U;"PERCENT"
10460 PRINT"WAGE INCREASE.  YOUR HOURLY WAGE RATE IS NOW $";S
10480 GOTO 10640
10490 IF (U(NR)-M(NR))*RND(0)>.5 THEN 10502
10500 U(NR)=M(NR):U=U(NR)
10501 GOTO 10440
10502 CLS
10503 PRINT@216,"WORKERS";:PRINT@282,"LOCAL";:PRINT@346,"10600";
10504 FOR X=1 TO 3:PRINT@540,"ON";:PRINT@600,"STRIKE";:IFX=3THEN10530
10505 PRINT@540,CHR$(194);:PRINT@600,CHR$(198);:FOR X1=1 TO 300:NEXT X1:NEXT X
10530 FOR X=1 TO 500:NEXT:M(7)=M(NR)-M(1):U(7)=U(1)-U(NR):DP=U(NR)-M(NR)
10540 IF M(7)>U(7) THEN SS(1)=(DP*(RND(6)*.1)) ELSE SS(1)=(DP*((RND(6)+3)*.1))
10550 SS(2)=M(NR)+SS(1):U=INT(SS(2)*100)*.01
10560 LS=RND(5)+RND(DP+1)
10590 CLS:PRINT"THE STRIKE LASTED FOR";LS;"DAYS.  THE ARBITRATOR"
10600 PRINT"HAS ORDERED A SETTLEMENT OF";U;" PERCENT."
10610 PRINT"THIS RESULTS IN A WAGE OF";
10620 S=INT(S*(100+U))*.01:PRINT USING FC;S
10621 PRINT"AS A RESULT OF THE STRIKE YOUR":PRINT
10623 GOSUB 10634
10624 T(4,YR)=T(4,YR)+X1:PRINT TAB(5) T$(4);" HAS INCREASED BY";X1
10625 GOSUB 10634
10626 T(5,YR)=T(5,YR)+X1:PRINT TAB(5)T$(5);" HAS INCREASED BY";X1
10627 IF PC<2 THEN 10630:IF LS>=7 THE PC=PC-2 ELSE GOTO 10629
10628 PRINT TAB(5)"CONSTRUCTION PROGRAM LOST ONE MILE":GOTO 10630
10629 PC=PC-1:PRINT TAB(5)"CONSTRUCTION PROGRAM LOST 1/2 MILE"
10630 PRINT:GOSUB10634:S(3,YR)=S(3,YR)+X1:PRINT TAB(5)S$(3);" HAS INCREASED BY";X1
10631 GOSUB 10634:S(4,YR)=S(4,YR)+X1:PRINT TAB(5)S$(4);" HAS INCREASED BY";X1
10633 PRINT:GOTO 10640
10634 IF LS>=7 THEN X1=RND(7)*.1 ELSE X1=RND(4)*.1
10635 RETURN:END
10640 INPUT"ENTER WHEN READY";Z
11000 CLS:PRINT TAB(15)"PERFORMANCE FOR YEAR";YR
11010 PRINT
11020 PRINT TAB(30)"YEAR";YR;TAB(40)"YEAR";YR-1;TAB(50)"PLAN"
11030 PRINT
```

```
11040 FOR X=2 TO 5
11050 PRINT T$(X);TAB(30)T(X,YR);TAB(40)T(X,YR-1);TAB(50)T(X,11)
11060 NEXT X
11070 PRINT:INPUT"TYPE '1' TO REVIEW THE STREET MAP, ELSE PRESS ENTER";Z
11071 CLS:IFZ=1 THEN 13000 ELSE 13330
13000 G2=0:G4=0:CLS:G1=G1+(PC/2)
13010 FOR X=1 TO 8
13020 IF X>5 THEN G5=64 ELSE G5=2
13030 IF X>5 THEN G6=.5 ELSE G6=.25
13040 IF X=4 OR X=6 THEN 13120
13050 FOR Y=A(X,1) TO A(X,2) STEP G5
13060 G2=G2+G6
13070 IF G2<=G1 PRINT@Y,"+";
13080 IF G2>G1 PRINT@Y,"-";
13090 NEXT Y
13100 NEXT X
13110 GOTO 13170
13120 FOR Y=A(X,1) TO A(X,2) STEP G5
13130 G4=G4+G6
13140 IF G4<=T(3,YR) PRINT@Y,"*";
13150 IF G4>T(3,YR) PRINT@Y,"#";
13160 GOTO 13090
13170 PRINT@13,"I-196";
13180 PRINT@30,"ASH";
13190 PRINT@46,"OAK";
13200 PRINT@128,"1ST";
13210 PRINT@384,"2ND";
13220 PRINT@640,"3RD";
13230 PRINT@704,"I-96";
13240 PRINT@896,"4TH";
13250 PRINT@242,"PRIMARIES";
13260 PRINT@311,"+=";G1;
13270 PRINT@375,"-=";44-G1;
13280 PRINT@498,"INTERSTATES";
13290 PRINT@567,"*=";T(3,YR);
13300 PRINT@631,"#=";16-T(3,YR);
13310 PRINT@960,"+,* = COMPLETE     -,# = INCOMPLETE";
13320 PRINT@1004,"PRESS ENTER";:INPUT Z
13330 CLS:PRINT TAB(15)"PERFORMANCE REVIEW FOR YEAR";YR:PRINT
13340 PRINT TAB(30)"YEAR";YR;TAB(40)"YEAR";YR-1;TAB(50)"PLAN"
13350 FOR X=1 TO 5
13351 IF X>1 THEN 13360
13352 PRINT S$(X);TAB(30);:PRINT USING FB;S(X,YR);:PRINT TAB(40);
13353 PRINT USING FB;S(X,YR-1);:PRINT TAB(50);:PRINT USING FB;S(X,11):GOTO13370
13360 PRINT S$(X);TAB(30)S(X,YR);TAB(40)S(X,YR-1);TAB(50)S(X,11)
13370 NEXT X
13380 PRINT:INPUT"PRESS ENTER";Z:CLS
14000 IF T(2,YR)<T(2,11) THEN 15100
14005 IF T(3,YR)<T(3,11) THEN 15100
14010 IF T(4,YR)>T(4,11) THEN 15100
14015 IF T(5,YR)>T(5,11) THEN 15100
14020 IF S(1,YR),S(1,11) THEN 15100
14025 IF S(2,YR)>S(2,11) THEN 15100
14030 IF S(3,YR)>S(3,11) THEN 15100
14035 IF S(4,YR)>S(4,11) THEN 15100
14040 CLS:PRINT CHR$(23):PRINT:PRINT"CONGRATULATIONS!"
14045 PRINT:PRINT"YOU HAVE SUCCESSFULLY COMPLETED THE TRANSPORTATION"
14046 PRINT"PLAN IN";YR;" YEARS.":PRINT
14050 IF YR>7 THEN 14060
14055 PRINT"YOUR PERFORMANCE HAS BEEN SO GOOD THAT YOU HAVE BEEN"
14056 PRINT"OFFERED A HIGHER-PAYING EXECUTIVE JOB IN THE PUBLIC SECTOR!"
14057 PRINT" ****** CONGRATULATIONS ******"
14060 FOR WAIT=1TO2000:NEXT
14070 CLS
14080 PRINT"DO YOU WISH TO PLAY AGAIN (Y/N)";
14090 INPUTZ$:IFZ$<>"N" THEN RUN ELSE PRINT"THANKS FOR PLAYING":END
```

Streets of the City

Streets of the City
Creative Computing
by Kenneth R Murray
CONGRATULATIONS! YOU HAVE BEEN NAMED TRANSPORTATION
DIRECTOR OF RIVER CITY, MICHIGAN, A CENTRAL CITY WITH
A DECLINING POPULATION AND WHICH HAS SUFFERED DETERIORATION
OF ITS TRANSPORTATION SERVICES OVER THE LAST SEVERAL YEARS.

PRIOR TO YOUR BEING HIRED, THE CITY COMMISSION ADOPTED
A TEN-TEAR TRANSPORTATION PLAN TO RESTORE SERVICES FOR
BOTH STREETS AND BUSES TO AN ADEQUATE LEVEL. IT WILL BE
YOUR RESPONSIBILITY TO CARRY OUT THIS PLAN.

FOR THE STREET FUND, YOU WILL NEED TO CONSTRUCT SEVERAL
MILES OF INTERSTATE HIGHWAYS AND RECONSTRUCT MAJOR LOCAL
STREETS (CALLED PRIMARIES). YOU WILL ALSO NEED TO IMPROVE
STREET CONDITIONS AND TRAFFIC SAFETY.

PRESS ENTER?
FOR THE TRANSIT AUTHORITY, YOU MUST REPLACE A
DELAPIDATED BUS FLEET, INCREASE RIDERSHIP, REDUCE THE
MAINTENANCE DOWNTIME, AND IMPROVE ON-SCHEDULE PERFORMANCE
(ALSO REFERRED TO AS SERVICE DELAY).

FOR ALL INDICES USED, THE HIGHER THE INDEX VALUE THE
WORSE THE CONDITION INDICATED. THE BUDGET NEEDS LISTED
ARE THE MINIMUMS NEEDED TO MAINTAIN THE INDEX AT ITS
PRESENT LEVEL; IMPROVING THE LEVEL REQUIRES BUDGETS THAT
ARE HIGHER THAN THE MINIMUM NEEDS.
PRESS ENTER?

YOUR GOALS FOR THE PLAN ARE AS FOLLOWS:

STANDARD	PRESENT	GOAL
PRIMARY ST. MILEAGE	107	151
INTERSTATE MILEAGE	0	16
STREET CONDITION INDEX	10.6	4
TRAFFIC SAFETY INDEX	8.9	3
RIDERSHIP	666,402	2,665,610
FLEET AGE	10.7	4
DOWNTIME	11.4	4
SERVICE DELAY	12.7	5

GOOD LUCK!
PRESS ENTER? @
?REDO
?
YOUR TRANSIT AUTHORITY SERVICE OPTIONS ARE:

    1.   ROUTES
    2.   HOURS OF OPERATION
    3.   DAYS OF SERVICE
    4.   FARE
    5.   TO CONTINUE

WHAT IS YOUR CHOICE? 4
THE FARE MAY BE CHANGED IN NICKEL UNITS, WITH A
MINIMUM FARE OF $.25 AND A MAXIMUM OF $1.00
DO NOT ENTER DOLLAR SIGN
CURRENT FARE = .35
NEW FARE =? .50
YOUR TRANSIT AUTHORITY SERVICE OPTIONS ARE:

    1.   ROUTES
    2.   HOURS OF OPERATION
    3.   DAYS OF SERVICE
    4.   FARE
    5.   TO CONTINUE

WHAT IS YOUR CHOICE? 5
                    PROPERTY TAX LEVY

	STREET FUND	TRANSIT AUTHORITY
OPERATING NEEDS	$7,217,030.	$1,416,170.
NON-TAX REVENUE	$2,645,400.	$1,594,290.
PROPERTY TAX NEEDED (MILLS)	$4,571,630.	-$178,116.

```
TOTAL PROPERTY TAX NEEDED (IN MILLS) = 5.3
WHAT PROPERTY TAX LEVY (0-10 MILLS) DO YOU PROPOSE? 7
THE CITY COMMISSION HAS APPROVED A LEVY OF 7 MILLS
HOW MANY MILLS ARE FOR THE STREET FUND? 5
             STREET FUND BUDGET DECISIONS FOR YEAR 1
OPERATIONS:                      CONSTRUCTION:
     AVAILABLE: $6,750,330.           AVAILABLE: $1,680,000.
     MAINT. NEED= $5,322,290.         COST PER HALF MILE UNIT:
     SAFETY NEED= $1,894,740.         PRIMARY RDS.=   $125,800.
                                      INTERSTATES=   $629,000.


YOU MAY TRANSFER UP TO  50 % FROM AN ACCOUNT
             1.  OPERATIONS TO CONSTRUCTION
             2.  CONSTRUCTION TO OPERATIONS
             3.  NO TRANSFER
? 3
             STREET FUND BUDGET DECISIONS FOR YEAR 1
OPERATIONS:                      CONSTRUCTION:
     AVAILABLE: $6,750,330.           AVAILABLE: $1,680,000.
     MAINT. NEED= $5,322,290.         COST PER HALF MILE UNIT:
     SAFETY NEED= $1,894,740.         PRIMARY RDS.=   $125,800.
                                      INTERSTATES=   $629,000.


ENTER CONSTRUCTION BY THE NUMBER OF HALF MILE UNITS;
ENTER MAINTENANCE AND SAFETY BY THOUSAND DOLLAR UNITS.
DO NOT USE COMMAS OR DOLLAR SIGNS


            PRIMARIES INTERSTATES    MAINTENANCE     SAFETY
LAST YR        0          0          $5,322,290.   $1,894,740.
THIS YR? 1
? 1
? 5400
? 1900
T
? 1900
YOUR MAINTENANCE AND SAFETY BUDGET EXCEEDS YOUR FUNDST
T
? 3
ARE YOU SURE (Y/N)? Y
? 5
ARE YOU SURE (Y/N)? Y
PRESS ENTER?
             TRANSIT BUDGET FOR YEAR 1
OPERATIONS                  BUS FLEET
     AVAILABLE $3,236,260.        AVAILABLE        $0.
     MAINT. NEED=  $341,379.      (COST PER BUS):
     OPERATIONS NEED= $1,074,790. ACQUISITION=  $140,000.
                                  SALE=      $75,000.
OPERATIONS TO THE BUS FLEET


HOW MANY BUSES DO YOU WISH TO SELL? 0
             TRANSIT BUDGET FOR YEAR 1
OPERATIONS                  BUS FLEET
     AVAILABLE $3,236,260.        AVAILABLE        $0.
     MAINT. NEED=  $341,379.      (COST PER BUS):
     OPERATIONS NEED= $1,074,790. ACQUISITION=  $140,000.
                                  SALE=      $75,000.


ENTER BUDGETS IN THOUSAND DOLLAR UNITS. DO NOT
USE COMMAS OR DOLLAR SIGNS


            MAINTENANCE   OPERATIONS    NEW BUSES
LAST YEAR     $233,899.   $1,074,790.       0
THIS YEAR? 300
? 1300
? 0
YOUR PRESENT WAGE IS 7.21 DOLLARS PER HOUR
THE UNION'S INITIAL OFFER IS FOR A 14 PERCENT INCREASE
WHAT IS YOUR RESPONSE?
```

Survival

Survival was written by Stewart F. Rush and originally appeared in *Creative Computing*, January 1982.

It is the year 1991. You have crash landed on the moon and have only 180 minutes of oxygen and 230 units of power remaining. You are at Mare Serenitatis and observe the long, eerie shadows being cast by the distant mountains across the barren landscape. The realization sinks in that you are in big trouble.

Game Description

Survival is an "adventure" type of game. With logic, skill, persistence, and a little bit of luck, it is possible to survive. The action takes place on the surface of the moon where you must assess the situation, explore the surroundings, avoid potential hazards, and gather needed resources.

It is a race against time. Many explorations are required before the total situation is revealed, and the resources and life-threatening hazards are discovered.

Only then, can the process of determining an optimum course of action begin.

Once you succeed in surviving, there is then the challenge to plan new survival sequences to minimize the total elapsed time.

The commands to move are NORTH, SOUTH, EAST, WEST, UP, and DOWN. These commands may be spelled out or entered as a single letter—N, S, E, W, U, and D.

Other commands consist of an action verb followed by a noun. Examples of these commands are:

GET ILLUMINATOR
DROP KNIFE
INVENTORY

The set of commands is relatively small, hence you may have to try several alternatives to find the one that works. All commands may be abbreviated to the first three letters. To exit the program, you may enter END or QUIT. There is no provision for saving a partially completed game.

Program Design

The program is relatively small as it was originally written to fit in a computer with 8K of memory.

The program is directed by a move matrix M. There is one vector for each location P in the game. Table 1 lists the significance of each vector in the matrix M.

If the vector element (1-6) contains a value of "0," then the move requested in that direction is invalid. If the vector element contains a "99," then the game is terminated.

The T$ vector contains the textual description of all of the various locations. As an example, the first three elements in the vector contain the description for location 1 in the M matrix. Looking at the line 9001, the seventh and eighth data items correspond to M(1,7) which has a value of 1, and M(1,8) which has a value of 3.

Table 2 lists the variables used in the program.

Table 3 lists each of the objects used in the program which are contained in the 0 vector. Normally the vector element in 0, for a given object, contains either the P location of that item, or a value of 99 indicating that the player is carrying that item.

Locations 1-18, and 38 normally require oxygen. All other locations are within the space station or the space craft. Locations 1-21, and 38 require a power unit or pack. All other locations are within the space station.

Changing the Complexity of the Game

Normally, the program permits the player to carry four items. One way the difficulty can be increased is by permitting only three items to be carried. In this case, a longer survival time results, and the following statements must be updated:

```
350 LET T2=275
360 LET P1=320
370 LET P2=75
730 IF T1>485 THEN 2960
740 IF T1>380 THEN 3840
2270 IF C>2 THEN 2390
```

Conclusion

This program, unlike other Adventures, contains no random events. The emphasis is on determining optimum move scenarios, resulting in minimum times and resource use. Each location described corresponds to an actual moon location taken from a *National Geographic* map of the moon.

We wish you many happy hours of exploration. As a benchmarks, the author's best survival time is 385 minutes, with a four-item carry limit. Here's to your survival!

Table 1.
M(P.1) = location to go to if direction is NORTH
M(P.2) = location to go to if direction is SOUTH
M(P.3) = location to go to if direction is EAST
M(P.4) = location to go to if direction is West
M(P.5) = location to go to if direction is UP
M(P.6) = location to go to if direction is DOWN
M(P.7) = pointer to first print line in TS vector
M(P.8) = pointer to last print line in TS vector

Table 2.
P - The current location.
R - The previous location (P for the previous location).
T1 - The current elapsed time.
T2 - the amount of oxygen remaining in the oxygen module.
P1 - The amount of power remaining in the power unit.
P2 - The amount of power remaining in the power pack.
V - The number of visits to the control center.
C - The number of items being carried.
F0 - Flag: oxygen in use.
F1 - Flag: Meteor shower.
F2 - Flag: Shed open.
F4 - Flag: Illuminator on.
F7 - Flag: Bomb deactivated.
F9 - Flag: Oxygen required in station.

Table 3.
0(1) - An electronic key.
0(2) - Sealant.
0(3) - An oxygen module.
0(4) - An illuminator.
0(5) - A robot.
0(6) - A deactivator.
0(7) - A nuclear bomb.
0(8) - A transporter unit.
0(9) - Dilithium crystals.
0(10) - A computer message.
0(11) - A power unit.
0(12) - A mirror.
0(13) - A coded badge.
0(14) - A power pack.

Survival

```
1 REM
5 REM MOON SURVIVAL PROGRAM
6 REM WRITTEN BY STEWART RUSH 3/12/81
8 REM
10 DIM T$(60)
20 DIM M(42,8)
30 DIM O(14)
40 DIM C$(3)
50 DIM D$(1)
60 REM
70 REM INITIALIZE TEXT AND MOVE MATRICES
80 REM
90 PRINT"WELCOME TO THE GAME OF SURVIVAL. WOULD
100 PRINT"YOU LIKE INSTRUCTIONS?
110 INPUT D$
120 IF D$="Y" THEN GOSUB 5050
122 FOR I=1 TO 14
124 READ O(I)
126 NEXT I
130 FOR I=1 TO 60
140 READ T$(I)
150 NEXT I
160 FOR I=1 TO 42
170 FOR J=1 TO 8
180 READ M(I,J)
190 NEXT J
200 NEXT I
205 RESTORE
210 REM
225 REM PROGRAM VARIABLE DEFINITION
235 REM P  = CURRENT POSITION        F0 = OXYGEN IN USE
240 REM T1 = CURRENT ELAPSED TIME     F1 = OPEN SHED
250 REM T2 = OXYGEN REMAINING         F2 = METEOR SHOWER
260 REM                               F3 = LASER DEFLECTED
265 REM V  = NO. OF COMPUTER READS    F4 = ILLUMINATOR ON
270 REM P1 = PWR IN POWER UNIT        F5 = DEACTIVATIOR EXPOSED
275 REM P2 = PWR IN POWER PACK        F7 = BOMB DEACTIVATED
280 REM C  = NO. OF ITEMS CARRIED     F9 = OXYGEN REQ'D IN STATION
290 REM
320 P=1
330 C=2
340 T1=0
350 T2=185
360 P1=230
370 P2=50
380 V=0
390 F0=1
570 F1=0
580 F2=0
585 F3=0
590 F4=0
595 F5=0
600 F7=0
610 F9=0
620 REM
630 REM DISPLAY CURRENT STATUS AND LOCATION INFO
640 REM
650 PRINT"ELAPSED TIME: ";T1;"MINUTES
660 IF O(11)=99 THEN PRINT"POWER UNIT: ";P1;"UNITS
670 IF O(14)=99 THEN PRINT"POWER PACK: ";P2;"UNITS
680 T1=T1+5
690 IF O(11)=99 AND P1>0 THEN P1=P1-5
700 IF O(14)=99 AND P2>0 THEN P2=P2-5
710 IF O(11)=99 AND P1=0 THEN 3680
720 IF O(14)=99 AND P2=0 THEN 3680
730 IF T1>400 THEN 2960
740 IF T1>350 THEN 3840
750 IF T1>200 THEN 3740
760 IF F0=1 THEN T2=T2-5
770 IF T2<0 THEN T2=0
780 IF F0=0 THEN 800
790 IF T2>0 THEN 840
800 IF F9=0 THEN 820
810 IF P>21 THEN 2900
820 IF P<18 THEN 2900
830 IF P=38 THEN 1700
840 IF P=38 THEN 3590
850 IF F0=1 THEN PRINT "OXYGEN REMAINING: ";T2;"MINUTES
```

```
860 PRINT "PRESENT LOCATION STATUS; YOU ARE"
870 FOR I=M(P,7) TO M(P,8)
880 PRINT T$(I)
890 NEXT I
900 PRINT "##"
910 REM
920 REM DISPLAY ANY OBJECTS PRESENT
930 REM
940 IF P=2 THEN 1920
950 FOR I = 1 TO 14
960 IF O(I)<>P THEN 990
970 GOSUB 4410
980 PRINT "THERE IS ";B$;" HERE."
990 NEXT I
1000 GOTO 2000
1010 REM
1020 REM READ AND PROCESS KEYBOARD RESPONSE
1030 REM
1040 INPUT B$
1050 I=0
1060 IF LEN(B$)<>1 GOTO 1320
1070 IF B$="N" THEN I=1
1080 IF B$="S" THEN I=2
1090 IF B$="E" THEN I=3
1100 IF B$="W" THEN I=4
1110 IF B$="U" THEN I=5
1120 IF B$="D" THEN I=6
1130 IF B$="Q" THEN 9999
1140 IF I=0 THEN 1570
1150 IF M(P,I)=0 THEN 1270
1160 IF M(P,I)=99 THEN 2940
1170 Q=M(P,I)
1180 IF P=12 THEN 3060
1190 IF P=13 THEN 3180
1200 IF P=22 THEN 3310
1210 IF P=23 THEN 3420
1220 IF P=29 THEN 3470
1230 R=P
1240 P=Q
1260 GOTO 650
1270 PRINT"YOU CAN'T GO IN THAT DIRECTION!"
1280 GOTO 1040
1290 REM
1300 REM PROCESS 2 OR MORE CHARACTER COMMANDS
1310 REM
1320 C$=B$
1321 C$=LEFT$(C$,3)
1330 IF C$="LOO" THEN 650
1340 IF C$="DES" THEN 650
1350 IF C$="GET" THEN 2190
1360 IF C$="TAK" THEN 2190
1370 IF C$="KEE" THEN 2190
1380 IF C$="DRO" THEN 2580
1390 IF C$="LEA" THEN 2580
1400 IF C$="PUT" THEN 2580
1410 IF C$="INV" THEN 2780
1420 IF C$="QUI" THEN 9999
1430 IF C$="END" THEN 9999
1440 IF C$="TRA" THEN 1750
1450 IF C$="DIG" THEN 1860
1460 IF C$="FUE" THEN 4030
1480 IF C$="REA" THEN 4250
1490 IF C$="DEA" THEN 3890
1500 IF C$="BLA" THEN 4110
1510 IF C$="UP" THEN 1640
1520 IF C$="DOW" THEN 1640
1530 IF C$="NOR" THEN 1640
1540 IF C$="SOU" THEN 1640
1550 IF C$="EAS" THEN 1640
1560 IF C$="WES" THEN 1640
1570 PRINT"INVALID COMMAND!"
1580 GOTO 1040
1590 PRINT"I CAN'T PROCESS YOUR REQUEST!"
1600 GOTO 1040
1640 D$=B$
1650 B$=D$
1660 GOTO 1070
1670 REM
```

```
1680 REM PROCESS ENTRY TO HANGER FROM AIR LOCK
1690 REM
1700 IF R<>39 THEN 2900
1710 GOTO 840
1720 REM
1730 REM PROCESS TRANSPORT COMMAND
1740 REM
1750 IF P<>36 THEN 1800
1760 IF O(8)=99 THEN 1590
1770 P=O(8)
1780 PRINT"BEAMING IN PROGRESS."
1790 GOTO 650
1800 IF P<>O(8) THEN 1590
1810 P=36
1820 GOTO 1780
1830 REM
1840 REM PROCESS DIG COMMAND
1850 REM
1860 IF P<>10 THEN 1590
1870 O(9)=10
1880 GOTO 940
1890 REM
1900 REM DROP ILLUMINATOR IF AT OVERLOOK
1910 REM
1920 IF O(4)<>99 THEN 950
1930 O(4)=100
1940 PRINT"YOU DROPPED YOUR ILLUMINATOR! YOU"
1950 PRINT"CANNOT RETRIEVE IT."
1960 GOTO 950
1970 REM
1980 REM PROCESS ROBOT
2000 IF O(5)=28 THEN O(5)=35
2010 IF O(5)=42 THEN O(5)=28
2020 IF O(5)=41 THEN O(5)=42
2030 IF O(5)=27 THEN O(5)=41
2040 IF O(5)=25 THEN O(5)=27
2050 IF O(5)<>35 THEN 2090
2060 IF P<>28 THEN 1010
2070 M(28,1)=35
2080 GOTO 1010
2090 IF O(5)<>32 THEN 1010
2100 IF P<>32 THEN 1010
2110 O(5)=25
2120 IF O(13)=99 THEN 1010
2130 PRINT"ROBOT FAILS TO RECOGNIZE YOU. IT
2140 PRINT"FIRES A PHASOR WEAPON AT YOU!
2150 GOTO 2980
2160 REM
2170 REM PROCESS GET OR TAKE COMMAND
2180 REM
2190 GOSUB 4590
2200 IF I>0 THEN 2260
2210 IF I<0 THEN 2240
2220 PRINT"I DON'T RECOGNIZE ";MID$(B$,J+1);"."
2230 GOTO 1040
2240 PRINT"WHAT ITEM?
2250 GOTO 1040
2260 IF O(I)<>P THEN 2370
2270 IF C>3 THEN 2390
2280 IF I=5 THEN 2410
2290 IF I=10 THEN 2430
2300 IF I=11 THEN 2460
2310 IF I=14 THEN 2490
2320 C=C+1
2330 O(I)=99
2340 IF I=3 THEN F0=1
2350 PRINT"O.K.
2360 GOTO 1040
2370 PRINT"THERE IS NO ";MID$(B$,J+1);"HERE!"
2380 GOTO 1040
2390 PRINT"YOU CAN'T CARRY ANY MORE!"
2400 GOTO 1040
2410 PRINT"YOU CAN'T CARRY A ROBOT!"
2420 GOTO 1040
2430 PRINT"YOU CAN'T GET THE MESSAGE, IT'S
2440 PRINT"ON THE TERMINAL SCREEN.
2450 GOTO 1040
2460 IF O(14)=99 THEN 2520
```

```
2470 O(11)=99
2480 GOTO 2320
2490 IF O(11)=99 THEN 2520
2500 O(14)=99
2510 GOTO 2320
2520 PRINT"YOU CAN'T HAVE MORE THAN ONE
2530 PRINT"POWER SUPPLY.
2540 GOTO 1040
2550 REM
2560 REM PROCESS DROP OR LEAVE COMMAND
2570 REM
2580 GOSUB 4590
2590 IF I>0 THEN 2620
2600 IF I<0 THEN 2240
2610 GOTO 2220
2620 IF O(I)<>99 THEN 2690
2630 C=C-1
2640 O(I)=P
2650 IF I=3 THEN F0=0
2660 IF I=11 THEN 2710
2670 IF I=14 THEN 2710
2680 GOTO 2350
2690 PRINT"YOU DON'T HAVE ":STR(B$,J+1);"!
2700 GOTO 1040
2710 IF P<22 THEN 2870
2720 IF P=38 THEN 2870
2730 IF F9=1 THEN 2870
2740 GOTO 2350
2750 REM
2760 REM PROCESS INVENTORY COMMAND
2770 REM
2780 FOR I=1 TO 14
2790 IF O(I)<>99 THEN 2820
2800 GOSUB 4410
2810 PRINT"YOU HAVE ";B$;"."
2820 NEXT I
2830 GOTO 1040
2840 REM
2850 REM PROGRAM TERMINATION PROCESSING
2860 REM
2870 PRINT"YOU HAVE NO POWER OR POWER PACK.
2880 PRINT"YOU HAVE FROZEN TO DEATH.
2890 GOTO 2990
2900 PRINT"OXYGEN REQUIRED HERE. NONE AVAILABLE.
2910 GOTO 2980
2920 PRINT"A NUCLEAR DETONATION HAS JUST OCCURED.
2930 GOTO 2980
2940 PRINT"YOU HAVE FALLEN TO YOUR DEATH.
2950 GOTO 2980
2952 PRINT"YOU HAVE BEEN ZAPPED BY THE LASER.
2954 GOTO 2980
2960 PRINT"THE MOON BASE HAS JUST BEEN DESTROYED
2970 PRINT"BY A LARGE ASTEROID.
2980 PRINT"YOU HAVE FAILED TO SURVIVE.
2990 PRINT"DO YOU WISH TO TRY AGAIN?
3000 INPUT D$
3010 IF D$="Y" THEN 122
3020 GOTO 9999
3030 REM
3040 REM PROCESS METEOR SHOWER
3050 REM
3060 IF M(P,I)<>13 THEN 1230
3070 IF F2=1 THEN 1230
3080 PRINT"THERE IS A METEOR SHOWER, YOUR SPACE
3090 PRINT"SUIT HAS DEVELOPED A LEAK!
3100 GOSUB 4890
3110 IF I<>2 THEN 2980
3120 PRINT"YOUR SUIT IS NOW SEALED.
3130 F2=1
3140 GOTO 1230
3150 REM
3160 REM PROCESS LOCKED SHED
3170 REM
3180 IF M(P,I)<>22 THEN 1230
3190 IF F1=1 THEN 1230
3200 PRINT"THE SHED IS LOCKED!
3210 GOSUB 4890
3220 IF I<>1 THEN 3260
3230 PRINT"YOU ARE IN THE SHED AIR LOCK.
3240 F1=1
3250 GOTO 1230
3260 PRINT"YOUR ATTEMPT FAILS "
3270 GOTO 1040
3280 REM
3290 REM PROCESS DARK VENTILATOR SHAFT
3300 REM
3310 IF M(P,I)<>23 THEN 1230
3320 IF F4=1 THEN 1230
3330 PRINT"IT IS DANGEROUS TO PROCEED IN THE DARK!
3340 GOSUB 4890
3350 IF I<>4 THEN 2940
3360 PRINT"THE SHAFT IS NOW ILLUMINATED.
3370 F4=1
3380 GOTO 1230
3390 REM
3400 REM PROCESS SHAFT WITH NO ILLUMINATION
3410 REM
3420 IF O(4)<>99 THEN 2940
3430 GOTO 1230
3440 REM
3450 REM PROCESS LASER BEAM
3460 REM
3470 IF M(P,I)<>37 THEN 1230
3480 IF F3=1 THEN 1230
3490 PRINT"THERE IS A LASER BEAM HERE. PASSAGE NOT
3500 PRINT"POSSIBLE WITH BEAM PRESENT.
3510 GOSUB 4890
3520 IF I<>12 THEN 2952
3530 PRINT"THE BEAM IS NOW DEFLECTED.
3540 F3=1
3550 GOTO 1230
3560 REM
3570 REM PROCESS BLOWN SEAL IN SPACE STATION
3580 REM
3590 IF R<>29 THEN 850
3600 IF F9=1 THEN 850
3610 F9=1
3620 PRINT"YOU HAVE JUST BLOWN THE AIR SEAL IN
3630 PRINT"THE SPACE STATION.
3640 GOTO 850
3650 REM
3660 REM POWER REQUIRED TESTING
3670 REM
3680 IF P<22 THEN 2870
3690 IF F9=1 THEN 2870
3700 GOTO 730
3710 REM
3720 REM EXPOSE DEACTIVATOR
3730 REM
3740 IF F5=1 THEN 760
3760 M(2,8)=M(2,7)+1
3770 M(14,8)=M(14,7)
3780 M(14,4)=2
3790 F5=1
3800 GOTO 760
3810 REM
3820 REM DETONATE BOMB
3830 REM
3840 GOTO 760
3860 REM
3870 REM DEACTIVATE BOMB
3880 REM
3890 IFO(6)<>99 THEN 3940
3900 IF O(7)<>99 THEN 3980
3910 F7=1
3920 PRINT"BOMB IS NOW DEACTIVATED.
3930 GOTO 1040
3940 PRINT"YOU HAVE NOTHING TO DO IT WITH!
3950 GOTO 1040
3960 PRINT"THERE IS NOTHING TO DO IT TO!
3970 GOTO 1040
3980 PRINT"YOU CAN'T DO IT FROM HERE!
3990 GOTO 1040
4000 REM
4010 REM FUEL ROCKET
4020 REM
```

```
4030 IF P<>19 THEN 3980
4040 IF O(9)<>99 THEN 3940
4050 O(9)=98
4060 PRINT"FUEL IS NOW LOADED.
4070 GOTO 1040
4080 REM
4090 REM BLASTOFF PROCESSING
4100 REM
4110 IF P<>21 THEN 3980
4120 IF O(9)<>98 THEN 4200
4130 IF F7=1 THEN 4160
4140 PRINT"REPAIRS NOT YET COMPLETE.
4150 GOTO 1040
4160 PRINT"CONGRATULATIONS. YOU HAVE JUST BLASTED
4170 PRINT"OFF AND ARE ON YOUR WAY TO EARTH.
4180 PRINT"YOUR ESCAPE TIME:"; T1;"MINUTES."
4190 GOTO 2990
4200 PRINT"YOUR SPACE CRAFT HAS NO FUEL!
4210 GOTO 1040
4220 REM
4230 REM COMPUTER READOUT PROCESSING
4240 REM
4250 IF P<>35 THEN 3980
4260 GOSUB 4590
4270 IF I<>10 THEN 3960
4280 IF V<>0 THEN 4320
4290 PRINT"BOMB DEACTIVATIOR LOCATED SOMEWHERE EAST"
4300 PRINT"OF SPACE STATION, ON MOON'S SURFACE.
4310 GOTO 4360
4320 IF V<>1 THEN 4350
4330 PRINT"LOCAL FUEL SORCE: DILITHIUM CRYSTAL."
4340 GOTO 4360
4350 PRINT"DILITHIUM FOUND IN SOFT SURFACES."
4360 IF F7=1 THEN PRINT"SPACECRAFT REPAIRS COMPLETED.
4365 V=V+1
4370 GOTO 1040
4380 REM
4390 REM SUBROUTINE TO DESCRIBE ITEMS AT LOCATION
4400 REM
4410 IF I=1 THEN B$="AN ELECTRONIC KEY"
4420 IF I=2 THEN B$="SEALENT"
4430 IF I=3 THEN B$="AN OXYGEN MODULE"
4440 IF I=4 THEN B$="AN ILLUMINATOR"
4450 IF I=5 THEN B$="A ROBOT"
4460 IF I=6 THEN B$="A DEACTIVATOR"
4470 IF I=7 THEN B$="A NUCLEAR BOMB"
4480 IF I=8 THEN B$="A TRANSPORTER UNIT"
4490 IF I=9 THEN B$="DILITHIUM CRYSTALS
4500 IF I=10 THEN B$="A COMPUTER MESSAGE"
4510 IF I=11 THEN B$="A POWER UNIT"
4520 IF I=12 THEN B$="A MIRROR"
4530 IF I=13 THEN B$="A CODED BADGE"
4540 IF I=14 THEN B$="A POWER PACK"
4550 RETURN
4560 REM
4570 REM SUBROUTING TO CONVERT AN ITEM TO A NUMERIC VALUE
4580 REM
4590 FOR J=1 TO LEN(B$)
4600 IF MID$(B$,J,1)=" " THEN 4640
4610 NEXT J
4620 I=-1
4630 RETURN
4640 C$=MID$(B$,J+1,3)
4650 I=0
4660 IF C$="ELE" THEN I=1
4670 IF C$="KEY" THEN I=1
4680 IF C$="SEA" THEN I=2
4690 IF C$="OXY" THEN I=3
4700 IF C$="MOD" THEN I=3
4710 IF C$="ILL" THEN I=4
4720 IF C$="ROB" THEN I=5
4730 IF C$="DEA" THEN I=6
4740 IF C$="NUC" THEN I=7
4750 IF C$="BOM" THEN I=7
4760 IF C$="TRA" THEN I=8
4770 IF C$="DIL" THEN I=9
4780 IF C$="CRY" THEN I=9
4790 IF C$="COM" THEN I=10
4800 IF C$="MES" THEN I=10
4810 IF C$="UNI" THEN I=11
4820 IF C$="MIR" THEN I=12
4830 IF C$="BAD" THEN I=13
4840 IF C$="PAC" THEN I=14
4850 RETURN
4860 REM
4870 REM SUBROUTINE TO PROCESS TRY COMMAND
4880 REM
4890 INPUT B$
4900 C$=B$
4910 IF C$="TRY" THEN 4950
4920 IF C$="USE" THEN 4950
4930 I=-1
4940 RETURN
4950 GOSUB 4590
4960 IF I<1 THEN 5050
4970 IF O(I)=99 THEN RETURN
4980 PRINT"YOU DON'T HAVE ";STR(B$,J+1);"!
4990 GOTO 4930
5000 PRINT"YOUR ATTEMPT FAILS!
5010 GOTO 4930
5020 REM
5030 REM PRINT INSTRUCTIONS
5040 REM
5050 PRINT"YOU HAVE CRASH LANDED ON THE
5060 PRINT"EARTH'S MOON. YOU HAVE LIMITED
5070 PRINT"SUPPLIES AND TIME IN WHICH TO
5080 PRINT"SURVIVE. TO TRAVEL, YOU MAY
5090 PRINT"ENTER DIRECTIVES SUCH AS NORTH
5100 PRINT"OR N, AS WELL AS S, E, W AND
5110 PRINT"U, AND D (UP AND DOWN). YOU
5120 PRINT"WILL ENCOUNTER VARIOUS ITEMS
5130 PRINT"AND SITUATIONS DURING YOUR
5140 PRINT"TRAVELS. TO COMMUNICATE, ENTER
5150 PRINT"COMMANDS (VERBS) FOLLOWED BY
5160 PRINT"OBJECT NAMES (IF APPLICABLE).
5170 PRINT"FOR EXAMPLE, GET KEY, LEAVE,
5180 PRINT"USE, AND INVENTORY.
5190 PRINT " "
5200 PRINT "ONCE YOU HAVE SURVIVED, THE
5210 PRINT"OBJECT THEN IS TO ACHIEVE THE
5220 PRINT"OPTIMUM SURVIVAL TIME.
5230 PRINT"   *** GOOD LUCK ***
5240 RETURN
6000 REM
6001 REM OBJECT LOCATIONS
6002 REM
6010 DATA 21,19,99,06,32,00,38
6020 DATA 35,00,35,99,33,34,37
7500 REM
7502 REM
7510 REM TEXT LOCATION DESCRIPTIONS
8001 DATA"AT MARE SERENITATUS. LONG EERIE SHADOWS"
8002 DATA"FROM DISTANT MOUNTAINS AND CRATERS CAST"
8003 DATA"THEMSELVES ACROSS THE BARREN LANDSCAPE."
8004 DATA"ON A PROMONTARY POINT ON THE RIM OF THE"
8005 DATA"CRATER POSIDONIUS, ONLY HALF VISIBLE."
8006 DATA"THERE IS TOTAL DARKNESS TO THE EAST."
8007 DATA"BETWEEN THE CRATERS OF DAWES AND PLINIUS."
8008 DATA"AT A PASS IN THE MOUNTAINS OF HAEMUS."
8009 DATA"AT A STEEP BASE OF THE CRATER MANILUS."
8010 DATA"AT MARE VAPORUM. THE APENNINES MTNS."
8011 DATA"RISE OMINOUSLY TO THE NORTH AND WEST."
8012 DATA"AT THE BASE OF THE AWESOME MT. EUDOXUS."
8013 DATA"INSIDE THE CRATER OF ARISTOTELES, THE"
8014 DATA"CRATER FLOOR IS LITTERED WITH ROCKS."
8015 DATA"IN LACUS SOMNORIUM, NORTH OF POSIDONIUS"
8016 DATA"AND NORTH EAST OF MARE SERENITATUS.
8017 DATA"AT THE BASE OF THE BURG CRATER IN LACUS"
8018 DATA"MORTIS. THE SURFACE IS VERY SOFT HERE."
8019 DATA"AT THE EASE SIDE OF THE VAST MARE OF"
8020 DATA"IMBRIUM. TO THE NORTH THE LOW ANGLE OF"
8021 DATA"THE SUN CASTS EERIE SHADOWS ON THE SOFT"
8022 DATA"SURFACE AND DISTANT MOUNTAINS TO THE
8023 DATA"EAST. TO THE WEST, THE MARE STRETCHES
8024 DATA"OUT OF SIGHT TO THE HORIZON.
```

Survival

```
8025 DATA"AT THE BASE OF THE CRATER OF PLATO. A          9004 DATA 01,05,03,00,00,00,08,08
8026 DATA"SHINY OBJECT IS SEEN TO THE WEST.              9005 DATA 04,00,03,06,00,00,09,09
8027 DATA"STANDING BEFORE A SMALL METAL SHED. A          9006 DATA 00,00,05,00,00,00,10,11
8028 DATA"SIGN READS: VENTILATOR SHAFT #2.               9007 DATA 08,01,09,11,00,00,12,12
8029 DATA"SOMEWHERE EAST OF MARE SERENITATUS.            9008 DATA 00,07,10,00,00,00,13,14
8030 DATA"THERE IS TOTAL DARKNESS.                       9009 DATA 10,02,14,07,00,00,15,16
8031 DATA"AT THE CRASH SITE OF A SPACE CRAFT.            9010 DATA 00,09,14,08,00,00,17,18
8032 DATA"THE SHIP ENTRANCE IS BEFORE YOU.               9011 DATA 12,15,07,16,00,00,19,24
8033 DATA"AT THE CENTER OF MARE IMBRIUM.                 9012 DATA 00,11,00,13,00,00,25,26
8034 DATA"IN THE AIR LOCK CHAMBER OF THE SHIP.           9013 DATA 00,16,12,22,00,00,27,28
8035 DATA"IN THE AFT CARGO AND FUEL STORAGE ROOM.        9014 DATA 99,99,99,99,00,00,29,30
8036 DATA"IN THE ENGINE ROOM OF THE SPACECRAFT.          9015 DATA 11,18,01,00,00,00,31,32
8037 DATA"IN THE CONTROL ROOM. THE SHIP'S CONSOLE        9016 DATA 17,16,07,16,00,00,33,33
8038 DATA"IS BEFORE YOU.                                 9017 DATA 16,17,11,17,00,00,33,33
8039 DATA"INSIDE A CARK SHED. A LADDER LEADS DOWN        9018 DATA 15,19,00,00,00,00,34,34
8040 DATA"INTO A LARGE METAL SHAFT.                      9019 DATA 18,00,20,00,00,00,35,35
8041 DATA"IN A VENTILATOR PASSAGE.                       9020 DATA 00,00,00,19,21,00,36,36
8042 DATA"AT A VENTILATOR OPENING. THROUGH THE           9021 DATA 00,00,00,00,00,20,37,38
8043 DATA"OPENING A LIT PASSAGEWAY CAN BE SEEN.          9022 DATA 00,00,13,00,00,23,39,40
8044 DATA"IN A LIGHTED SPACE STATION CORRIDOR.           9023 DATA 24,00,00,00,22,00,41,41
8045 DATA"IN THE SPACE STATION INFIRMARY.                9024 DATA 25,23,00,00,00,00,42,43
8046 DATA"IN THE RECREATION ROOM AND LIBRARY.            9025 DATA 27,26,33,32,24,00,44,44
8047 DATA"IN THE MESS HALL. ABANDONED FOOD TRAYS         9026 DATA 25,00,30,31,00,00,44,44
8048 DATA"ARE STILL ON THE TABLES.                       9027 DATA 34,25,41,00,00,00,44,44
8049 DATA"IN THE STORAGE ROOM AND SUPPLY AREA.           9028 DATA 00,29,42,36,00,00,44,44
8050 DATA"IN THE SLEEPING QUARTERS.                      9029 DATA 28,38,43,37,00,00,44,44
8051 DATA"IN AN ELEVATOR AT SUBSURFACE LEVEL.            9030 DATA 00,00,00,26,00,00,45,45
8052 DATA"IN AN ELEVATOR AT SURFACE LEVEL.               9031 DATA 00,00,26,00,00,00,46,46
8053 DATA"IN THE STATION CONTROL CENTER.                 9032 DATA 00,00,25,00,00,00,47,48
8054 DATA"IN THE TRANSPORTER ROOM.                       9033 DATA 00,00,00,25,00,00,50,50
8055 DATA"IN THE SPACE STATION LABORATORY.               9034 DATA 00,27,00,00,00,00,49,49
8056 DATA"IN THE HANGER AREA. THE LAUNCH AREA            9035 DATA 00,28,00,00,24,00,53,53
8057 DATA"IS JUST SOUTH OF HERE.                         9036 DATA 00,00,28,00,00,00,54,54
8058 DATA"IN AN AIR LOCK CHAMBER BETWEEN THE             9037 DATA 00,00,29,00,00,00,55,55
8059 DATA"CHANGING AREA AND THE HANGER.                  9038 DATA 29,00,39,00,00,00,56,57
8060 DATA"IN A SPACE SUIT CHANGING AREA.                 9039 DATA 40,00,00,38,00,00,58,59
8500 REM                                                 9040 DATA 00,39,00,29,00,00,60,60
8501 REM MOVEMENT AND TEXT POINTER MATRIX                9041 DATA 00,00,00,27,42,00,51,51
8502 REM                                                 9042 DATA 00,00,00,28,00,41,52,52
9001 DATA 07,04,02,15,00,00,01,03                        9999 END
9002 DATA 09,03,14,01,00,00,04,06
9003 DATA 02,05,14,04,00,00,07,07
```

```
WELCOME TO THE GAME OF SURVIVAL. WOULD           ##
YOU LIKE INSTRUCTIONS?                           ? N
? Y                                              ELAPSED TIME: 5 MINUTES
YOU HAVE CRASH LANDED ON THE                     POWER UNIT: 225 UNITS
EARTH'S MOON. YOU HAVE LIMITED                   OXYGEN REMAINING: 175 MINUTES
SUPPLIES AND TIME IN WHICH TO                    PRESENT LOCATION STATUS: YOU ARE
SURVIVE. TO TRAVEL, YOU MAY                      AT THE BASE OF THE AWESOME MT. EUDOXUS.
ENTER DIRECTIVES SUCH AS NORTH                   ##
OR N, AS WELL AS S. E. W AND                     ? N
U. AND D (UP AND DOWN). YOU                      ELAPSED TIME: 10 MINUTES
WILL ENCOUNTER VARIOUS ITEMS                     POWER UNIT: 220 UNITS
AND SITUATIONS DURING YOUR                       OXYGEN REMAINING: 170 MINUTES
TRAVELS. TO COMMUNICATE, ENTER                   PRESENT LOCATION STATUS: YOU ARE
COMMANDS (VERBS) FOLLOWED BY                     INSIDE THE CRATER OF ARISTOTELES. THE
OBJECT NAMES (IF APPLICABLE).                    CRATER FLOOR IS LITTERED WITH ROCKS.
FOR EXAMPLE. GET KEY. LEAVE,                     ##
USE, AND INVENTORY.                              ? E
ONCE YOU HAVE SURVIVED. THE                      ELAPSED TIME: 15 MINUTES
OBJECT THEN IS TO ACHIEVE THE                    POWER UNIT: 215 UNITS
OPTIMUM SURVIVAL TIME.                           OXYGEN REMAINING: 165 MINUTES
    *** GOOD LUCK ***                            PRESENT LOCATION STATUS: YOU ARE
ELAPSED TIME: 0 MINUTES                          AT THE BASE OF THE BURG CRATER IN LACUS
POWER UNIT: 230 UNITS                            MORTIS. THE SURFACE IS VERY SOFT HERE.
OXYGEN REMAINING: 180 MINUTES                    ##
PRESENT LOCATION STATUS: YOU ARE                 ? DIG
AT MARE SERENITATUS. LONG EERIE SHADOWS          THERE IS DILITHIUM CRYSTALS HERE.
FROM DISTANT MOUNTAINS AND CRATERS CAST          ? GET CRYSTALS
THEMSELVES ACROSS THE BARREN LANDSCAPE.          O.K.
```

Survival

```
? INVENTORY
YOU HAVE AN OXYGEN MODULE.
YOU HAVE DILITHIUM CRYSTALS.
YOU HAVE A POWER UNIT.
? S
ELAPSED TIME:  30 MINUTES
POWER UNIT:  200 UNITS
OXYGEN REMAINING:  150 MINUTES
PRESENT LOCATION STATUS: YOU ARE
AT MARE SERENITATUS. LONG EERIE SHADOWS
FROM DISTANT MOUNTAINS AND CRATERS CAST
THEMSELVES ACROSS THE BARREN LANDSCAPE.
##
? S
ELAPSED TIME:  35 MINUTES
POWER UNIT:  195 UNITS
OXYGEN REMAINING:  145 MINUTES
PRESENT LOCATION STATUS: YOU ARE
AT A PASS IN THE MOUNTAINS OF HAEMUS.
##
? S
ELAPSED TIME:  40 MINUTES
POWER UNIT:  190 UNITS
OXYGEN REMAINING:  140 MINUTES
PRESENT LOCATION STATUS: YOU ARE
AT A STEEP BASE OF THE CRATER MANILUS.
##
?
```

Trucker

Trucker was written by Richard R. Galbraith and first appeared in the March 1981 issue of *Creative Computing*.

Tucker is a program which simulates the problems facing a long-haul truck driver. Ideally, you can make a good living hauling freight coast-to-coast without exceeding the legal load limit. If all goes well, you can obey the speed limits and stop each night for eight hours sleep and still make the time schedule. On a good trip you will be able to earn well over $1,000. However, even the best drivers run into occasional streaks of bad luck and may barely break even.

Bad weather, road construction, or a flat tire can place you behind schedule and eat up your profits. You may try to increase your profits by skimping on sleep, driving fast, or carrying an overweight load. However, pushing too hard raises the risk of a traffic accident, and you will be fined if you are caught breaking the law.

Your Truck

You are driving an 18-wheel tractor-trailer combination that can hold 50,000 pounds of cargo (10,000 pounds more than the legal limit). You are buying your truck through a bank loan that requires payment of $1,955 per month, or $85 for each working day. This amount includes reserves for taxes and insurance.

Your truck has a 200-gallon fuel tank and gets 4.5 miles per gallon of diesel fuel. Your mileage decreases when you drive faster or slower than 55 miles per hour. Your fuel gauge is accurate to within 5 gallons and your speedometer is accurate to within 3 miles per hour.

Accidents

It is extremely unlikely that you will be involved in a traffic accident in good weather if you drive at a reasonable speed and get enough rest. The danger increases dramatically if you drive at an excessive rate of speed, fail to slow down in fog or a blizzard, or continue driving after you have become fatigued. An exhausted driver speeding through a snow storm is asking for trouble.

There is always the danger of losing time due to a flat tire. This danger can be reduced by purchasing retreads or more expensive tires before you start your trip, and by promptly replacing your spare tire after a flat.

Speeding

The speed limit is 55 miles per hour unless otherwise posted. Generally, Smokey will allow some leeway before pulling you over, but the faster you go the more likely you are to attract his attention. There are also a couple of places along the way where a radar speed trap may be in operation with strict enforcement.

Whenever you get a traffic ticket, you will lose time as you wait to pay your fine at the Justice of the Peace. If you receive more than three traffic tickets, you lose your Interstate Commerce Commission driver's license.

Truck Stops

Every three or four hours you will approach a truck stop. Each stop will take at least one hour while you get coffee, fuel and a spare tire if necessary. The price of diesel fuel and tires will vary unpredictably; diesel fuel will average about $1.00 per gallon.

Truck stops are also the only places where you can sleep. You may choose when to sleep, but, if you attempt to sleep during the day, you will be disturbed by traffic noise.

Cargo

You can select one of three types of cargo to haul for each trip:

1. U.S. Mail: This contract will pay $.0475 per pound, or $1,900 for a 40,000 pound load upon delivery.

2. Freight Forwarding: This contract pays $.05 pound, or 2,000 for a load. However, there is a 10% penalty that is subtracted if you are more than 12 hours late in delivering your freight.

3. Oranges: This contract will pay $.065 per pound of good oranges delivered to New York, which amounts to $2,600 for a standard load. You are required to run the air-conditioning unit in your trailer in order to keep the oranges from rotting or freezing. This uses 7 gallons of diesel fuel per hour while you sleep.

Routes

You can choose one of three routes: the northern route, the middle route or the southern route. Let's look at each route in detail:

Northern Route

This route is the shortest but also the riskiest. You will leave from Los Angeles on Interstate 15 and drive through Las Vegas and Denver. You then take Interstate 80 through Nebraska, northern Ohio and Pennsylvania. The total mileage is 2,710. You will pay a total of $195 in tolls and have one chance in eight of avoiding weighing stations. The danger of bad weather is high, and the speed limit is vigorously enforced.

MiddleRoute

The middle route follows old Route 66 from Los Angeles through northern Arizona and Oklahoma into St. Louis. Then you cut over to the Pennsylvania Turnpike and follow through to New York. The total distance to New York is 2,850 miles. The toll road portions will cost you $240 in fees. This route has fewer Smokies watching your speed and the weather conditions are much more favorable than the Northern route. However, watch the weight in your trailer since there are usually several truck scales in operation.

Southern Route

This route takes you from Los Angeles on Interstate 10 through Arizona, New Mexico, and Texas. You then follow Interstate 20 to Atlanta before heading north to Washington, D.C. The last leg of your journey follows Interstate 95 up the Atlantic coast. The mileage is 3120; much longer than the other routes. However, it is the safest route because you avoid much of the bad weather. Tolls amount to only $95 and you will run into fewer police and fewer truck scales. If you cannot resist the temptation to take on an over-weight cargo or if you have a lead foot, this is the best route for you to take.

Trucker

```
10 REM--INDEPENDENT TRUCKER SIMULATION
20 REM--BY CREATIVE COMPUTING
30 REM--5/23/84
70 DIM MT(2), MP(2,25), MP$(2,25), MR$(2,25), ZM(2,25), D$(6), NT$(4)
80 CLS
85 PRINT"                 INDEPENDENT TRUCKER SIMULATION"
90 NT$(1)="First":NT$(2)="Second":NT$(3)="Third":NT$(4)="Fourth"
92 DS$(0)="Monday":DS$(1)="Tuesday":DS$(2)="Wednesday"
94 DS$(3)="Thursday":DS$(4)="Friday":DS$(5)="Saturday":DS$(6)="Sunday"
300 PRINT@784,"DO YOU WANT TO SEE INSTRUCTIONS";
310 INPUT Z$:IF LEFT$(Z$,1)="N" OR LEFT$(Z$,1)="n" THEN 1000 ELSE 6000
1000 CLS:XC=0:MF=0:HL=2:HS=7:HR=0:GOSUB2100
1010 PRINT@128," "
1020 PRINT"You are at the Los Angeles Trucking Terminal"
1030 PRINT"Three types of cargo are available:"
1040 PRINTTAB(5)"1--ORANGES  (highest profit IF they don't spoil)"
1050 PRINTTAB(5)"2--FREIGHT FORWARDING   (penalty for late delivery)"
1060 PRINTTAB(5)"3--U.S. MAIL  (lowest rate, but no hurry to arrive)"
1070 PRINT"The cargo is due in New York BY 4 pm on Thursday."
1075 INPUT"Which type of cargo do you want";CT
1080 IF CT<1 OR CT>3 INPUT"PICK A NUMBER: 1, 2, OR 3";CT:GOTO1080
1090 INPUT"How many pounds will you carry (40000 is the LEGAL limit)";WL
1100 IF WL<25000 PRINT"You can't make a living on half a load.":GOTO 1090
1110 PRINT:PRINTTAB(5)"They are loading your truck now."
1120 RESTORE
1140 FOR RT=0 TO 2
1150 READ NP, MT(RT)
1160 FOR I=1 TO NP
1170 READ MP(RT,I), MP$(RT,I), MR$(RT,I), ZM(RT,I)
1180 NEXT I,RT
1190 TC=10:WF=190:NP=1:TS=1:SL=55:XN=XN+1:XC=190
1200 IF WL>50000 THEN WL=50000 ELSE 1220
1210 PRINT"50,000 pounds of cargo has filled your trailer!"
1211 FOR I=1 TO 750:NEXTI
1220 HR=HR+1:CLS:GOSUB2100:PRINT@128,""
1225 PRINT"You have nearly a full tank (cost of fuel: $ 190).":PRINT
1230 INPUT"Two of your tires are worn.  Do you want replacements";Z$
1240 IF LEFT$(Z$,1)="N" OR LEFT$(Z$,1)="n" THEN 1350
1250 PRINT"A NEW tire costs $200.    A RETREAD costs $100.":PRINTTAB(5);
1260 INPUT"Which type do you want";Z$:PRINTTAB(5);:Z$=LEFT$(Z$,1)
1270 INPUT"How many";T
1280 IF T=3 IF Z$="N" OR Z$="n" THEN TS=2:T=2:XC=XC+200
1290 IF T<0 OR T>2 THEN 1330
1300 IF T=0 THEN 1350
1310 IF Z$="R" OR Z$="r" THEN TC=TC-3*T:XC=XC+100*T:GOTO1350
1320 IF Z$="N" OR Z$="n" THEN TC=TC-4*T:XC=XC+200*T:GOTO1350
1330 PRINT"I did not understand your answers.":PRINT"Let's try again:"
1340 PRINTTAB(5);:GOTO1230
1350 PRINT:PRINT"You may choose the Northern, Middle or Southern route."
1360 INPUT"   Which route do you choose";Z$:Z$=LEFT$(Z$,1)
1365 IF Z$="N" OR Z$="n" THEN RT=1:RH=4:GOTO 1600
1370 IF Z$="M" OR Z$="m" THEN RT=0:RH=2:GOTO 1600
1375 IF Z$="S" OR Z$="s" THEN RT=2:RH=1:GOTO 1600
1380 PRINT"Please, answer: NORTH, MIDDLE, or SOUTH !"
1385 GOTO1360
1400 REM***
1410 AF= SP[2 * CD * CR
1420 IF AF> RND(0)*1E7 GOTO 4000
1430 AF= SQR(MF+100)*TC
1440 IF AF> RH*25000*RND(0)  GOSUB 2600
1450 IF SP> SL-RH+10  GOSUB 2300
1460 HR= HR+1:HL=HL+1
1470 IF SL<40 THEN SL=55
1480 T=ABS(55-SP):IF T>12 THEN T=12.5
1490 T1= SP/(4.5 -0.2*T)
1500 WF= WF -T1:IF WF<0 GOSUB 2500
1510 MF= MF+SP
1520 IF MF> MT(RT) THEN 5000
1530 FOR I=1 TO 250:NEXT I
1550 CLS:GOSUB 2100
1560 PRINT@64,"Approximate FUEL:";INT(WF-5)+RND(10);TAB(36)"SPEED:";SP
1570 PRINTTAB(8)"Odometer:";MF;TAB(30)"Miles to go:";MT(RT)-MF
1580 PRINT
1590 REM** MILEPOST
1600 IF MP(RT,NP)<= MF GOTO 3100 ELSE PRINT"Cruising on ";MR$(RT,NP)
1610 GOSUB 3000:PRINT"You are feeling ";CD$
1620 GOSUB 2800:PRINT"Current weather: ";CR$
1630 NS= NS+1:IF NS> 3 GOSUB 1700
```

```
1640 INPUT"How fast do you wish to go";SP
1650 IF SP< 20 PRINT"YOU HAVE TO GO AT LEAST 20 -- ";:GOTO 1640
1660 IF SP> INT(1.5*SL) THEN SP= INT(1.5*SL) ELSE 1670
1665 PRINT"You can only get the old rig to go";SP;"mph on this road."
1670 GOTO 1400
1700 REM**
1710 INPUT"TRUCK STOP AHEAD.   Do you want to stop";Z$
1720 IF LEFT$(Z$,1)="N" OR LEFT$(Z$,1)="n" THEN NS=1:HL=HL+1:RETURN
1730 IF LEFT$(Z$,1)<>"Y" AND LEFT$(Z$,1)<>"y" INPUT"YES or NO";Z$:GOTO1720
1740 T= 85 +INT(35*RND(0))
1750 PRINT"Diesel fuel costs";T;"cents a gallon."
1760 INPUT"   How many gallons do you want";T1
1770 IF T1>0 PRINT"PAY";:PRINTUSING"$$###.##";T*T1/100:XC=XC+T*T1/100:WF=WF+T1
1780 PRINT"So far, you have spent ";:PRINT "$";XC
1790 IF WF > 201 PRINT"The tank holds 200 gallons--";INT(WF-200);"gallons spilled!
1795 WF=200
1800 IF TS>0 THEN 1900
1810 T= 200 +INT(50*RND(0)):T1=100 +INT(70*RND(0))
1820 PRINT"A NEW tire costs $";T;"    a RETREAD costs $";T1
1830 INPUT"     Do you want to buy a tire";Z$
1840 IF LEFT$(Z$,1)="N" OR LEFT$(Z$,1)="n" THEN 1900
1850 INPUT"     Choose:  New or Retread";Z$
1860 IF LEFT$(Z$,1)="N" OR LEFT$(Z$,1)="n" THEN XC=XC+T:TS=2:GOTO1900
1870 IF LEFT$(Z$,1)="R" OR LEFT$(Z$,1)="r" THEN XC=XC+T1:TS=1:GOTO1900
1880 PRINT"I DID NOT UNDERSTAND YOUR ANSWERS.":GOTO1830
1900 HR= HR+1:NS=0
1910 INPUT"Do you want to get some sleep";Z$
1920 IF LEFT$(Z$,1)="N" OR LEFT$(Z$,1)="n"  GOSUB 2100:GOTO 2020
1930 INPUT"     How many hours of rest";T
1940 IF T<1 GOTO 2020
1945 IF T>10 THEN PRINT"NOBODY NEEDS THAT MUCH SLEEP" ELSE 1950
1946 FOR TDT = 1 TO 2000:NEXT:GOTO1930
1950 DH= HR -24*INT(HR/24)
1960 HR= HR+T:FORI=1 TO 125*T:NEXTI:IFCT=1 THEN WF=WF-7*T
1965 IFWF<0 THEN WF=0:GOSUB2570
1970 IFDH<21 OR DH>12 THEN GOTO 1980
1975 T=INT(T/2+.6)
1976 PRINT"Thanks to the daytime noise, you got only";T;"hours of real sleep."
1980 HS=HS+T
1990 IF T>3 THEN HL=0 ELSE HL=HL/2
2010 GOSUB2100:PRINT"Time to hit the road again."
2015 PRINT"You now have ";WF;"gallons of fuel."
2016 INPUT"Do you want to buy more";Z$
2017 IF LEFT$(Z$,1)="Y" OR LEFT$(Z$,1)="y" THEN 1740
2020 IF SL<55 PRINT"REMEMBER, the current speed limit is";SL;"mph."
2025 RETURN
2100 REM*** DISPLAY DAY & TIME
2110 DH=HR+8
2120 DT=INT(DH/24):DH=DH -24*DT
2130 IF DT>6 THEN DT=DT-7:GOTO2130
2140 DM$="am"
2150 IF DH=12 THEN DM$="noon":GOTO 2200
2160 IF DH>12 THEN DH=DH-12:DM$="pm"
2170 IF DH=0 THEN DH=12:DM$="midnight"
2200 T=PEEK(&H4020):T1=PEEK(&H4021)
2210 PRINT@0,"            Day: ";DS$(DT);TAB(37)"Time:";DH;DM$
2220 POKE &H4020,T:POKE &H4021,T1
2230 RETURN
2300 REM** SPEEDING
2310 IF (SP-SL-5)[2< 900*RND(0) RETURN
2320 PRINT"SMOKEY is behind you with his lights on.    PULL OVER!"
2350 NT=NT+1:PRINT"See the JUSTICE of the PEACE for your ";NT$(NT);" offense"
2360 PRINT"     Wait";NT;"hours for your hearing"
2370 HR=HR+NT:HL=HL+NT
2380 IF NT>3 THEN 2430
2390 T=NT*RND(5):T1= 5*(RT+NT*RND(4))
2400 PRINT"     FINE is ";:PRINTUSING"$###";T1;
2401 PRINT" plus $";T;"for each MPH over the limit."
2410 PRINT"     PAY $";:PRINT DD$;T1+T*(SP-SL):XC=XC+T1+T*(SP-SL)
2420 FOR I=1 TO 1000:NEXTI:RETURN
2430 PRINT"  You are sentenced to 30 Days in jail for reckless driving."
2440 FOR I=1 TO 500:NEXTI
2450 PRINT"Your I.C.C. Driver's License is revoked !"
2460 GOTO5500
2500 REM** OUT OF GAS
2510 T1=T1+WF:WF=0:SP=0
2520 T=(4.5 -0.2*T)*T1:MF=MF+T
2530 PRINT"After";T;"more miles, you ran out of fuel  (DUMMY !!)"
```

```
2540 PRINT"   It cost $ 200 to get a barrel of diesel delivered."
2550 WF=55:T1=RND(5):HR=HR+T1:XC=XC+200:HL=HL+T1
2560 PRINTTAB(5)"   You also wasted";T1;"hours by your carelessness."
2570 IF CT=1 THEN CX=CX+RND(3)
2575 PRINT"   Sitting with the refer unit off is damaging the oranges."
2580 FOR I=1 TO 500:NEXTI
2590 RETURN
2600 REM**   FLAT TIRE
2620 PRINT"You just blew a tire !!"
2630 IF TS=0 THEN 2700
2640 TC=TC -2*TS:TS=0
2650 T=RND(2):IF T=1 THEN T$="outside" ELSE T$="inside"
2660 PRINT"   It took";T;"hours to change the ";T$;" tire.":HR=HR+T:HL=HL+T+1
2670 FOR I=1 TO 750:NEXTI:RETURN
2700 REM   NO SPARE
2710 PRINT"Since your spare has already been used, you have to call a tow  ";
2715 PRINT"truck from town to deliver a new tire to you."
2720 PRINT"   This service cost $ 400 and took 4 hours."
2730 HR=HR+4:HL=HL+4:XC=XC+400
2740 FOR I=1 TO 1000:NEXTI:RETURN
2800 REM**   ROAD CONDITIONS
2810 AF=(3000 + MF)*RND(0):ON (RT+1) GOTO 2870,2820,2910
2820 IF AF<3300 AND CR<>50 THEN 2960
2830 IF AF>4800 THEN 2965
2840 IF AF>4600 THEN 2970
2850 IF AF>3800 THEN 2975
2860 GOTO2985
2870 IF AF<3400 AND CR<>50 THEN 2960
2880 IF AF>4900 THEN 2965
2890 IF AF>4700 THEN 2970
2900 IF AF>4200 IF RND(3)=1 THEN 2975 ELSE 2980
2905 GOTO2985
2910 IF AF<4000 AND CR<>50 THEN 2960
2920 IF AF>5700 THEN 2965
2930 IF AF>5500 THEN 2970
2940 IF AF>4400 THEN 2980
2950 GOTO2985
2960 CR=1:CR$="CLEAR & DRY":RETURN
2965 CR=50:CR$="B-L-I-Z-Z-A-R-D  !!":RETURN
2970 CR=10:CR$="FOG -- Limited visibility":RETURN
2975 CR=5:CR$="LIGHT SNOW":RETURN
2980 CR=5:CR$="RAIN":RETURN
2985 CR=3:CR$="CLEAR, but roadway is wet":RETURN
3000 REM** CONDITION OF DRIVER
3010 IF HL>19 OR HR/HS>4 THEN CD=100:CD$="..E.X.H.A.U.S.T.E.D..":RETURN
3020 IF HL<3 AND CSNG(HR/HS)<2.3 THEN CD=1:CD$="RESTED & REARING TO GO.":RETURN
3030 IF HL<8 AND CSNG(HR/HS)<2.5 THEN CD=2:CD$="FINE":RETURN
3040 IF HL<12 AND HR/HS<=3 THEN CD=4:CD$="   B O R E D":RETURN
3050 IF HL<16 AND HR/HS<=3 THEN CD=8:CD$="   T I R E D  !!":RETURN
3060 CD=25:CD$="FATIGUED...You're getting sleepy":RETURN
3100 REM*** MILEPOST
3110 PRINT"You have just passed ";MP$(RT,NP)
3120 ZH=ZM(RT,NP):SL=55
3130 ON INT(ZH) GOSUB 3210,3310,3360,3410,3500,3710,3860
3140 NP=NP+1:IF INT(ZH)=8 THEN 5000 ELSE 1600
3210 PRINT"Time Zone changes -- Set clock ahead one hour"
3220 HR=HR+1:GOSUB 2100
3230 RETURN
3310 T=100*(ZH-INT(ZH))
3320 PRINT"STOP!   PAY TOLL of ";:PRINTUSING"$##.##";T
3330 XC=XC+T
3340 RETURN
3360 IF RND(0)< ZH -INT(ZH) RETURN
3370 PRINT"CONSTRUCTION AHEAD !!":FOR I=1 TO 500:NEXTI
3380 PRINT"SLOW DOWN -- SPEED LIMIT 35 mph":SL=35
3390 RETURN
3410 IF RND(0)< ZH -INT(ZH) RETURN
3420 T=SP +RND(5) -2
3430 PRINT"You were just clocked by RADAR at";T;"mph"
3440 IF T> SL+3 GOSUB 2320 ELSE PRINT"   No ticket this time."
3450 RETURN
3500 IF ZH=INT(ZH) IF RND(0)<.5 THEN 3520 ELSE RETURN
3510 IF RND(0)< ZH -INT(ZH) RETURN
3520 PRINT"WEIGHING STATION OPEN  --  TRUCKS MUST STOP":FOR I=1 TO 500:NEXTI
3530 PRINT"Scale weighs truck with cargo, fuel & driver: ";
3540 T=19000 +WL +7*WF +25*RND(10)
3550 PRINTUSING"##,###";T;:PRINT" POUNDS."
3560 T=INT(T-60000)
```

```
3570 IF T<1 PRINT"     You're O.K.":RETURN
3580 IF ZH=5.00 THEN 3630
3590 T1=RND(4)+2:PRINT"     Overweight fine is $ 200 plus";T1;"cents/pound"
3600 XC=XC+100+(T*T1)/100
3610 PRINT"Pay fine of";:PRINT 200+(T*T1)/100
3620 RETURN
3630 REM
3640 PRINT"You are not allowed to enter Lousiana with that load."
3650 PRINT"     Take a 200 mile detour through Arkansas with 45 mph limit."
3660 SL=45:MR$(RT,12)="Arkansas County Roads"
3670 FOR I=12 TO 25:MP(RT,I)=MP(RT,I)+200:NEXTI
3680 MT(RT)=MT(RT)+200
3690 RETURN
3710 IF RND(0)< ZH -INT(ZH) RETURN
3720 T=RND(6)
3730 PRINT"A ROCK SLIDE has blocked the Alleghany Tunnel entrance"
3740 PRINT"     The highway Department will have it cleared in";T;"hours"
3750 HR=HR+T:FORI=1TO 200*T:NEXTI:IF CT=1 THEN WF=WF-7*T:IF WF<=1 GOSUB3820
3760 IF T>1 THEN T1=INT(T/2 +.5) ELSE T1=0
3770 IF T1>3 THEN HL=0 ELSE IF T1>0 HL=HL/2
3780 HS=HS+T1
3790 PRINT"     While waiting, you got";T1;"hours of sleep"
3800 GOSUB 2100:RETURN
3820 PRINT"     You ran out of gas while waiting":T=0:GOSUB2540
3830 RETURN
3860 IF CT>1 RETURN
3870 IF RND(0)< ZH - INT(ZH) RETURN
3880 PRINT"The trailer refrigeration unit has failed endangering the cargo"
3890 PRINT"     Repairs take 2 hours and cost $ 100"
3900 CX=CX +RND(4):HR=HR+2:HL=HL+2:XC=XC+100
3910 GOSUB2100
3920 RETURN
4000 REM**
4020 FOR I=1 TO 6
4030 CLS:FOR J=1 TO 60:NEXTJ
4040 PRINT@400,CHR$(23);"C R A S H  !!"
4050 FOR J=1 TO 60:NEXTJ,I
4060 PRINT
4070 IF CD=100 OR (CD=25 AND SP<65) PRINT"You fell asleep at the wheel":GOTO4130
4080 IFCR=50PRINT"You drove into a snow-filled ditch.":GOTO4130
4090 IF CR=10 PRINT"You rear-ended a Pick-up with no tail lights":GOTO 4130
4100 IF SP>65 PRINTTAB(8)"SPEED KILLS !":END
4110 IF CR>2 PRINT"You hit a slick spot and skidded off the road.":GOTO4130
4120 PRINT"A drunk driver rammed your rig":PRINTTAB(8)"TOUGH LUCK !"
4130 PRINT:FORI=1TO500:NEXTI
4140 PRINT"You lose your truck & profits":PRINT
4150 PRINT:INPUT"Do you want to start over";Z$
4160 IF LEFT$(Z$,1)="N" OR LEFT$(Z$,1)="n" THEN CLS:END
4170 XP=0:CLS:GOTO 1000
5000 REM**
5010 FOR I=1 TO 5
5020 CLS:FOR J=1 TO 60:NEXTJ
5030 PRINT@152,"WELCOME":PRINT@286,"TO":PRINT@408,"NEW YORK"
5040 FOR J=1 TO 60:NEXTJ,I
5050 FOR I=1 TO 250:NEXTI:CLS
5100 GOSUB2100:PRINT@64,""
5110 T=HR -INT(HR/24):IF T<10 OR T>21 THEN 5140
5120 PRINT"The warehouse is closed for the night.  Come back tomorrow."
5130 T=24-T:HR=HR+T:FOR I=1 TO 1000:NEXTI:GOSUB 2100
5140 PRINT:T=INT(HR/24):T1=HR -24*T
5150 PRINT"You completed the trip in";T;"days";
5160 IF T1>1 PRINT" &";T1;"hours." ELSE PRINT
5170 PRINT"     Trip expenses totaled ";:PRINT DC$;XC
5175 IF T1>0 THEN T=T+1
5180 T1=85*T +85:PRINT"     Truck payments, Insurance & Taxes cost ";:PRINT T1
5190 XC=XC+T1:PRINT
5200 ON CT GOTO 5220,5310,5360
5220 T1=(T-4)*RND(3):IF T1>0 THEN CX=CX+T1
5230 IFCX>6PRINT"Your oranges have spoiled. Take them away!":XT=-50:GOTO5400
5240 PRINT"Collect six-and-a-half cents per pound for good oranges."
5250 XT=.065*WL:PRINT"     Total for the load: ";:PRINT XT
5260 IF CX<1 THEN 5400
5270 PRINT"     Part of the load is damaged.  Subtract ";:PRINT 5*CS;:PRINT"%"
5280 XT=XT -XT*CX/20:PRINT"     Net Payment is ";:PRINT XT
5290 GOTO5400
5310 XT=.06*WL:PRINT"Collect five cents a pound for freight."
5320 PRINT"     Total for load = ";:PRINT XT
5330 IFHR<90 THEN 5400
```

Trucker

```
5340 CX=2:PRINT"    You're late!!  Subtract ten percent penalty.":GOTO5280
5360 PRINT"Postmaster pays 4.75 cents per pound on delivery.":XT=.0475*WL
5365 CX=0:GOTO5290
5400 PRINT:XT=XT-XC:XP=XP+XT:IF XT<0 THEN 5470
5410 PRINT"Your Net Profit this trip was ";:PRINT XT
5420 IF XT>1000 PRINT"    G O O D    W O R K  !!"
5430 IF XN>1 PRINT"    Your Average Profit has been";:PRINT XP/XN
5440 IF XT<200 OR XP/XN<250 PRINT"   You'd make more money washing dishes !"
5450 PRINT:PRINT:INPUT"Do you want to make another trip";Z$
5460 IF LEFT$(Z$,1)<>"N" AND LEFT$(Z$,1)<>"n" THEN RUN ELSE CLS:END
5470 PRINT"BAD TRIP. . . You lost";:PRINT ABS(XT)
5480 IF XP>=0 GOTO 5430
5490 PRINT"    You are BANKRUPT !!!"
5500 REM -- LOSE TRUCK, END GAME
5520 PRINT:PRINT"Your rig has been repossessed."
5530 PRINT:END
5590 FOR I=1 TO 2:NEXTI:RETURN
6000 CLS
6010 PRINTTAB(5)"This is a simulation of the problems facing a long haul"
6020 PRINT"truck driver.  Ideally, you can make a good living hauling"
6030 PRINT"freight coast-to-coast without exceeding the legal load limit."
6040 PRINT"If all goes well, you can obey the speed limits, stop for"
6050 PRINT"8 hours sleep each night and still meet the schedule.":PRINT
6060 PRINTTAB(5)"Bad weather, road construction or flat tires may throw"
6070 PRINT"you behind schedule & eat up your profits.  You may try to"
6080 PRINT"increase your profits by skimping on sleep, driving fast, or"
6090 PRINT"carrying an overweight load.  However, pushing too hard raises"
6100 PRINT"the risk of a traffic accident, and you will be fined if you"
6110 PRINT"are caught breaking the law.":PRINT
6120 GOSUB8900:CLS
6130 PRINTTAB(26)"YOUR TRUCK":PRINT
6140 PRINTTAB(5)"You are driving an 18-wheel tractor trailer combination"
6150 PRINT"that can hold 50,000 pounds of cargo (10,000 more than the"
6160 PRINT"legal limit).  You are buying your truck through a bank loan"
6170 PRINT"that requires payment of $ 1,955 per month (including"
6180 PRINT"reserves for taxes & insurance).  This works out to $ 85 for"
6190 PRINT"each working day."
6200 PRINTTAB(5)"You have a 200 gallon fuel tank and get 4.5 miles per"
6210 PRINT"gallon of diesel oil.  Your mileage decreases when you drive"
6220 PRINT"either faster or slower than 55.  Your fuel gauge is accurate"
6230 PRINT"to within 5 gallons, and your speedometer is accurate to"
6240 PRINT"within 3 miles per hour.":PRINT
6250 GOSUB 8910:CLS
6260 PRINTTAB(26)"ACCIDENTS":PRINT
6270 PRINTTAB(5)"It is extremely unlikely that you will be involved in"
6280 PRINT"a traffic accident in good weather if you drive at a reasonable"
6290 PRINT"speed and get enough rest.  The danger increases dramatically"
6300 PRINT"if you drive at an excessive rate of speed, fail to slow down"
6310 PRINT"in fog or a blizzard, or continue driving after you become"
6320 PRINT"fatigued.  An exhausted driver speeding through a snow storm"
6330 PRINT"is asking for trouble."
6340 PRINTTAB(5)"There is always the danger of losing time because of"
6350 PRINT"a flat tire.  You can reduce the danger by starting the trip"
6360 PRINT"buying some retreads or more expensive new tires, and"
6370 PRINT"promptly replacing your spare after a flat."
6380 GOSUB 8910:CLS
6390 PRINTTAB(26)"SPEEDING":PRINT
6400 PRINTTAB(5)"The speed limit is 55 unless posted otherwise.  Generally,"
6410 PRINT"the police allow some leeway before pulling you over.  The"
6420 PRINT"faster you go the more likely you are to attract Smokey's"
6430 PRINT"attention.  There are also a couple of places along the way"
6440 PRINT"where a RADAR speed trap may be in operation with strict"
6450 PRINT"enforcement.":PRINT
6460 PRINTTAB(5)"Whenever you get a ticket, you will lose time as you wait"
6470 PRINT"to pay your fine at the Justice of the Peace.  Also, if you"
6480 PRINT"collect more than 3 tickets your Interstate Commerce"
6490 PRINT"commission driver's license will be revoked."
6500 GOSUB 8910:CLS
6510 PRINTTAB(24)"TRUCK STOPS":PRINT
6520 PRINTTAB(5)"Every three or four hours, you will approach a truck"
6530 PRINT"stop.  Each stop will take at least 1 hour, to get coffee,"
6540 PRINT"fuel, and a spare tire if necessary.  The price of diesel"
6550 PRINT"fuel and tires will vary unpredictably, but diesel will"
6560 PRINT"average about one dollar per gallon.":PRINT
6570 PRINTTAB(5)"Truck stops are also the only places where you can"
6580 PRINT"stop to sleep.  You may choose when to sleep, but attempts"
6590 PRINT"to sleep during the day will be interrupted by the traffic"
6600 PRINT"noise."
```

```
6610 GOSUB 8910:CLS
6620 PRINTTAB(28)"CARGO":PRINT
6630 PRINT"You can choose one of three types of cargo for each trip:"
6640 PRINTTAB(5)"U.S. MAIL:  The contract pays 4.75 cents per pound,"
6650 PRINT" or $ 1,900 for a 40,000 lb. load, whenever you deliver."
6660 PRINTTAB(5)"FREIGHT FORWARDING:  Pays five cents a pound, or"
6670 PRINT"$ 2,000 for a load.  However, there is a ten percent penalty"
6680 PRINT"subtracted if you are more than 12 hours late."
6690 PRINTTAB(5)"ORANGES:  Require running the air-conditioning unit in"
6700 PRINT"your trailer to keep them from freezing or rotting, so you"
6710 PRINT"will burn 7 gallons of diesel per hour while you sleep."
6720 PRINT"You will be paid six-and-one-half cents per pound of good"
6730 PRINT"oranges delivered to New York.  That's $ 2,600 for a standard"
6740 PRINT"load."
6750 GOSUB 8910:CLS
6760 PRINTTAB(27)"ROUTES":PRINT
6770 PRINT"You can choose one of three routes.  The Northern is the"
6780 PRINT"shortests, but riskiest.  The Southern is the longest and"
6790 PRINT"safest.":PRINT
6800 PRINTTAB(21)"NORTHERN ROUTE"
6810 PRINTTAB(5)"Leave Los Angeles on Interstate 15.  Drive through"
6820 PRINT"Las Vegas, & Denver.  Then follow Interstate 80 through"
6830 PRINT"Nebraska, Northern Ohio & Pennsylvania.  Total distance is"
6840 PRINT"2,710 miles.  You will pay $ 195 in tolls, and have one"
6850 PRINT"chance in eight of avoiding weighing stations.  The danger"
6860 PRINT"of bad weather is high and the speed limit is vigorously"
6870 PRINT"enforced."
6880 GOSUB 8910:CLS
6890 PRINTTAB(26)"MIDDLE ROUTE":PRINT
6900 PRINTTAB(5)"The middle route follows old Route 66 through"
6910 PRINT"northern Arizona and Oklahoma into St. Louis.  From there"
6920 PRINT"you cut over to the Pennsylvania Turnpike.  Total distance"
6930 PRINT"to New York is 2,850 miles.  The toll road portions will cost"
6940 PRINT"you an extra $ 240 in fees.  This route has fewer police"
6950 PRINT"watching your speed and better weather than the Northern"
6960 PRINT"route.  However, watch your weight because there are"
6970 PRINT"usually several truck scales in operation."
6980 GOSUB 8910:CLS
6990 PRINTTAB(26)"SOUTHERN ROUTE":PRINT
7000 PRINTTAB(5)"The Southern route takes you on Interstate 10 through"
7010 PRINT"Arizona, New Mexico & Texas.  Then you follow Interstate 20"
7020 PRINT"to Atlanta before heading north to Washington D.C.  The"
7030 PRINT"last leg of your journey follows Interstate 95 up the Atlantic"
7040 PRINT"seaboard.  This route is the longest, at 3120 miles."
7050 PRINT"However, you avoid most of the bad weather and pay only $ 95"
7060 PRINT"in tolls.  You also will run into fewer police and fewer"
7070 PRINT"truck scales.  If you can't resist the temptation to take on"
7080 PRINT"an over-weight cargo or if you have a lead foot, then the"
7090 PRINT"southern route offers your best bet."
7100 GOSUB 8910:CLS
7110 PRINTTAB(26)"FINAL TIPS"
7120 PRINTTAB(5)"You've seen a long explanation and may be confused"
7130 PRINT"by now.  But don't worry, the game is easy to play.  After"
7140 PRINT"you have tried a few trips, you may want to review the"
7150 PRINT"explanations again to pick up hints for improving your"
7160 PRINT"profits.  On a good trip you will be able to earn over $1,000."
7170 PRINT"However, even the best drivers will run into occasional"
7180 PRINT"streaks of bad luck and barely break even."
7190 PRINTTAB(5)"When you play, the computer reports current conditions"
7200 PRINT"and events, and asks you to make decisions.  You simply"
7210 PRINT"type your answer then hit 'ENTER'.  For word answers, you"
7220 PRINT"can save time by typing only the first letter of the word."
7230 GOSUB 8910
7240 GOTO 1000
7990 END
8900 REM**
8910 PRINT@916,"PRESS ENTER TO CONTINUE";
8920 Z$=INKEY$:IF Z$=""THEN 8920 ELSE RETURN
9000 REM***   DATA
9030 DATA 21,2850
9040 DATA 90,BARSTOW,I-15 in California,7.80
9050 DATA225,NEEDLES,I-40 in California,1
9060 DATA 440,FLAGSTAFF,I-40 in Arizona,3.65
9070 DATA 620,GALLUP,I-40 in Arizona,5.5
9080 DATA 760,ALBUQUERQUE,I-40 in New Mexico,3.35
9090 DATA 930,TUCUMCARI,I-40 in New Mexico,1
9100 DATA 1040,AMARILLO,I-40 in Texas,7.80
9110 DATA 1155,OKLAHOMA Border,I-40 in Texas,5.5
```

```
9120 DATA 1305,OKLAHOMA CITY,I-40 in Oklahoma,2.65
9130 DATA 1530,MISSOURI Border,Oklahoma Turnpike,2.40
9140 DATA 1815,ST. LOUIS,I-44 in Missouri,0
9150 DATA 1980,TERRE HAUTE,I-70 in Illinois,5.5
9160 DATA 2050,INDIANAPOLIS,I-70 in Indiana,0
9170 DATA 2115,OHIO Border,I-70 in Indiana,1
9180 DATA 2220,COLUMBUS,I-70 in Ohio,5.5
9190 DATA 2350,WHEELING West Virginia,I-70 in Ohio,4.25
9200 DATA 2410,NEW STANTON,I-70 in Pennsylvania,6.75
9210 DATA 2570,HARRISBURG,Pennsylvania Turnpike,3.75
9220 DATA 2760,NEW JERSEY Border,Pennsylvania Turnpike,2.95
9230 DATA 2840,HOLLAND TUNNEL,I-70 in New Jersey,2.40
9240 DATA 9999,NEW YORK,New York Streets,0
9255 DATA 18,2710
9260 DATA 90,BARSTOW,I-15 in California,7.80
9270 DATA 245,LAS VEGAS,I-15 in California,1
9280 DATA 365,UTAH BORDER,I-15 in Nevada,0
9290 DATA 500,end of Interstate,I-15 in Utah,3.20
9300 DATA 555,SALINA,US-89 in Utah,4.50
9310 DATA 760,GRAND JUNCTION,I-70 in Utah,5.40
9320 DATA 1010,DENVER,I-70 in Colorado,3.75
9330 DATA 1190,NEBRASKA Border,I-76 in Colorado,1
9340 DATA 1450,OMAHA,I-80 in Nebraska,5.50
9350 DATA 1590,DEMOINES,I-80 in Iowa,4.75
9360 DATA 1750,ILLINOIS Border,I-80 in Iowa,5.6
9370 DATA 1910,GARY,I-80 in Illinois,2.50
9380 DATA 2050,OHIO Border,Indiana Turnpike,2.45
9390 DATA 2215,CLEVELAND,Ohio Turnpike,2.80
9400 DATA 2280,PENSYLVANIA Border,I-80 in Ohio,4.16
9410 DATA 2615,EAST STROUDSBERG,I-80 in Pennsylvania,3.33
9420 DATA 2675,WASHINGTON BRIDGE,I-80 in New Jersey,2.20
9430 DATA 9999,NEW YORK,City Streets,0
9450 DATA 25,3120
9460 DATA 75,PALM SPRINGS,I-10 in California,0
9470 DATA 225,BLYTHE,I-10 in California,1
9480 DATA 375,PHOENIX,I-10 in Arizona,0
9490 DATA 495,TUCSON,I-10 in Arizona,7.9
9500 DATA 650,LORDSBURG,I-10 in Arizona,5.75
9510 DATA 795,EL PASO,I-10 in New Mexico,0
9520 DATA 965,PECOS,I-10 in Texas,1
9530 DATA 1080,ODESSA,I-20 in Texas,0
9540 DATA 1250,ABILENE,I-20 in Texas,3.80
9550 DATA 1439,DALLAS,I-20 in Texas,0
9560 DATA 1610,LOUISIANA Border,I-20 in Texas,5.00
9570 DATA 1785,VICKSBURG,I-20 in Louisiana,0
9580 DATA 1965,ALABAMA Border,I-20 in Mississippi,1
9590 DATA 2100,BIRMINGHAM,I-20 in Alabama,4.25
9600 DATA 2200,GEORGIA Border,I-20 in Alabama,0
9610 DATA 2255,ATLANTA,I-20 in Georgia,0
9620 DATA 2320,CAROLINA Border,I-85 in Georgia,5.75
9630 DATA 2565,GREENSBORO,I-85 in North Carolina,3.80
9640 DATA 2680,VIRGINIA Border,I-85 in North Carolina,7.85
9650 DATA 2775,RICHMOND,I-85 in Virginia,0
9660 DATA 2880,WASHINGTON D.C.,I-95 in Virginia,0
9670 DATA 2920,BALTIMORE,I-95 in Maryland,2.30
9680 DATA 2990,NEW JERSEY Border,I-95 in Deleware,2.25
9690 DATA 3110,HOLLAND TUNNEL,New Jersey Turnpike,2.40
9700 DATA 9999,NEW YORK,City Streets,0
```

```
            INDEPENDENT TRUCKER SIMULATION
DO YOU WANT TO SEE INSTRUCTIONS? N
          Day: Monday              Time: 8 am

You are at the Los Angeles Trucking Terminal
Three types of cargo are available:
     1--ORANGES  (highest profit IF they don't spoil)
     2--FREIGHT FORWARDING   (penalty for late delivery)
     3--U.S. MAIL  (lowest rate, but no hurry to arrive)
The cargo is due in New York BY 4 pm on Thursday.
Which type of cargo do you want? 2
How many pounds will you carry (40000 is the LEGAL limit)? 45000

     They are loading your truck now.
          Day: Monday              Time: 9 am

You have nearly a full tank (cost of fuel: $ 190).
```

Trucker

Two of your tires are worn.
    Do you want replacements? Y
A NEW tire costs $200.   A RETREAD costs $100.
    Which type do you want? N
    How many? 3

You may choose the Northern, Middle or Southern route.
    Which route do you choose? M
Cruising on I-15 in California
You are feeling RESTED & REARING TO GO.
Current weather: CLEAR & DRY
How fast do you wish to go? 65
            Day: Monday   Time: 10 am
Approximate FUEL: 167   SPEED: 65
        Odometer: 65   Miles to go: 2785

Cruising on I-15 in California
You are feeling FINE
Current weather: CLEAR & DRY
How fast do you wish to go? 65
            Day: Monday   Time: 11 am
Approximate FUEL: 137   SPEED: 65
        Odometer: 130   Miles to go: 2720

You have just passed BARSTOW
Cruising on I-40 in California
You are feeling FINE
Current weather: CLEAR & DRY
How fast do you wish to go? 70
            Day: Monday   Time: 12 noon
Approximate FUEL: 103   SPEED: 70
        Odometer: 200   Miles to go: 2650

Cruising on I-40 in California
You are feeling FINE
Current weather: CLEAR & DRY
TRUCK STOP AHEAD.   Do you want to stop? N
How fast do you wish to go? 60
            Day: Monday   Time: 1 pm
Approximate FUEL: 84   SPEED: 60
        Odometer: 260   Miles to go: 2590

You have just passed NEEDLES
Time Zone changes -- Set clock ahead one hour
            Day: Monday   Time: 2 pm
Cruising on I-40 in Arizona
You are feeling FINE
Current weather: CLEAR & DRY
How fast do you wish to go? 65
            Day: Monday   Time: 3 pm
Approximate FUEL: 64   SPEED: 65
        Odometer: 325   Miles to go: 2525

Cruising on I-40 in Arizona
You are feeling   B O R E D
Current weather: CLEAR & DRY
How fast do you wish to go? 55
            Day: Monday   Time: 4 pm
Approximate FUEL: 50   SPEED: 55
        Odometer: 380   Miles to go: 2470

Cruising on I-40 in Arizona
You are feeling   B O R E D
Current weather: CLEAR & DRY
TRUCK STOP AHEAD.   Do you want to stop? Y
Diesel fuel costs 97 cents a gallon.
    How many gallons do you want? 150
PAY $145.50
So far, you have spent $ 935.5
Do you want to get some sleep? N
            Day: Monday   Time: 5 pm
How fast do you wish to go? 55
            Day: Monday   Time: 6 pm
Approximate FUEL: 186   SPEED: 55
        Odometer: 435   Miles to go: 2415

Cruising on I-40 in Arizona
You are feeling   B O R E D

Current weather: CLEAR & DRY
How fast do you wish to go? 65
            Day: Monday   Time: 7 pm
Approximate FUEL: 162   SPEED: 65
        Odometer: 500   Miles to go: 2350

You have just passed FLAGSTAFF
Cruising on I-40 in Arizona
You are feeling   B O R E D
Current weather: CLEAR & DRY
How fast do you wish to go? 63
            Day: Monday   Time: 8 pm
Approximate FUEL: 139   SPEED: 63
        Odometer: 563   Miles to go: 2287

Cruising on I-40 in Arizona
You are feeling   T I R E D !!
Current weather: CLEAR & DRY
How fast do you wish to go? 60
            Day: Monday   Time: 9 pm
Approximate FUEL: 123   SPEED: 60
        Odometer: 623   Miles to go: 2227

You have just passed GALLUP
WEIGHING STATION OPEN   -- TRUCKS MUST STOP
Scale weighs truck with cargo, fuel & driver:
    64,910 POUNDS.
        Overweight fine is $ 200 plus 3 cents/pound
Pay fine of 347.3
Cruising on I-40 in New Mexico
You are feeling   T I R E D !!
Current weather: CLEAR & DRY
TRUCK STOP AHEAD.   Do you want to stop? Y
Diesel fuel costs 85 cents a gallon.
    How many gallons do you want? 177
PAY $150.45
So far, you have spent $ 1333.25
The tank holds 200 gallons-- 99 gallons spilled!
Do you want to get some sleep? Y
    How many hours of rest? 8
            Day: Tuesday   Time: 6 am
Time to hit the road again.
You now have 200 gallons of fuel.
Do you want to buy more? N
How fast do you wish to go? 65
            Day: Tuesday   Time: 7 am
Approximate FUEL: 178   SPEED: 65
        Odometer: 688   Miles to go: 2162

Cruising on I-40 in New Mexico
You are feeling RESTED & REARING TO GO.
Current weather: CLEAR & DRY
How fast do you wish to go? 65
            Day: Tuesday   Time: 8 am
Approximate FUEL: 149   SPEED: 65
        Odometer: 753   Miles to go: 2097

Cruising on I-40 in New Mexico
You are feeling RESTED & REARING TO GO.
Current weather: CLEAR & DRY
How fast do you wish to go? 90
You can only get the old rig to go 82 mph on
    this road.
            Day: Tuesday   Time: 9 am
Approximate FUEL: 106   SPEED: 82
        Odometer: 835   Miles to go: 2015

You have just passed ALBUQUERQUE
CONSTRUCTION AHEAD !!
SLOW DOWN -- SPEED LIMIT 35 mph
Cruising on I-40 in New Mexico
You are feeling FINE
Current weather: CLEAR & DRY
How fast do you wish to go? 82
You can only get the old rig to go 52 mph on
    this road.
            Day: Tuesday   Time: 10 am
Approximate FUEL: 89   SPEED: 52
        Odometer: 887   Miles to go: 1963

Trucker

Cruising on I-40 in New Mexico
You are feeling FINE
Current weather: CLEAR & DRY
TRUCK STOP AHEAD.   Do you want to stop? Y
Diesel fuel costs 96 cents a gallon.
      How many gallons do you want? 111
PAY $106.56
So far, you have spent $ 1439.81
The tank holds 200 gallons-- 4 gallons spilled!
Do you want to get some sleep? N
              Day: Tuesday   Time: 11 am
How fast do you wish to go? 90
You can only get the old rig to go 82 mph on
    this road.
              Day: Tuesday   Time: 12 noon
Approximate FUEL: 161   SPEED: 82
        Odometer: 969   Miles to go: 1881

You have just passed TUCUMCARI
Time Zone changes -- Set clock ahead one hour
              Day: Tuesday   Time: 1 pm
Cruising on I-40 in Texas
You are feeling FINE
Current weather: CLEAR & DRY
How fast do you wish to go? 80
SMOKEY is behind you with his lights on.
PULL OVER!
See the JUSTICE of the PEACE for your First offense
    Wait 1 hours for your hearing
    FINE is $ 20 plus $ 2 for each MPH over the limit.
    PAY $ 70
              Day: Tuesday   Time: 3 pm
Approximate FUEL: 118   SPEED: 80
        Odometer: 1049   Miles to go: 1801

You have just passed AMARILLO
Cruising on I-40 in Texas
You are feeling FINE
Current weather: CLEAR & DRY
How fast do you wish to go? 65
              Day: Tuesday   Time: 4 pm
Approximate FUEL: 91   SPEED: 65
        Odometer: 1114   Miles to go: 1736

Cruising on I-40 in Texas
You are feeling   B O R E D
Current weather: CLEAR & DRY
How fast do you wish to go? 65
              Day: Tuesday   Time: 5 pm
Approximate FUEL: 70   SPEED: 65
        Odometer: 1179   Miles to go: 1671

You have just passed OKLAHOMA Border
WEIGHING STATION OPEN -- TRUCKS MUST STOP
Scale weighs truck with cargo, fuel & driver:
    64,494 POUNDS.
      Overweight fine is $ 200 plus 6 cents/pound
Pay fine of 469.64
Cruising on I-40 in Oklahoma
You are feeling   B O R E D
Current weather: CLEAR, but roadway is wet
TRUCK STOP AHEAD.   Do you want to stop? Y
Diesel fuel costs 101 cents a gallon.
      How many gallons do you want? 130
PAY $131.30
So far, you have spent $ 2010.75
Do you want to get some sleep? NNO
              Day: Tuesday   Time: 6 pm
How fast do you wish to go? 65
              Day: Tuesday   Time: 7 pm
Approximate FUEL: 172   SPEED: 65
        Odometer: 1244   Miles to go: 1606

Cruising on I-40 in Oklahoma
You are feeling   B O R E D
Current weather: CLEAR & DRY
How fast do you wish to go? 65
              Day: Tuesday   Time: 8 pm
Approximate FUEL: 145   SPEED: 65

Odometer: 1309   Miles to go: 1541

You have just passed OKLAHOMA CITY
STOP!   PAY TOLL of $65.00
Cruising on Oklahoma Turnpike
You are feeling   B O R E D
Current weather: CLEAR & DRY
How fast do you wish to go? 70
              Day: Tuesday   Time: 9 pm
Approximate FUEL: 113   SPEED: 70
        Odometer: 1379   Miles to go: 1471

Cruising on Oklahoma Turnpike
You are feeling   T I R E D !!
Current weather: CLEAR & DRY
How fast do you wish to go? 60
              Day: Tuesday   Time: 10 pm
Approximate FUEL: 94   SPEED: 60
        Odometer: 1439   Miles to go: 1411

Cruising on Oklahoma Turnpike
You are feeling   T I R E D !!
Current weather: CLEAR, but roadway is wet
TRUCK STOP AHEAD.   Do you want to stop? Y
Diesel fuel costs 115 cents a gallon.
      How many gallons do you want? 106
PAY $121.90
So far, you have spent $ 2197.65
The tank holds 200 gallons-- 1 gallons spilled!
Do you want to get some sleep? Y
      How many hours of rest? 8
              Day: Wednesday   Time: 7 am
Time to hit the road again.
You now have 200 gallons of fuel.
Do you want to buy more? N
How fast do you wish to go? 65
              Day: Wednesday   Time: 8 am
Approximate FUEL: 172   SPEED: 65
        Odometer: 1504   Miles to go: 1346

Cruising on Oklahoma Turnpike
You are feeling RESTED & REARING TO GO.
Current weather: CLEAR & DRY
How fast do you wish to go? 65
              Day: Wednesday   Time: 9 am
Approximate FUEL: 151   SPEED: 65
        Odometer: 1569   Miles to go: 1281

You have just passed MISSOURI Border
STOP!   PAY TOLL of $40.00
Cruising on I-44 in Missouri
You are feeling RESTED & REARING TO GO.
Current weather: CLEAR, but roadway is wet
How fast do you wish to go? 65
              Day: Wednesday   Time: 10 am
Approximate FUEL: 127   SPEED: 65
        Odometer: 1634   Miles to go: 1216

Cruising on I-44 in Missouri
You are feeling FINE
Current weather: CLEAR & DRY
How fast do you wish to go? 65
              Day: Wednesday   Time: 11 am
Approximate FUEL: 97   SPEED: 65
        Odometer: 1699   Miles to go: 1151

Cruising on I-44 in Missouri
You are feeling FINE
Current weather: CLEAR & DRY
TRUCK STOP AHEAD.   Do you want to stop? N
How fast do you wish to go? 65
              Day: Wednesday   Time: 12 noon
Approximate FUEL: 72   SPEED: 65
        Odometer: 1764   Miles to go: 1086

Cruising on I-44 in Missouri
You are feeling FINE
Current weather: CLEAR & DRY
How fast do you wish to go? 65

```
              Day: Wednesday          Time: 1 pm
Approximate FUEL: 46                  SPEED: 65
              Odometer: 1829     Miles to go: 1021

You have just passed ST. LOUIS
Cruising on I-70 in Illinois
You are feeling FINE
Current weather: RAIN
How fast do you wish to go? 55
              Day: Wednesday          Time: 2 pm
Approximate FUEL: 32                  SPEED: 55
              Odometer: 1884     Miles to go: 966

Cruising on I-70 in Illinois
You are feeling   B O R E D
Current weather: CLEAR & DRY
TRUCK STOP AHEAD.   Do you want to stop? Y
Diesel fuel costs 103 cents a gallon.
      How many gallons do you want? 168
PAY $173.04
So far, you have spent $ 2410.69
Do you want to get some sleep? N
              Day: Wednesday          Time: 3 pm
How fast do you wish to go? 65
              Day: Wednesday          Time: 4 pm
Approximate FUEL: 174                 SPEED: 65
              Odometer: 1949     Miles to go: 901

Cruising on I-70 in Illinois
You are feeling   B O R E D
Current weather: CLEAR & DRY
How fast do you wish to go? 65
              Day: Wednesday          Time: 5 pm
Approximate FUEL: 147                 SPEED: 65
              Odometer: 2014     Miles to go: 836

You have just passed TERRE HAUTE
WEIGHING STATION OPEN  --  TRUCKS MUST STOP
Scale weighs truck with cargo, fuel & driver:
      65,211 POUNDS.
      Overweight fine is $ 200 plus 6 cents/pound
Pay fine of 512.66
Cruising on I-70 in Indiana
You are feeling   B O R E D
Current weather: FOG -- Limited visibility
How fast do you wish to go? 55
              Day: Wednesday          Time: 6 pm
Approximate FUEL: 139                 SPEED: 55
              Odometer: 2069     Miles to go: 781

You have just passed INDIANAPOLIS
Cruising on I-70 in Indiana
You are feeling   B O R E D
Current weather: CLEAR & DRY
How fast do you wish to go? 65
              Day: Wednesday          Time: 7 pm
Approximate FUEL: 111                 SPEED: 65
              Odometer: 2134     Miles to go: 716

You have just passed OHIO Border
Time Zone changes -- Set clock ahead one hour
              Day: Wednesday          Time: 8 pm
Cruising on I-70 in Ohio
You are feeling   T I R E D  !!
Current weather: CLEAR & DRY
TRUCK STOP AHEAD.   Do you want to stop? Y
Diesel fuel costs 115 cents a gallon.
      How many gallons do you want? 90
PAY $103.50
So far, you have spent $ 2926.85
Do you want to get some sleep? Y
      How many hours of rest? 8
              Day: Thursday           Time: 5 am
Time to hit the road again.
You now have  200 gallons of fuel.
Do you want to buy more? N
How fast do you wish to go? 65
              Day: Thursday           Time: 6 am
Approximate FUEL: 176                 SPEED: 65
```

```
Odometer: 2199        Miles to go: 651

Cruising on I-70 in Ohio
You are feeling RESTED & REARING TO GO.
Current weather: CLEAR & DRY
How fast do you wish to go? 65
              Day: Thursday           Time: 7 am
Approximate FUEL: 148                 SPEED: 65
              Odometer: 2264     Miles to go: 586

You have just passed COLUMBUS
Cruising on I-70 in Ohio
You are feeling RESTED & REARING TO GO.
Current weather: B-L-I-Z-Z-A-R-D  !!
How fast do you wish to go? 55
              Day: Thursday           Time: 8 am
Approximate FUEL: 132                 SPEED: 55
              Odometer: 2319     Miles to go: 531

Cruising on I-70 in Ohio
You are feeling FINE
Current weather: CLEAR, but roadway is wet
How fast do you wish to go? 65
              Day: Thursday           Time: 9 am
Approximate FUEL: 113                 SPEED: 65
              Odometer: 2384     Miles to go: 466

You have just passed WHEELING West Virginia
You were just clocked by RADAR at 64 mph
SMOKEY is behind you with his lights on.
PULL OVER!
See the JUSTICE of the PEACE for your Second
      offense
      Wait 2 hours for your hearing
      FINE is $ 20 plus $ 6 for each MPH over the
      limit.
      PAY $ 80
Cruising on I-70 in Pennsylvania
You are feeling FINE
Current weather: RAIN
TRUCK STOP AHEAD.   Do you want to stop? N
How fast do you wish to go? 82
SMOKEY is behind you with his lights on.
      PULL OVER!
See the JUSTICE of the PEACE for your Third
      offense
      Wait 3 hours for your hearing
      FINE is $ 30 plus $ 9 for each MPH over the
      limit.
      PAY $ 273
              Day: Thursday           Time: 3 pm
Approximate FUEL: 70                  SPEED: 82
              Odometer: 2466     Miles to go: 384

You have just passed NEW STANTON
Cruising on Pennsylvania Turnpike
You are feeling   B O R E D
Current weather: CLEAR & DRY
How fast do you wish to go? 65
              Day: Thursday           Time: 4 pm
Approximate FUEL: 44                  SPEED: 65
              Odometer: 2531     Miles to go: 319

Cruising on Pennsylvania Turnpike
You are feeling   T I R E D  !!
Current weather: CLEAR & DRY
How fast do you wish to go? 65
              Day: Thursday           Time: 5 pm
Approximate FUEL: 18                  SPEED: 65
              Odometer: 2596     Miles to go: 254

You have just passed HARRISBURG
Cruising on Pennsylvania Turnpike
You are feeling   T I R E D  !!
Current weather: CLEAR, but roadway is wet
TRUCK STOP AHEAD.   Do you want to stop? Y
Diesel fuel costs 113 cents a gallon.
      How many gallons do you want? 182
PAY $205.66
```

Trucker

So far, you have spent $ 3485.51
Do you want to get some sleep? N
        Day: Thursday   Time: 6 pm
How fast do you wish to go? 65
        Day: Thursday   Time: 7 pm
Approximate FUEL: 173   SPEED: 65
     Odometer: 2661   Miles to go: 189

Cruising on Pennsylvania Turnpike
You are feeling T I R E D !!
Current weather: CLEAR, but roadway is wet
How fast do you wish to go? 60
        Day: Thursday   Time: 8 pm
Approximate FUEL: 155   SPEED: 60
     Odometer: 2721   Miles to go: 129

Cruising on Pennsylvania Turnpike
You are feeling T I R E D !!
Current weather: CLEAR & DRY
How fast do you wish to go? 65
        Day: Thursday   Time: 9 pm
Approximate FUEL: 135   SPEED: 65
     Odometer: 2786   Miles to go: 64

You have just passed NEW JERSEY Border
STOP!   PAY TOLL of $95.00
Cruising on I-70 in New Jersey
You are feeling FATIGUED...You're getting sleepy
Current weather: CLEAR & DRY
How fast do you wish to go? 64
        Day: Thursday   Time: 10 pm
Approximate FUEL: 105   SPEED: 64
     Odometer: 2850   Miles to go: 0

You have just passed HOLLAND TUNNEL
STOP!   PAY TOLL of $40.00
Cruising on New York Streets
You are feeling FATIGUED...You're getting sleepy
Current weather: CLEAR & DRY
TRUCK STOP AHEAD.   Do you want to stop? N

How fast do you wish to go? 20
WELCOME
TO
NEW YORK
WELCOME
TO
NEW YORK
WELCOME
TO
NEW YORK
WELCOME
TO
NEW YORK
WELCOME
TO
NEW YORK
        Day: Thursday   Time: 11 pm

You completed the trip in 3 days & 15 hours.
   Trip expenses totaled 3620.51
   Truck payments, Insurance & Taxes cost 425

Collect five cents a pound for freight.
   Total for load = 2700

BAD TRIP. . . You lost 1345.51
   You are BANKRUPT !!!

Your rig has been repossessed.

How To Write An Adventure Game

by Greg Hassett

As I gazed back at the crystal bridge that I had just crossed, I could hear water rushing nearby. My brass lantern was getting dim, and I knew that I would have to rest soon. The wisps of white mist danced before my eyes as if alive, and a sudden cold chill ran up my spine. I had with me a diamond necklace which I was determined to keep. A nasty dwarf emerged from the gloom. He threw a sharp knife at me! I grabbed my axe and heaved it at him. His body vanished in a cloud of greasy black smoke. My lamp was now out; I would have to search for batteries tomorrow in the dark. So I put my necklace in my small leather sack and called it a day.

I did not lie down on the cavern floor and go to sleep. I merely turned off my home computer. I had been play a game called "Adventure." In this game, you explore a network of caves and pits in search of priceless treasure. This game is not the type of game which is mastered in an hour. It may take days, weeks, or even months to complete an Adventure.

This "original Adventure," developed at Stanford University a few years back by Willie Crowther and Don Woods, required large amounts of disk storage space. This made it very difficult to convert to run on a personal computer. However, other versions of Adventure have sprung up in the past year that are specifically designed to fit in the smaller machines.

To play Adventure, you enter commands to the computer in one- or two-word sentences in what seems to be English. A typical command might be "INSERT COIN" or "GET NECKLACE." To move about, you use commands such as "GO NORTH" or enter a new "location," and a new room description will be displayed. An example of such a description might be:

I AM IN A RADIANT CAVERN FORTY FEET HIGH. THE WALLS AND FLOORS ARE MADE OF SMOOTH MARBLE. THE POOLS OF CLEAR WATER ON THE FLOOR INDICATE AN OPENING HIGH ABOVE ME. UP ON THE CEILING GLOWS AN EERIE RED LIGHT.

AROUND ME I SEE: POOLS OF WATER. SMALL PLASTIC VIAL. . . .

Later on in the game, the vial might come in handy for holding some liquid, etc., so in this situation it might be wise to "GET VIAL."

The one thing that I feel makes Adventuring so interesting is the clues that are given as you explore.

Knowing that clues exist is one thing; isolating them and figuring out what they mean is quite another. In Adventure, clues exist *everywhere.* They are in the room descriptions, the object descriptions. Let's say you enter a room where there are many stalactites, but no stalagmites on the floor. This in itself is clue. If you think about it, stalagmites could be worn off if creatures lived there and walked through the cavern.

But stalactites would not be destroyed because most creatures cannot reach them.

Then there are the type of clues which have to be decoded. As an example, take the clue "MAGIC BREAK WORD BOTTLE BIMBO." This clue makes no sense at first glance. But then you notice that if you read alternate words of the clue, it deciphers into "MAGIC WORD BIMBO" and "BREAK BOTTLE."

Magic words are very popular in Adventure. A common use for these words is movement. They might be the only way to get to a completely different area of the Adventure. For example, in one Adventure the magic word "BIMBO" will magically take you from being lost in a maze of caves to a small jungle on the other side of an island. And there is no other way to get there.

In this way, Adventure is like a good mystery novel, with you being the ace detective. On the other hand, Adventure can be nerve-wracking, frustrating, and the source of serious insomnia! Adventure is a sort of puzzle . . . you have to fit *all* the pieces together to make it work.

I was first introduced to Adventure a few years back on a Digital Equipment Corporation PDP-11/70. I took an immediate liking to the game, but I didn't own a computer. When I purchased my Radio Shack TRS-80, I immediately set out to write an Adventure. The result was my first original Adventure, *Journey to the Center of the Earth*. When I found out I could sell this, I wrote six other Adventures: *The House of Seven Gables, Entry into King Tut's Tomb, Sorcerer's Castle, Voyage to Atlantis, Enchanted Island,* and *Enchanted Island-Plus* (a machine-language version with additional features).

If there's one thing that's more habit-forming than playing Adventures, it's writing them.

Writing Adventures

What follows is an attempt to outline the basic structure of the way an Adventure can be written in Basic.

The first step in writing a Basic Adventure is coming up with the plot. This means answering the questions:

"Where will the Adventure take place?"

"What will be the main purpose of the Adventure?"

"In what kind of world is this supposedly happening?"

"What types of obstacles will the player have to overcome?"

"How is the player going to get by these obstacles?"

Once these five questions are answered in your mind, you begin to draw the map of the Adventure. The general form of the map is shown in Figure 1. Once you have about 40 rooms (more if you are in machine language), you are ready to begin keying in the DATA. The way I do this is in the form:

line# DATA "room description",n,e,s,w,u,d

where line# is the Basic statement number, "room description" is the description of the room, n is the room north of it, e is the room east of it, s is the room south of it, etc. If n,e,s,w,u,or d are set to zero, then there is no way to go from that room in the corresponding direction.

The objects are set up somewhat differently. They are in the form:

line# DATA "object", (room),(value)

where line# is the Basic statement number, "object" is the description of the object, (room) is the room where the object resides at the start of the Adventure, and (value) [if the Adventure has treasures and points] is the number of points that the object is worth. If (room) is set to zero, then the object is currently nowhere. For instance, if a trap door is only revealed after the command "MOVE RUG" is executed, the starting room for the "TRAP DOOR" is zero. Later on, after the rug is moved, the trap door's room gets set to some number other than zero.

During the initial setup of the Adventure, the program READs all of this DATA into arrays P(x), P(x,y), OB$(x), and OB(x,y). P$(x) holds the room description of room x. P(x,y) holds the room adjacent to room x in direction y. Direction 1 = North, direction 2 = East, direction 3 = South, direction 4 = West, direction 5 = Up, and direction 6 = Down. Also, after all of the room and object DATA has been read, the program proceeds to READ the vocabulary tables into arrays NO$(x) and VB$(x). The vocabulary is stored in this manner:

line# DATA noun1,noun2,noun3,
noun4, . . . noun x

line#2 DATA verb1, verb2, verb3,
verb4, . . . verbx

where line# and line#2 are Basic statement numbers, noun1–nounx are the vocabulary entries to be read into NO$(x) [nouns], and verb1–verbx are the vocabulary entries to be read into VB$(x) [verbs].

When the player enters a new room, the short routine in Listing 1 is executed. This will print the room description, its contents, and all possible directions leading out.

Parsing

Now that the Data Structure has been discussed, it becomes necessary to explain the parsing routine. This is the routine which will take the player's input, divide it into a verb/noun combination, compare it with the vocabulary tables, and return with two numbers, stored in the variables VB and NO, each representing the offset in the vocabulary array. For instance, let's assume that "EAT" is verb number 28 [VB$(28)="EAT"] and "CHAIR" is noun number 12 [NO $(12)= "CHAIR"]. If the player inputs "EAT CHAIR" as his command, the parsing routine would get called, and upon return, NO would equal 12 and VB would equal 28. The main part of the program would then deal with these two numbers. Depending on the number stored in VB upon return from the parsing routine, the main part of the program would then jump to a verb routine.

Verb Routines

Each verb has its own special "verb routine" which is called by a large ON GOTO statement executed after the parsing routine. For each verb, there are usually only a few nouns which would make sense. For instance, for the "EAT" routine, "CHAIR" would have no meaning. In all probability, only the

noun "FOOD" would make any sense with "EAT." If any other noun was entered, the message "DON'T BE RIDICULOUS" would be output, and control would return to the input/parsing routine. If the noun *was* "FOOD," then the room# for the food would be set to zero [the food is nonexistent once it has been eaten] and the message "MMM, GOOD." would be output. Control would then be transferred back to the input/parsing routine.

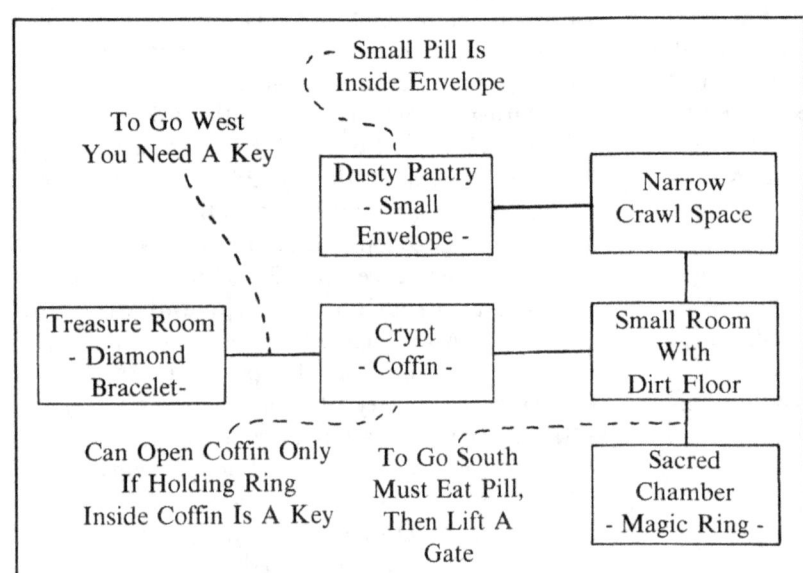

Figure 1: A typical portion of an Adventure map. Note that to get into the treasure room for the diamond bracelet, you must get the magic ring. To get the magic ring, you must eat the pill, then lift a gate. To eat the pill, you must open the envelope found in the dusty pantry.

```
1000 'BASIC ROUTINE TO DISPLAY ROOM & ITS CONTENTS
1010 '
1020 'UPON ENTRY:
1030 '    CP=THE CURRENT PLACE IN THE ADVENTURE
1040 '    LO=THE MAXIMUM NUMBER OF OBJECTS IN THE ADVENTURE
1050 '    D$(1)='NORTH' , D$(2)='SOUTH' , D$(3)='EAST'
1060 '    D$(4)='WEST'  , D$(5)='UP'    , D$(6)='DOWN'
1070 '
1080 '
1090 CLS 'CLEAR SCREEN
1100 PRINT P$(CP) 'PRINT THE ROOM DESCRIPTION
1110 FOR I=1 TO LO 'THIS ROUTINE WILL PRINT ALL OBJECTS IN ROOM
1120 IF OB(I,0)=CP THEN PRINT OB$(I) 'IN ROOM? YES... PRINT IT
1130 NEXT I 'GO ON TO THE NEXT OBJECT
1140 FOR I=1 TO 6 'THIS ROUTINE WILL PRINT ALL POSSIBLE DIRECTIONS
1150 IF P(CP,I) <> 0 THEN PRINT D$(I) 'NOT ZERO? YES, PRINT D$(I)
1160 NEXT I 'GO ON TO NEXT DIRECTION
1170 PRINT STRING$(63,'-') 'PRINT BAR ACROSS SCREEN
1180 RETURN 'RETURN
```

Listing 1—Basic listing of how the "display room" routine works. Note that all arrays must be set up as described in the text. The OB(x,0) array holds the room # of object x. Note line 1120, where this value is compared with the current room number. Each object is "tested" in this fashion.

Adventures in Videoland

by David Lubar

Frame One: *Editorial meetings, luck runs out, and a sweep through the Augean stables.*

With the right misuse of eye contact, it's possible to survive a meeting intact and leave without any awesome assignments. The meeting in question was almost over when the words, "I've been saving the best assignment for last," put a choke hold on my spirit of survival. No doubt, the phrase was aimed in my direction. Realizing that the meaning of "best" varies considerably, depending on who is doing the besting, I tore my gaze from the toy robots on the bookshelf and waited to see what the boss had in mind. Since previous assignments had run the range from covering conferences to reviewing printers, there was no way to predict what might come. The suspense was short-lived.

"I want you to write a videodisc adventure," the boss said in the casual manner usually associated with phrases such as "please pass the butter."

"Need it by tomorrow?" I asked.

"For January." End of topic.

Could be fun, I thought, though I had never written an adventure or toyed with the fringes of video technology. This project would require three-part harmony between an Apple computer, a Pioneer Laserdisc player, and an Aurora Systems Interface. A vague suspicion that I was in over my head prompted a stroll down to the software department. After trying all available personnel, it was obvious that no one there could be talked into whitewashing the fence. Looked like the job was mine. Since the November issue was still under construction, I put the video project on temporary hold, hoping the subconscious would start the work.

Frame Two: *Dissected disc, death of procrastination, and the birth of a framework.*

November doesn't last forever. The harbinger of flying time came in the form of a memo. While I had been blithely trying to forget the project, the boss had been busy. He had taken side one of the movie *Rollercoaster* and compiled two pages of notes listing the frame numbers for every scene. At this point, it dawned on me that he really wanted the program. I got down to work, keeping an eye open for an easy way out.

The first problem was figuring a way to write the program in Basic while avoiding the long delays associated with that language. Taking a shot at modular programming, I started by writing units that would handle essential tasks, such as gathering and parsing input, in an efficient manner. Since actual work with the disc player and interface would require a trip to the boss's house, I wanted to finish as much of the programming as possible before taking the act up to the Fortress of Solitude. This situation, coupled with the eternal search for the easy way out, gave birth to the adventure framework, described at the end of this chapter. Since the idea is fairly simple, and has most likely been developed more than once in the past, I make no claims of great originality here.

The framework handles all the procedures that are common to most adventures. It is, in essence, a gofer, keeping track of a player's moves and the location of objects, and handling common commands such as "GET" and "DROP." By plugging in a couple buckets full of variables, any adventurous realm could be defined. The task of creating a specific adventure now seemed less monstrous (and next year, when they invent the neutrino disc, I'll be able to write a neutrino adventure in record time).

Frame Three: *Onward to Olympus, empathy for hermits, and getting down to the hard stuff.*

I hit the mansion on the hill early one Monday morning, ready to wrestle with technology. The boss flipped a handful of switches, powering up computer, disc player, television, and stereo, while dimming lights throughout the neighborhood. After showing me how to use the interface and disc player, the boss left for the office, and I was on my own. Being alone in someone else's house is a rather strange experience, which I will not dwell on here. It should suffice to say that I trod gently so as not to risk breaking the carpet.

The first and easiest task was watching the movie. This not only helped pass the time, but gave me a glimpse of scenes that could be used in the adventure. *Rollercoaster,* for those of you who missed the movie, concerns an extortionist who plants bombs on rollercoaster tracks, merry-go-rounds, and other fun places. The movie occupies five sides of three discs. The side used for the adventure contains good scenes of carnival rides and explosions, making it highly suitable for an action adventure.

Having checked out the scenery, I started getting acquainted with the interface. The software included a short machine-language driver that could be called from Basic. Instructions went from computer to interface via the USR command. As the video-disc obeyed my commands, I felt like Archimedes lunging from the tub. This was POWER. I was the demigod of the disc, making it fulfill my every whim. It all seemed too easy. I could search for frames, play sequences, switch from computer to video display, do almost anything except make it roll over and beg.

As is the way in life, there was rain on this parade. Since the precipitation occurred later that day, I won't go into it now. With spirits still undampened, I started mapping the adventure, trying to create a scenario that could best exploit the available video. Thanks to the framework, the rooms and objects were plugged in fairly quickly. While the game wouldn't have the magnitude of Crowther and Wood's colossal cave, it would have enough locations to allow the player to get lost once or twice before catching on.

Frame Four: *The problem with adventures, an emergency guide to dairy substitutes, and the coming of the rain.*

The problem with the average adventure is that it is linear, frustrating, and ultimately boring. The first one is fun, the second entertaining, but after that the novelty wears thin. I realized I could either put a lot of hard work behind my feelings on the subject and pro-

duce a different sort of adventure, or rely on the novelty of the video to save the day. Following the sage advice of Occam's Razor and other convenient laws of laziness, I took the easy way out and stuck with the standard adventure format.

This sort of work definitely called for vast quantities of coffee, which led to the following discovery. If you are ever out of milk and sugar, but have peppermint stick ice cream in the freezer, try some in the coffee. It's not bad.

Having mapped the adventure, I was ready to add some video. As a start, I decided to display a still frame or sequence for each location. I wrote a short parser that would take strings of command codes and send them to the interface. The routine can be found starting at line 40000 in the main program. (If the code at 40000 is replaced with a RETURN, the game can be played without a videodisc, though lack of visuals makes it as exciting as watching salt dissolve.)

Once the visuals were defined, I tried a test run. After giving instructions, the game displayed a scene of the carnival midway. So far, so good. I went east. The disc player whirred. The wrong picture came up. A few tests produced the following realization: the computer is a lot faster than the disc player. If you send commands to search for frame 12345, you might get frame 135. To compensate for this, I added delays to the video parser. Now that the disk had time to digest the whole command, another problem appeared. Commands are not buffered by the interface; they are executed immediately. Sinking into the mind of the disc player, the process goes something like this: *Hey, I gotta search for frame 20123. O.K., I'm on my way. Half-way there. Getting closer. Almost there. Hey, a PLAY command. Here goes.* Thus Mr. Disc doesn't care if the search is finished. The PLAY command takes priority, giving whatever scene was under the beam at the moment. Enter more delay loops. End result: no matter how quickly the main code executes, there are inevitable delays associated with calling frames from the videodisc.

Frame Five: *Meat on the bones, shooting ducks, and an end to modularity.*

With the rooms mapped out and the video stuffed in, the next task was to add all those conditional actions that turn an adventure from a Sunday drive into a real game. In the real world, most problems have more than one solution. In an ideal adventure, any intelligent input should be greeted with an intelligent response. Any attempt to introduce such reality into a program would probably lead to either insanity or an OUT OF MEMORY error. Keeping this in mind, I first added routines to check for any commands that were required for the player to win. Any such input caused the program to jump to the appropriate subroutine. Had all this been planned out beforehand, these subroutines would be neatly organized into meaningful groups. Since I was creating as I went along, the structure of the program suffered somewhat.

To add a bit of spice to the game, I tossed in some more video scenes to go along with special actions. If the player tries his hand at the shooting gallery, he sees metal ducks being flattened. If he tampers with a certain box, he is rewarded with a view of the rollercoaster being blown off the tracks.

By the end of the second day, the game was approaching finished form. All correct moves were recognized, and some incorrect moves produced special responses. So much for the easy part.

Frame Six: *Error checks, custom changes, and the true meaning of déjà vu.*

While the programmer in the role of game creator must try to anticipate various inputs, the programmer in the role of debugger has to create all possible situations. This can be a rather tedious process. Seeing the same scenes over and over is rather akin to drowning. Eventually, self-preservation overcame perfectionism, and I decided that all the bugs were eliminated. Though this is never true, the thought can be comforting. Leaving the message "Play me" on the diskette sleeve, I packed it in for the day.

I was eager to learn the boss's reaction to the program. "Not bad," he told me the next day, "though I do have a few changes to suggest."

I looked at the three pages of notes, feeling some empathy for the ancient mariner, Sisyphus, and other bearers of long sentences. A close inspection reavealed that most of the changes would not be difficult. "I'll take a shot at it," I told him, trying not to give signs of relief.

Back at the Fortress, I plugged in the changes and started another round of error checks. By the end of the afternoon, I could close my eyes and see rollercoasters. But the program was finished. In an odd way, the project had almost been fun.

Frame Seven: *Conclusions, the future of video, and the meaning of it all.*

Naturally, there is a post natal pleasure associated with the completion of any programming task. After the glow dims, some questions remain. Was the project worth doing? Did it accomplish the desired functions? The main goal was to try an experiment with a fairly new technology. Here I feel partial failure. The new medium was used in an old way. Beyond the video scenes, the program is just another adventure. It was as if I had been given Vulcan's forge and used it to produce a souped-up Ford Pinto. Despite the racing stripes and whitewalls, it's still a compact car. But the exercise has convinced me of the potential power of the video–computer connection. The fusion of these two devices will produce some spectacular results. Rather than add to existing concepts, people will create applications that open new areas, merging computers and video rather than just tacking picture to program. The rollercoaster ride has just begun.

An Adventure Framework

There are two key parts to the framework; the input routine and the partial parser. Rather than use an INPUT statement, each character is obtained with GET. This has several advantages. First, each character can be checked on entry. Second, commas won't cause an EXTRA IGNORED error message. Finally, there is plenty of time between each character to process the preceding one. With INPUT, the program receives the whole phrase at once and any processing has to be done after the user has hit return. To separate a two-word phrase, the program would have to search through the input string for a space, adding to the delay time. On the other hand the GET routine can immediately identify a space and define anything prior to it as the first word of input. The rest of the routine just traps illegal characters and checks for controls such as the back arrow or return. For back arrows, the routine erases characters as the cursor crosses them.

The input routine accepts one or two words, but no more. In its present form, it accepts only letters. It could be easily modified to recognize other characters if required. Upon returning from the input routine, there is a horrendous ON A GOSUB command with twenty-six parameters for the variable A. This causes the program to branch to different lines depending on the first letter of the command. While such a solution might be considered inelegant, it cuts down the delay considerably. Once the branch has been made, the program has just a few possible keywords for which to check.

Next, I took the basic concepts encountered in an adventure (moving, picking up, and dropping objects, examining objects, and looking at a location), and designed the framework in such a way that objects and rooms could be changed with little effort. For movement, I limited the program to four directions; adding up and down would be easy if required later. The rooms were given two identifiers, a number from 1 to 26 and the corresponding letter of the alphabet. For each room, there is a string containing the rooms that can be reached by going north, east, south, and west. Disallowed directions are marked by a null character.

This information, stored in an array called RS, serves not only to determine where a person would end up, but also for printing visible exits.

There are two other string arrays associated with rooms. The RM$ array contains a brief description of each room. RD$ contains a complete description. By separating them, it is possible to print a full description the first time a person enters a room, and a short description if he returns. (I ended up printing the full description each time since most weren't that long.)

Objects are also held in an array, OB$, and another array, OB, contains the location of each object. OB holds either a room number, a zero if the person has the object, or a negative number if the object is out of play. This is the same sort of technique used in most Basic adventures.

One further concept was the use of variables for what I consider "furniture." This would cover objects that can't be taken but can be examined. Furniture is contained in the array FR$, its description is in FD$, and FL contains it location. If the value of FL is zero, that furniture can occur in any location. For example, if all rooms have walls, FR$ would be WALL, FD$ might be "IT IS MADE OF STONE AND CONTAINS NO CRACKS OR MARKINGS" and FL would be 0. Since the routines for LOOK and TAKE check through both objects and furniture, these two sets of arrays must have the same value, even if the higher numbers of one set aren't used.

The rest is reasonably straightforward. Once rooms and objects have been taken care of, routines need only be added to handle special situations. Note that the LOOK routine checks to see whether an object is either in the player's possession or in the same room as he. This avoids the frustration encountered when a player wants to examine something and is told he isn't carrying it. The general framework, with dummy room and object definitions, is given in Listing 2 for those who might want to construct their own adventures.

The Roller Coaster Game Explained   *by David H. Ahl*

"Over my dead body you will!" This was the response I got from David Lubar when I suggested running a map of the *Rollercoaster* game with the information as to what is found in each spot.

His reasoning was that the game could be played by someone whether they had a videodisc player or not. The only difference is that a person with a videodisc player and interface would be able to see the motion sequences where other players would merely have them described by the computer program.

My reasoning was that this is the first computer/videodisc game ever published and that if it is going to be part of the entertainment wave of the future, we ought to share as much information about it as possible.

My reasoning prevailed and, thus, you are reading this article. Mr. Lubar was last heard saying, "Mutter, mutter, you're the publisher."

Flash Back

Ever since I saw an experimental videodisc player from Phillips/MCA in 1975 and published three articles about video discs in March of 1976, I have been enthusiastic about the medium. More recently, I have gotten very excited about the possibilities for computer programs which take advantage of the videodisc. Many educators and people involved in industrial training are working in similar directions. However, my thoughts were more in the area of home entertainment.

In particular, I imagined an adventure-type game based on the movie *Jaws*. I haven't quite worked out the entire scenario, however, I envision a scene where a shark is about to attack and is swimming toward you with his jaws wide open when the screen goes blank and you are asked for a decision. Make the right decision, and the shark would back off, probably in reverse slow motion and you would see it recede into the ocean. Make the wrong decision and, of course, you get eaten and lose the game. Or, you might invoke magic which would transform you to an entirely different time and place. If you did this, you might or might not lose some of the objects you have gained and you might be posed with an entirely different yet of problems based on your new location.

I envisioned using portions of the soundtrack with only the computer output visible on the screen. I also saw opportunities for the player to put in his own search coordinates (a frame number) not knowing, of course, what was there beforehand. Based on what he finds in a particular location, he must continue the game from that point. Thus, I envisioned a very open-ended type of game as opposed to the completely structured adventures and other games that exist today.

Can it all be done? I think so. We are, of course, starting in a much more structured way. However, I believe that this game will give you some idea of what the capabilities are of marrying the computer with the videodisc.

How the Game Works

After showing the appropriate title graphics, the player is told that a madman has planted a bomb on a rollercoaster. At this point a 10-second scene of the bomb being planted is shown. A message flashes back which states that you, the player, are being sent to stop the saboteur. At this point a 10-second sequence of a plane landing is shown followed by some additional introductory messages.

After this, you find yourself in a central area of the midway. (See diagram.) Some of the video sequences (both still frames and motion sequences) are activated by going to a new place in the game-playing area. Other video sequences are activated by picking up an object or giving some other command. For example, the command "Wear Uniform" triggers a still frame of the groundskeeper in a uniform.

Still other video sequences are triggered as part of a sequence of events over which a player has no control. For example, if you crawl too far out on the coaster track, you are shown a scene of the empty track follwed by a computer message that says "The sound of the coaster is getting very loud." This is immediately followed by a scene of the coaster passing by after knocking you unconcious. This triggers one of the alternate end-of-game routines and you are given the opportunity to play again.

Possible Extensions

The mind boggles with the possible extensions to a videodisc/computer game. For example, the way the game is written now, the bomb explodes if the player tampers with the electronic device in the Aid Station. A possible alternative: by turning the knob on the device you discover that it is an alien time warp machine and that it reverses time for ten seconds. You might see the rollercoaster going backwards or people walking backwards on the midway for the next ten seconds. Used in the adventure, you might have to find a detonator, take it to the Aid Station and explode the bomb, make time go backwards and un-explode the bomb in order to find out on what frequency the detonator works so that you are able to construct a jammer.

Of course, there are many, many possible extensions. One side of the videodisc has over 50,000 individual frames on it and the disc of *Rollercoaster* that we used for this adventure, has over 120 separate motion sequences on the first side. Thus, it should be apparent that we are just scratching the surface with the game as it currently exists.

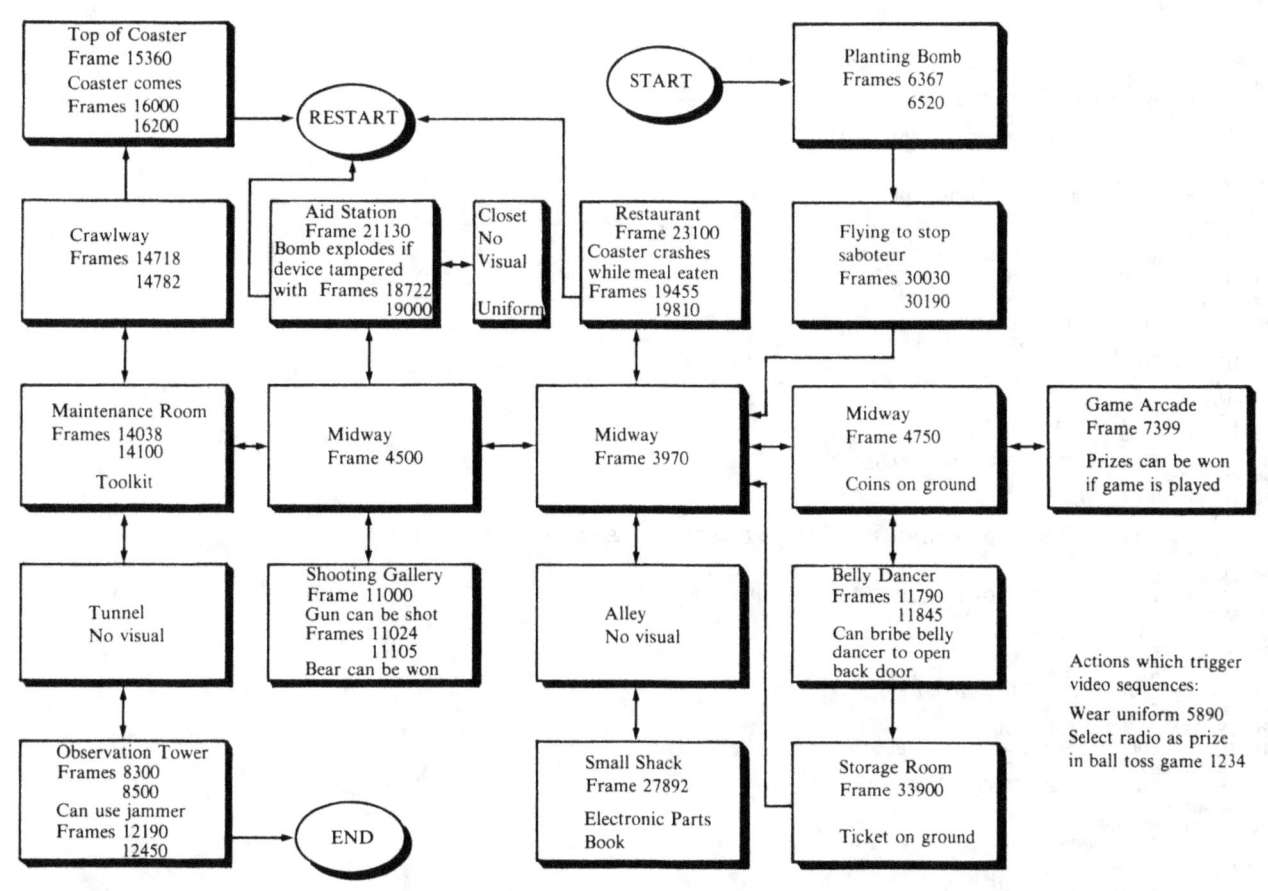

Location Map of Rollercoaster Videodisc/Computer Game

```
   1 GOSUB 30000: REM   INITIALIZE
   2 GOSUB 34000: REM INSTRUCTIONS
   3 GOSUB 22000: REM DISPLAY 1ST ROOM
  10 GOSUB 1000: REM INPUT ROUTINE
  30 IF NOT SPACE THEN
        V$=A$
  40 IF A$=" " THEN 10
  45 PRINT: PRINT
  50 IF ASC(V$)=32 AND LEN(V$)>1 THEN
        V$=RIGHT$(V$,LEN(V$)-1): A$=RIGHT$(A$,LEN(A$)-1): GOTO 50
  60 IF LEN(V$)=LEN(A$) THEN
        NFLAG=0: GOTO 90
  70 N$=RIGHT$(A$,LEN(A$)-LEN(V$))
  80 IF ASC(N$)=32 AND LEN(N$)>1 THEN
        N$=RIGHT$(N$,LEN(N$)-1): GOTO 80
  85 IF N$=" " THEN
        NFLAG=0
  90 A=ASC(V$)-64
 100 IF A<1 OR A>26 THEN 10
 110 ON A GOSUB 10100,10200,10300,10400,10500,10600,10700,10800,10900,11000,
        11100,11200,11300,11400,11500,11600,11700,11800,11900,12000,12100,12200,
        12300,12400,12500,12600
 120 IF NOT KW THEN
        PRINT "I DON'T KNOW HOW TO DO THAT": KW=1
 125 T=T+1:
        IF T>150 THEN
        INVERSE: PRINT "I THINK TIME JUST RAN OUT": NORMAL: T=0: VC$=
        "S16000SXP": GOSUB 40000: GOTO 50000
 130 PRINT: GOTO 10
1000 A$=" ": SPACE=0: N$=" ": V$=" ": NFLAG=1
1010 GET B$:
        IF ASC(B$)=13 THEN
        RETURN
1020 IF ASC(B$)=8 AND SPACE AND RIGHT$(A$,1)=" " THEN
        SPACE=0
1025 IF LEN(A$)=1 AND B$=" " THEN 1010
1030 IF ASC(B$)=8 AND LEN(A$)>1 THEN
        A$=LEFT$(A$,LEN(A$)-1): PRINT B$;" ";B$;: GOTO 1010
1040 IF B$=" " AND NOT SPACE THEN
        V$=A$: SPACE=1: GOTO 1060
1050 IF ASC(B$)<65 OR ASC(B$)>91 THEN 1010
1060 PRINT B$;
1070 A$=A$+B$
1080 GOTO 1010
9999 REM FOLLOWING ROUTINES ACT ON THE INPUT. KW IS  KEYWORD FLAG
10100 KW=0: RETURN
10200 IF A$="BREAK BOX" THEN 53000
10210 IF A$="BREAK DOOR" THEN
        PRINT "TOO SOLID TO EVEN TRY": RETURN
10299 KW=0: RETURN
10300 KW=0: RETURN
10400 IF V$="DROP" AND NFLAG THEN 26000
10499 KW=0: RETURN
10500 IF A$="E" THEN
        D=2: GOTO 20000
10501 IF V$="EXAMINE" AND NFLAG THEN 27000
10599 KW=0: RETURN
10600 IF A$="FIND BATTERIES" THEN
        PRINT "TRY THE BEAR": RETURN
10610 IF V$="FIND" THEN
        PRINT "I CAN'T HELP YOU": RETURN
10699 KW=0: RETURN
10700 IF V$="GO" THEN 19000
10710 IF A$="GIVE COINS" AND L=5 THEN 43000
10720 IF A$="GIVE TICKET" AND L=16 THEN 48000
10799 KW=0: RETURN
10800 IF V$="HELP" THEN
        PRINT
        "JUST KEEP MOVING AND EXAMINING THINGS, AND AVOID DANGEROUS PLACES. ":
        RETURN
10899 KW=0: RETURN
10900 IF A$="I" OR A$="INV" OR A$="INVENTORY" THEN 24000
10999 KW=0: RETURN
11000 IF V$="JAM" THEN 54000
11099 KW=0: RETURN
11100 IF V$="KILL" THEN
        PRINT "THAT IS BEYOND MY POWER. ": RETURN
11199 KW=0: RETURN
11200 IF A$="LOOK" THEN 22000
11210 IF V$="LOOK" AND NFLAG THEN 27000
11299 KW=0: RETURN
11300 IF A$="MAKE JAMMER" THEN 55000
11399 KW=0: RETURN
11400 IF A$="N" THEN
        D=1: GOTO 20000
11499 KW=0: RETURN
11500 IF A$="OPEN BEAR" THEN
        PRINT "TWO BATTERIES JUST FELL ": PRINT "OUT OF THE BACK. ": PRINT
        "THEY'RE ON THE GROUND": OB(11)=L: RETURN
11599 KW=0: RETURN
```

```
11600 IF (V$="PUT" OR V$="PLACE") AND NFLAG THEN 28000
11610 IF V$="PLAY" AND L=6 THEN 43000
11620 IF V$="PLAY" AND L=16 THEN 48000
11630 IF (A$="PUSH BUTTON" OR A$="PRESS BUTTON") AND L=2 THEN 53000
11699 KW=0: RETURN
11700 IF A$="QUIT" THEN
        END
11799 KW=0: RETURN
11800 IF (A$="READ BOOK") AND (OB(4)=0 OR OB(4)=L) THEN
        PRINT "YOU NOW KNOW HOW TO MAKE A": PRINT "JAMMER FROM A RADIO": BK=1:
        RETURN
11810 IF A$="READ TICKET" THEN
        A$="LOOK TICKET": GOTO 27000
11899 KW=0: RETURN
11900 IF A$="S" THEN
        D=3: GOTO 20000
11910 IF V$="SHOOT" THEN 43000
11920 IF A$="SHOW TICKET" AND L=16 THEN 48000
11999 KW=0: RETURN
12000 IF V$="TAKE" AND NFLAG THEN 25000
12010 IF (A$="TURN KNOB" OR A$="TURN DIAL") AND L=2 THEN 53000
12099 KW=0: RETURN
12100 IF A$="USE JAMMER" THEN 54000
12199 KW=0: RETURN
12200 IF A$="VISIT DANCER" THEN
        PRINT "SHE DOESN'T WANT TO SEE YOU": RETURN
12299 KW=0: RETURN
12300 IF A$="W" THEN
        D=4: GOTO 20000
12310 IF (A$="WEAR UNIFORM") AND (OB(9)=0 OR OB(9)=L) THEN
        VC$="S5890SX": GOSUB 40000:
        FOR I=1 TO 1000:
        NEXT I:
        VC$="X": GOSUB 40000: PRINT "IT FITS WELL AND MAKES A GOOD": PRINT
        "DISGUISE": KW=1: RETURN
12399 KW=0: RETURN
12400 KW=0: RETURN
12500 KW=0: RETURN
12600 POP: STOP: REM DEBUGGING AID.  INPUT OF Z STOPS PROGRAM.
19000 REM   PARSER FOR DIRECTION
19010 D=ASC(N$): D=(D=78)+(D=69)*2+(D=83)*3+(D=87)*4:
        IF NOT D THEN
        PRINT "I NEED A DIRECTION. ": RETURN
20000 REM MOVE ROUTINE:D=DIRECTION:R=ROOM MOVED INTO:L=PRESENT LOCATION
20060 R=ASC(MID$(R$(L),D,1))-64
20070 IF NOT R THEN
        PRINT "YOU CAN'T GO THAT WAY": RETURN
20080 L=R
22000 IF RND(1)>.6 AND A$="LOOK" THEN
        VC$="S2550SX":
        FOR I=1 TO LEN(VC$):
          A=USR(ASC(MID$(VC$,I,1))):
          FOR J=1 TO 400:
          NEXT J:
        NEXT I:
        FOR I=1 TO 4000:
        NEXT I:
        A=USR(ASC("X"))
22001 IF V$(L)<>"" THEN
        VC$=V$(L): GOSUB 40000:
        FOR I=1 TO 4000:
        NEXT I:
        V$(L)="": VC$="XZ": GOSUB 40000
22005 PRINT "YOU ARE IN ";
22010 PRINT RM$(L): PRINT RD$(L): PRINT "THIS LOCATION CONTAINS ";: F1=0
22020 FOR I=1 TO NO
22030    IF OB(I)=L THEN
            PRINT OB$(I): F1=1
22040 NEXT I:
        IF NOT F1 THEN
        PRINT "NOTHING"
22050 PRINT "VISIBLE EXITS: ";
22060 FOR I=1 TO 4
22070    IF MID$(R$(L),I,1)<>"@" THEN
            PRINT DIR$(I);"  ";: F1=1
22080 NEXT I:
        IF NOT F1 THEN
        PRINT "DON'T EXIST"
22081 PRINT:
        IF L=5 THEN 41000
22082 IF L=8 THEN 47000
22083 IF L=15 THEN 47100
22084 IF L=18 THEN
        PRINT
        "YOU FOLLOW A WINDING PATH, FINALLY        RETURNING TO FAMILIAR GROUND":
        L=1: GOTO 22000
22085 IF L=9 THEN 49000
22090 RETURN
24000 F1=0: PRINT "YOU ARE CARRYING":
        FOR I=1 TO NO
```

```
24010    IF OB(I)=0 THEN
             PRINT OB$(I): F1=1
24020 NEXT I:
      IF NOT F1 THEN
          PRINT "NOTHING"
24030 RETURN
25000 F1=0: F2=0:
      FOR I=1 TO NO
25005    IF N$=OB$(I) AND OB(I)=0 THEN
             PRINT "YOU ALREADY HAVE THE ";N$: RETURN
25010    IF (N$=OB$(I) OR N$="ALL" OR N$="EVERYTHING") AND (OB(I)=(L)) THEN
             OB(I)=0: PRINT OB$(I);" TAKEN": F1=1
25020    IF N$=OB$(I) THEN
             F2=1
25025 NEXT I
25030 IF F1=0 AND F2=0 AND N$<>"ALL" AND N$<>"EVERYTHING" THEN
          PRINT "I CAN'T TAKE THE ";N$: RETURN
25035 IF F1=0 AND F2=0 THEN
          PRINT "THERE IS NOTHING HERE I CAN TAKE."
25040 IF F1=0 AND F2=1 THEN
          PRINT "I DON'T SEE IT HERE."
25060 RETURN
26000 F1=0:
      FOR I=1 TO NO
26010    IF (OB$(I)=N$ OR N$="ALL" OR N$="EVERYTHING") AND (OB(I)=(0))
            THEN OB(I)=L: F1=1
26020 NEXT I
26030 IF NOT F1 THEN
          PRINT "YOU CAN'T DROP WHAT YOU AREN'T CARRYING": RETURN
26040 PRINT "OK": RETURN
27000 F1=0:
      FOR I=1 TO NO
27010    IF (OB(I)=0 OR OB(I)=L) AND (OB$(I)=N$) THEN
             F1=1: PRINT OD$(I):
             IF OD$(I)="" THEN
                 PRINT "I SEE NOTHING IMPORTANT.": RETURN
27020    IF (FL(I)=(L) OR FL(I)=0) AND (FR$(I)=N$) THEN
             F1=1: PRINT FD$(I):
             IF FD$(I)="" THEN
                 PRINT "NOTHING EXTRAORDINARY HERE": RETURN
27030    IF F1 THEN
             RETURN
27040 NEXT I
27050 PRINT "I CAN'T DESCRIBE THAT"
27060 RETURN
28000 FOR I=1 TO NO
28010    IF N$<>OB$(I) OR OB(I)<>0 THEN
             NEXT I:
             PRINT "YOU AREN'T CARRYING THE ";N$: RETURN
28090 PRINT "WHERE?"
28095 T$=N$
28100 GOSUB 1000
28102 N$=T$
28105 PRINT
28106 IF A$=" DOWN" THEN 26000
28110 IF V$<>" IN" AND V$<>" ON" THEN
          PRINT "I CAN'T DO THAT": RETURN
28115 T$=RIGHT$(A$,LEN(A$)-LEN(V$))
28116 IF LEFT$(T$,1)=" " AND LEN(T$)>1 THEN
          T$=RIGHT$(T$,LEN(T$)-1)
28117 IF T$="FLOOR" OR T$="TABLE" THEN 26000
28120 FOR I=1 TO NO
28130    IF T$<>OB$(I) OR (OB(I)<>L AND OB(I)<>0) THEN
             NEXT I:
             PRINT "THE ";T$;" ISN'T HERE": RETURN
28140 PRINT "OK":
      IF (T$="RADIO" OR T$="JAMMER") AND N$="BATTERIES" THEN
          B=1
28200 RETURN
30000 DIM OB(12),OB$(12),RM$(18),RD$(18),R$(18),OD$(12),FR$(12),FL(12),FD$(12),
      V$(18)
30001 RM$(1)="THE MIDWAY": RM$(2)="THE FIRST AID STATION": RM$(3)="THE MIDWAY":
      RM$(4)="THE MIDWAY": RM$(5)="A RESTAURANT": RM$(6)="A SHOOTING GALLERY"
30002 RM$(7)="A MAINTAINANCE ROOM": RM$(8)="THE BELLY DANCER'S TENT": RM$(9)=
      "THE TOP OF THE ROLLER COASTER": RM$(10)="A CLOSET"
30003 RM$(11)="AN ALLEY": RM$(12)="THE OBSERVATION TOWER": RM$(13)=
      "A CRAWLWAY": RM$(14)="A STORAGE ROOM": RM$(15)="A SMALL SHACK": RM$(16)=
      "A GAME BOOTH": RM$(17)="A NARROW TUNNEL": RM$(18)=
      "A DARK, TWISTING PATH"
30010 R$(1)="EDKC": R$(2)="@JC@": R$(3)="B@FG": R$(4)="@PHA": R$(5)="@@@@":
      R$(6)="C@@@": R$(7)="MC@@": R$(8)="D@N@": R$(9)="@@M@"
30011 R$(10)="@@@B": R$(11)="A@@@": R$(12)="@@@@": R$(13)="I@G@": R$(14)=
      "@@@R": R$(15)="K@@@": R$(16)="@@@D": R$(17)="G@L@": R$(18)="@@@@"
30020 L=1: NO=12
30030 OB$(1)="COINS": OB$(2)="TOOLKIT": OB$(3)="TICKET": OB$(4)="BOOK": OB$(5)=
      "LAMP": OB$(6)="TOWELS": OB$(7)="POSTER": OB$(8)="BEAR"
30031 OB$(9)="UNIFORM": OB$(10)="RADIO": OB$(11)="BATTERIES": OB$(12)="JAMMER"
30040 OB(1)=4: OB(2)=7: OB(3)=14: OB(4)=15: OB(5)=-1: OB(6)=-1: OB(7)=-1:
      OB(8)=-1
30045 OB(9)=10: OB(10)=-1: OB(11)=-1: OB(12)=-1
```

```
30050 DIR$(1)="NORTH": DIR$(3)="SOUTH": DIR$(2)="EAST": DIR$(4)="WEST"
30060 RD$(1)=
      "WHICH STRETCHES TO THE EAST AND WEST. A RESTAURANT IS TO THE NORTH"
30061 RD$(2)=
      "CONTAINING STRANGE EQUIPMENT. LIGHTS    FLASH FROM AN ELECTRONIC BOX"
30062 RD$(3)=
      "AN AID STATION IS TO THE NORTH. THE       SOUND OF GUNFIRE COMES FROM A SH
      OOTING  GALLERY TO THE SOUTH. "
30063 RD$(4)="FROM A TENT TO THE SOUTH YOU HEAR EXOTICMUSIC"
30064 RD$(5)="THE ROOM IS CROWDED BUT YOU SEE AN EMPTYTABLE IN THE CORNER"
30065 RD$(6)="A SIGN READS '3 SHOTS FOR 25 CENTS'"
30066 RD$(7)=
      "THERE ARE DOORS TO THE NORTH AND SOUTH. THE NORTHERN DOOR IS OPEN. YOU C
      AN HEAR THE ROLLER COASTER. "
30067 RD$(8)="SHE STOPS AND LOOKS AT YOU"
30068 RD$(9)="A DANGEROUS PLACE TO BE. "
30069 RD$(10)="": RD$(11)=
      "THERE IS A DOOR LEADING TO A SMALL ROOM TO THE SOUTH"
30070 RD$(12)=
      "BELOW, YOU CAN SEE THE WHOLE CARNIVAL.   THE TOP OF THE ROLLER COASTER IS
          IN      SIGHT. "
30071 RD$(13)=
      "THE PASSAGE LEADS NORTH TO THE TOP OF    THE ROLLER COASTER. THE NOISE IS
          QUITE  LOUD"
30072 RD$(14)=
      "THE DOOR IS LOCKED BEHIND YOU, BUT THEREIS A WINDOW TO THE WEST"
30073 RD$(15)=
      "THE ROOM IS LITTERED WITH FRAGMENTS OF  ELECTRONIC PARTS, BUT NONE OF IT
      IS      SALVAGEABLE.  A GUARD BLOCKS YOUR PATH"
30074 RD$(16)="A SIGN SAYS, '50 CENTS A BALL. WINNER'S CHOICE.'"
30075 RD$(17)="THE PASSAGE LEADS SOUTH TO THE TOP OF   THE OBSERVATION TOWER"
30100 OD$(1)="TWO DIMES AND A NICKEL": OD$(2)=
      "IT CONTAINS EVERYTHING NEEDED FOR SMALL ELECTRONIC REPAIRS"
30101 OD$(4)="THE TITLE IS 'RADIO FREQUENCY JAMMING   TECHNIQUES": OD$(5)=
      "IT IS VERY GAUDY": OD$(6)="NICE AND FLUFFY": OD$(7)=
      "WHOOPIE--IT'S THE DALLAS CHEERLEADERS": OD$(8)=
      "WHEN YOU PUSH THE BUTTON ON ITS BACK, ITSAYS 'I WUV YOU'"
30102 OD$(3)=
      "IT SAYS, 'GOOD FOR 1 FREE GAME AT THE    BALL TOSS, COURTESY OF CREATIVE
              COMPUTING, THE #1 MAGAZINE OF SOFTWARE  AND APPLICATIONS.'"
30200 FR$(1)="BOX": FD$(1)=
      "IT IS FIRMLY ATTACHED TO THE TABLE. THERE ARE KNOBS AND A BUTTON ON IT":
      FL(1)=(2)
30201 FR$(2)="RIFLE": FL(2)=6: FD$(2)="IT IS CHAINED TO THE COUNTER"
30202 FR$(3)="GUN": FL(3)=6: FD$(3)="IT IS CHAINED TO THE COUNTER"
30300 V$(1)="S3970SPX": V$(2)="S21130SX": V$(3)="S4500SX": V$(4)="S4750SX"
30310 V$(5)="S23100SX": V$(6)="S11000SX": V$(7)="S14038SPXA": V$(8)=
      "S11790SPX": V$(9)="S15360SXP"
30320 V$(10)="": V$(12)="S8300SPX": V$(13)="S14718SPX": V$(14)="S33900SX":
      V$(15)="S27892SX": V$(16)="S7399SX"
30330 V$(17)="": V$(18)=""
30400 KW=1
31000 IF PEEK(3*256)<>32 THEN
          PRINT "D^BLOAD VIDEO.CODE": POKE 10,76: POKE 11,9: POKE 12,3
32000 RETURN
34000 VC$="S6367S": GOSUB 40000: TEXT: HOME: REM GET TO FIRST VIDEO FRAME AHEAD
      OF TIME. PLAYER SHOULD BE ON BEFORE RUNNING PROGRAM
34001 PRINT "WHAT IS YOUR FIRST NAME?": GOSUB 1000: NA$=A$
34010 PRINT: PRINT "YOU HAVE JUST RECEIVED AN ANONYMOUS": PRINT
      "TIP THAT A BOMB HAS BEEN PLANTED": PRINT "ON A ROLLER COASTER. ":
      FOR I=1 TO 1000:
      NEXT I
34011 VC$="S6367S": GOSUB 40000:
      FOR I=1 TO 2000:
      NEXT I:
      VC$="PX": GOSUB 40000:
      FOR I=1 TO 15200:
      NEXT I
34012 VC$="XZ": GOSUB 40000
34015 PRINT: PRINT "YOU ARE CALLED TO INVESTIGATE AND FLY": PRINT
      "OFF TO STOP THE SABOTEUR. ":
      FOR I=1 TO 1000:
      NEXT I
34016 VC$="S30030S": GOSUB 40000:
      FOR I=1 TO 6000:
      NEXT I:
      VC$="PX": GOSUB 40000:
      FOR I=1 TO 9000:
      NEXT I
34017 VC$="XZ": GOSUB 40000
34018 PRINT
34020 PRINT "ON HIS SIDE, HE HAS THE BRILLIANCE OF": PRINT
      "AN INSANE MIND, AND THE AID OF ALLIES": PRINT
      "WHO ARE DETERMINED TO SEE THAT YOU FAIL"
34030 PRINT: PRINT "ON YOUR SIDE, YOU HAVE CUNNING, ": PRINT
      "TRAINING, AND DEDICATION"
34055 PRINT: PRINT "YOU HAVE INFILTRATED THE PARK  WITH": PRINT
      "THE KNOWLEDGE THAT THE SABOTEUR": PRINT "WILL STRIKE SOMETIME TONIGHT":
      PRINT: PRINT "ALL YOU NEED DO IS STOP HIM. "
34056 PRINT: INVERSE: PRINT "PRESS ANY KEY TO CONTINUE";: GET A$: NORMAL: HOME
```

Adventures in Videoland

```
34060 PRINT "BY GIVING THE RIGHT COMMAND, YOU CAN ": PRINT
      "MOVE, EXAMINE OBJECTS, AND PERFORM ": PRINT "OTHER ACTIONS"
34070 PRINT "I UNDERSTAND TWO-WORD COMMANDS SUCH AS": PRINT
      "'DROP BOOK' OR 'TAKE KNIFE'.": PRINT
      "TO MOVE, YOU CAN SIMPLY ENTER 'N' FOR": PRINT "NORTH, ETC."
34080 PRINT: PRINT "AT TIMES, I WILL AWAIT YOUR COMMAND": PRINT
      "IN OTHER SITUATIONS, I WILL PRESENT YOU": PRINT
      "WITH A CHOICE OF ACTIONS": PRINT "BUT SUCCESS OR FAILURE IS UP TO YOU."
34090 PRINT: INVERSE: PRINT "PRESS ANY KEY TO BEGIN. MAY LUCK BE": PRINT
      "WITH YOU, ":NA$: GET A$: NORMAL: PRINT: RETURN
40000 FOR I=1 TO LEN(VC$):
      A=USR(ASC(MID$(VC$,I,1)))
40010   IF MID$(VC$,I,1)="S" AND I>1 THEN
          FOR J=1 TO 6500:
          NEXT J
40020   FOR J=1 TO 400:
          NEXT J:
      NEXT I:
      RETURN
41000 PRINT: PRINT "A WAITER APPROACHES AND ASKS IF YOU": PRINT
      "WOULD LIKE A SEAT": PRINT: PRINT "SINCE YOU MISSED LUNCH TODAY, YOU":
      PRINT "ARE HUNGRY"
41010 PRINT: PRINT "DO YOU WANT TO EAT?": GOSUB 1000
41020 IF A$<>" NO" AND A$<>" YES" THEN
          PRINT "PLEASE ANSWER YES OR NO": GOTO 41010
41025 PRINT
41030 IF A$=" NO" THEN
          PRINT "THE WAITER CALLED YOU A STIFF": PRINT "AND THREW YOU OUT": L=3:
          GOTO 22000
41040 PRINT: PRINT "YOU ARE SERVED A DELICIOUS MEAL": PRINT
      "UNFORTUNATELY, THE SERVICE IS": PRINT "RATHER SLOW": VC$="S19455SPX":
      GOSUB 40000:
      FOR I=1 TO 12000:
      NEXT I:
      VC$="XZ": GOSUB 40000
41045 PRINT
41050 PRINT "THE BOMB WENT OFF AND THE BOMBER ESCAPED":
      FOR I=1 TO 3000:
      NEXT I:
      GOTO 50000
43000 IF OB(1)<>0 THEN
          PRINT "THE MAN BEHIND THE COUNTER TELLS": PRINT
          "YOU, 'IF YOU WANNA PLAY YOU GOTTA PAY.'": RETURN
43010 PRINT "YOU HAND OVER THE COINS AND PICK": PRINT "UP THE GUN": OB(1)=-1
43020 VC$="S11024SXP": GOSUB 40000:
      FOR I=1 TO 3000:
      NEXT I:
      VC$="XZ": GOSUB 40000
43030 PRINT "GOOD SHOOTING": PRINT "HE HANDS YOU A TEDDY BEAR": OB(8)=0
43035 PRINT "A PASSERBY LOOKS AT THE BEAR AND": PRINT
      "SAYS, 'MODERN NONSENSE. WHAT EVER      HAPPENED TO SIMPLE STUFFED ANIMA
      LS?'": PRINT "HE SHAKES HIS HEAD AND LEAVES."
43040 RETURN
47000 PRINT:
      IF OB(8)<>0 THEN
          PRINT "SHE SAYS YOU CAN'T COME IN UNLESS YOU HAVE A PRESENT FOR HER":
          PRINT "SHE PUSHES YOU OUT. ": L=4: GOTO 22000
47005 IF OB(8)=-2 THEN
          PRINT
          "SHE SAYS, 'YOU THINK ONE PRESENT ENTITLES YOU TO COME IN HERE ANY TIME
          YOU WANT?'": PRINT "SHE TURNS HER BACK AND IGNORES YOU.": RETURN
47010 PRINT "SHE LETS YOU IN AND EYES THE BEAR. ": PRINT
      "DO YOU WANT TO GIVE IT TO HER? ": GOSUB 1000
47020 PRINT:
      IF A$<>" Y" AND A$<>" YES" THEN
          PRINT "SHE THROWS YOU OUT": L=4: GOTO 22000
47030 OB(8)=-2: PRINT "SHE UNLOCKS THE DOOR TO THE SOUTH"
47040 RETURN
47100 IF OB(9)<>0 THEN
          PRINT "HE SAYS, 'EMPLOYEES ONLY' AND THROWS YOU OUT": L=11: GOTO 22000
47110 PRINT "HE SEES YOUR UNIFORM AND LETS YOU IN"
47120 RETURN
48000 IF OB(3)<>0 THEN
          PRINT "YOU CAN'T AFFORD THE GAME": RETURN
48010 PRINT "YOU HAND OVER THE TICKET AND THROW THE  BALL.": PRINT "G^G^G^":
      PRINT "IT'S A WINNER.": PRINT "YOU HAVE A CHOICE OF FOUR PRIZES:"
48020 PRINT "A LAMP, TOWELS, RADIO, OR POSTER."
48030 PRINT "WHICH DO YOU WANT?": GOSUB 1000
48040 A$=RIGHT$(A$,LEN(A$)-1):
      FOR I=5 TO 10
48050   IF OB$(I)=A$ THEN
          OB(I)=0: PRINT: PRINT "IT'S YOURS":
          IF A$="RADIO" THEN
              VC$="S1234SX": GOSUB 40000:
              FOR I=1 TO 1000:
              NEXT I:
              VC$="X": GOSUB 40000: RETURN
48060 NEXT I:
      PRINT: PRINT "PLEASE ANSWER WITH LAMP, RADIO OR TOWEL.": GOTO 48030
```

Adventures in Videoland

```
49000 INVERSE: SPEED=200: PRINT "IF YOU LOOK BACK, YOU'LL NOTICE": PRINT
      "A CAR SPEEDING TOWARD YOU": VC$="S16000SXPAAXZ"
49010 NORMAL: SPEED=255: GOSUB 40000: GOTO 50000
50000 HOME: VTAB 10: PRINT "IT IS ONE YEAR LATER": PRINT
      "THE ROLLER COASTER HAS BEEN REBUILT": PRINT
      "THE SABOTEUR PLANS TO DESTROY IT AGAIN": PRINT
      "WOULD YOU LIKE TO TRY TO SAVE IT?"
50010 GOSUB 1000: PRINT
50020 IF A$=" YES" OR A$=" Y" THEN
      GOSUB 30001: GOTO 22000
50030 IF A$<>" N" AND A$<>" NO" THEN
      PRINT "YES OR NO":: GOSUB 1000: PRINT: GOTO 50020
50040 END
53000 PRINT "UH OH, I THINK THAT WAS A MISTAKE": VC$="S18722S2SXPAAAAXZ": GOSUB
      40000: PRINT "YOU SET OFF THE BOMB":
      FOR I=1 TO 2000:
      NEXT I:
      GOTO 50000
54000 IF L<>12 THEN
      PRINT "YOU AREN'T IN LINE OF SIGHT WITH": PRINT "THE ROLLER COASTER":
      RETURN
54010 IF OB(12) THEN
      PRINT "YOU DON'T HAVE A JAMMER": RETURN
54020 IF NOT B THEN
      PRINT "IT DOESN'T WORK. MAYBE IT NEEDS BATTERIES": RETURN
54030 VC$="S12190SPX": GOSUB 40000:
      FOR I=1 TO 8000:
      NEXT I:
      VC$="XZ": GOSUB 40000
54040 HOME: VTAB 10: HTAB 12: INVERSE: SPEED=100: PRINT "CONGRATULATIONS":
      NORMAL: PRINT: HTAB 6: PRINT "YOU SAVED THE ROLLER COASTER": SPEED=255:
      END
55000 IF NOT BK THEN
      PRINT "YOU DON'T KNOW HOW": RETURN
55010 IF OB(10)<>0 THEN
      PRINT "SOMETHING VITAL IS MISSING": RETURN
55020 IF OB(2)<>0 THEN
      PRINT "YOU DON'T HAVE THE REQUIRED TOOLS": RETURN
55030 PRINT "CONGRATULATIONS, YOU NOW HAVE A ": PRINT "JAMMER": OB(10)=-1:
      OB(12)=0: RETURN
```

Adventure Framework

This is not *a playable game as is. It is a framework
handling common Adventure features.*

```
 1 GOSUB 30000: REM  INITIALIZE
 2 TEXT: HOME
 3 GOSUB 22000
 4 HTAB 1
10 GOSUB 1000
30 IF NOT SPACE THEN
   V$=A$
40 IF A$=" " THEN 10
45 PRINT: PRINT
50 IF ASC(V$)=32 AND LEN(V$)>1 THEN
   V$=RIGHT$(V$,LEN(V$)-1): A$=RIGHT$(A$,LEN(A$)-1): GOTO 50
60 IF LEN(V$)=LEN(A$) THEN
   NFLAG=0: GOTO 90
70 N$=RIGHT$(A$,LEN(A$)-LEN(V$))
80 IF ASC(N$)=32 AND LEN(N$)>1 THEN
   N$=RIGHT$(N$,LEN(N$)-1): GOTO 80
85 IF N$=" " THEN
   NFLAG=0
90 A=ASC(V$)-64
100 IF A<1 OR A>26 THEN 10
110 ON A GOSUB 10100,10200,10300,10400,10500,10600,10700,10800,10900,11000,
    11100,11200,11300,11400,11500,11600,11700,11800,11900,12000,12100,12200,
    12300,12400,12500,12600
120 PRINT
130 PRINT: GOTO 10
1000 A$=" ": SPACE=0: N$=" ": V$=" ": NFLAG=1
1010 GET B$:
     IF ASC(B$)=13 THEN
     RETURN
1020 IF ASC(B$)=8 AND SPACE AND RIGHT$(A$,1)=" " THEN
     SPACE=0
1025 IF LEN(A$)=1 AND B$=" " THEN 1010
1030 IF ASC(B$)=8 AND LEN(A$)>1 THEN
     A$=LEFT$(A$,LEN(A$)-1): PRINT B$;" ";B$;: GOTO 1010
1040 IF B$=" " AND NOT SPACE THEN
     V$=A$: SPACE=1: GOTO 1060
1050 IF ASC(B$)<65 OR ASC(B$)>91 THEN 1010
1060 PRINT B$;
1070 A$=A$+B$
1080 GOTO 1010
10100 RETURN
10200 RETURN
10300 RETURN
```

```
10400 IF V$="DROP" AND NFLAG THEN 26000
10499 RETURN
10500 IF A$="E" THEN
          D=2: GOTO 20000
10501 IF V$="EXAMINE" AND NFLAG THEN 27000
10599 RETURN
10600 RETURN
10700 IF V$="GO" THEN 19000
10799 RETURN
10800 RETURN
10900 IF A$="I" OR A$="INV" OR A$="INVENTORY" THEN 24000
10999 RETURN
11000 RETURN
11100 RETURN
11200 IF A$="LOOK" THEN 22000
11210 IF V$="LOOK" AND NFLAG THEN 27000
11299 RETURN
11300 RETURN
11400 IF A$="N" THEN
          D=1: GOTO 20000
11499 RETURN
11500 RETURN
11600 RETURN
11700 RETURN
11800 RETURN
11900 IF A$="S" THEN
          D=3: GOTO 20000
11999 RETURN
12000 IF V$="TAKE" AND NFLAG THEN 25000
12099 RETURN
12100 RETURN
12200 RETURN
12300 IF A$="W" THEN
          D=4: GOTO 20000
12399 RETURN
12400 RETURN
12500 RETURN
12600 POP: STOP: REM DEBUGGING AID.  INPUT OF Z STOPS PROGRAM
19000 REM PARSER FOR GO DIRECTION
19010 D=ASC(N$): D=(D=78)+(D=69)*2+(D=83)*3+(D=87)*4:
          IF NOT D THEN
             PRINT "I NEED A DIRECTION.": RETURN
20000 REM MOVE ROUTINE:D=DIRECTION:R=ROOM MOVED INTO:L=PRESENT LOCATION
20060 R=ASC(MID$(R$(L),D,1))-64
20070 IF NOT R THEN
          PRINT "YOU CAN'T GO THAT WAY": RETURN
20080 L=R
22000 REM LOOK ROUTINE
22005 PRINT "YOU ARE IN ";
22010 PRINT RM$(L): PRINT RD$(L): PRINT "THE ROOM CONTAINS ";: F1=0
22020 FOR I=1 TO NO
22030   IF OB(I)=L THEN
             PRINT OB$(I): F1=1
22040 NEXT I:
          IF NOT F1 THEN
             PRINT "NOTHING"
22050 PRINT "VISIBLE EXITS: ";
22060 FOR I=1 TO 4
22070   IF MID$(R$(L),I,1)<>"@" THEN
             PRINT DIR$(I);" ";: F1=1
22080 NEXT I:
          IF NOT F1 THEN
             PRINT "DON'T EXIST"
22090 RETURN
24000 F1=0: PRINT "YOU ARE CARRYING":
          FOR I=1 TO NO
24010   IF OB(I)=0 THEN
             PRINT OB$(I): F1=1
24020 NEXT I:
          IF NOT F1 THEN
             PRINT "NOTHING"
24030 RETURN
25000 F1=0: F2=0:
          FOR I=1 TO NO
25005   IF N$=OB$(I) AND OB(I)=0 THEN
             PRINT "YOU ALREADY HAVE THE ";N$: RETURN
25010   IF (N$=OB$(I) OR N$="ALL" OR N$="EVERYTHING") AND (OB(I)=(L)) THEN
             OB(I)=0: PRINT OB$(I);" TAKEN": F1=1
25020   IF N$=OB$(I) THEN
             F2=1
25025 NEXT I
25030 IF F1=0 AND F2=0 AND N$<>"ALL" AND N$<>"EVERYTHING" THEN
          PRINT "I CAN'T TAKE THE ";N$: RETURN
25035 IF F1=0 AND F2=0 THEN
          PRINT "THERE IS NOTHING HERE I CAN TAKE."
25040 IF F1=0 AND F2=1 THEN
          PRINT "I DON'T SEE IT HERE."
25060 RETURN
26000 F1=0:
          FOR I=1 TO NO
```

Adventures in Videoland

```
26010   IF (OB$(I)=N$ OR N$="ALL" OR N$="EVERYTHING") AND (OB(I)=(0)) THEN
           OB(I)=L: F1=1
26020 NEXT I
26030 IF NOT F1 THEN
           PRINT "YOU CAN'T DROP WHAT YOU AREN'T CARRYING": RETURN
26040 PRINT "OK": RETURN
27000 F1=0:
        FOR I=1 TO NO
27010   IF (OB(I)=0 OR OB(I)=L) AND (OB$(I)=N$) THEN
           F1=1: PRINT OD$(I):
           IF OD$(I)="" THEN
             PRINT "I SEE NOTHING IMPORTANT.": RETURN
27020   IF (FL(I)=(L) OR FL(I)=0) AND (FR$(I)=N$) THEN
           F1=1: PRINT FD$(I):
           IF FD$(I)="" THEN
             PRINT "NOTHING EXTRAORDINARY HERE": RETURN
27030   IF F1 THEN
           RETURN
27040 NEXT I
27050 PRINT "I CAN'T DESCRIBE WHAT ISN'T HERE"
27060 RETURN
30000 DIM OB(26),OB$(26),RM$(26),RD$(26),R$(26),OD$(26),FR$(26),FL(26),FD$(26)
30001 RM$(1)="A DIMLY LIT HALL": RM$(2)="A DARK HALL": RM$(3)=
        "A VERY DARK HALL": RM$(4)="MONTY HALL": RM$(5)=
        "THE DARKEST HALL OF ALL": RM$(6)="A PITCH BLACK HALL"
30002 RM$(7)="THE CELLAR": RM$(8)="THE ATTIC": RM$(9)="THE BEDROOM": RM$(10)=
        "THE LIVING ROOM": RM$(11)="THE CELLAR STAIRS": RM$(12)="A TUNNEL":
        RM$(13)="THE PARLOR"
30003 RM$(14)="A BATHROOM": RM$(15)="THE WINE CELLAR": RM$(16)=
        "THE BILLIARDS ROOM": RM$(17)="A THRONE ROOM": RM$(18)="A HALLWAY"
30004 RM$(19)="A BALCONY": RM$(20)="THE PORCH": RM$(21)="THE LIBRARY": RM$(22)=
        "THE BLUE ROOM": RM$(23)="THE GREEN ROOM": RM$(24)="THE PINK ROOM":
        RM$(25)="THE YELLOW ROOM": RM$(26)="THE ROSE ROOM"
30010 R$(1)="BCGF": R$(2)="@EA@": R$(3)="EDHA": R$(4)="@@IC": R$(5)="P@CB":
        R$(6)="@A@@": R$(7)="AH@@": R$(8)="CI@G": R$(9)="D@JH"
30011 R$(10)="I@K@": R$(11)="J@LN": R$(12)="K@@@": R$(13)="ON@@": R$(14)=
        "@K@M": R$(15)="G@M@": R$(16)="Q@E@": R$(17)="R@P@"
30012 R$(18)="@SQ@": R$(19)="@T@R": R$(20)="@@US": R$(21)="T@V@": R$(22)=
        "UW@@": R$(23)="@XYV": R$(24)="@@ZW": R$(25)="WZ@@": R$(26)="X@@Y"
30020 L=1: NO=26
30030 OB$(1)="BATTERIES": OB$(2)="KNIFE": OB$(3)="DETONATOR": OB$(4)="WATCH":
        OB$(5)="WALLET": OB$(6)="COINS"
30031 OB$(7)="HAT": OB$(8)="BALL": OB$(9)="CAR": OB$(10)="GLASS": OB$(11)=
        "RUG": OB$(12)="CARPET": OB$(13)="LETTER": OB$(14)="KNIFE": OB$(15)=
        "GUN"
30032 OB$(16)="AXE": OB$(17)="DAGGER": OB$(18)="PAINT": OB$(19)="HAMMER":
        OB$(20)="SAW": OB$(21)="BOX": OB$(22)="RAZOR": OB$(23)="PIN": OB$(23)=
        "CARTON": OB$(24)="PLUG": OB$(25)="MALLET": OB$(26)="CHAIN"
30040 FOR I=1 TO NO:
        OB(I)=I:
        NEXT I
30050 DIR$(1)="NORTH": DIR$(3)="SOUTH": DIR$(2)="EAST": DIR$(4)="WEST"
30060 RD$(1)="A SMALL WATERFALL TRICKLES TO THE FLOOR, WETTING EVERYTHING":
        RD$(2)="THERE IS AN ODOR OF DEATH HERE"
30100 OD$(1)="PLAIN DURACELLS": OD$(2)="IT IS RUSTY": OD$(3)=
        "IT APPEARS TO BE HOME MADE": OD$(5)="IT IS EMPTY"
30200 FR$(1)="WATERFALL": FD$(1)="IT IS COLD AND WET": FL(1)=1: FR$(2)="WALL":
        FD$(2)="JUST AN ORDINARY WALL": FL(2)=0
30201 FR$(3)="FLOOR": FL=0
32000 RETURN
```

115

Helpful Tips For Playing Adventure Games

If an Adventure is getting you very frustrated, the best thing to do is shut down the machine and try again a little bit later. If you are determined to get by the frustrating obstacle, call up a friend. He/she might have some ideas which you would never think of. If no friends are available, apply as much common sense as possible. If this fails as well, try obscure reasoning and make irrational decisions.

Watch out for any words in "quotes" or with *stars* around them. These usually are clues. Any clue can be figured out if enough thought is put into it. Try reversing all of the letters of a particular clue. It can transform something as obscure as ARBADAC ARBA into something meaningful like "ABRA CADABRA."

Remember that not every obstacle can be overcome! A window that cannot be opened or broken is probably just there to confuse the player. So, if it seems impossible to get by, it probably is.

Another reason why you may not be able to get by an obstacle is that you do not have the necessary resources! For instance, to break a window, you may need a hammer! If you have never encountered the hammer before, you may not even know that it exists, and you may spend more time trying to get by it without the hammer than you will spend finding the hammer!

Do not be afraid to try things that are seemingly stupid! In many cases a command that seems dumb turns out to be the way to overcome the obstacle.

Periodically (every 15 minutes or so) save your game out to tape or disk with the command "SAVE" or "SAVE GAME." This will insure that in the case of a fatal accident you only lose about 15 minutes Adventuring. Make absolutely sure that you save your game before trying things with unknown results, such as drinking strange bubbling liquids or jumping off a cliff.

www.ingramcontent.com/pod-product-compliance
Lightning Source LLC
Chambersburg PA
CBHW081132170526
45165CB00008B/2646